Reading Beyond the Alphabet

Innovations in Lifelong Literacy

Editors

Brij Kothari
P.G. Vijaya Sherry Chand
Michael Norton

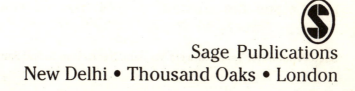

Sage Publications
New Delhi • Thousand Oaks • London

First published in 2003 by

Sage Publications India Pvt Ltd
B-42 Panchsheel Enclave
New Delhi 110 017

Sage Publications Inc
2455 Teller Road
Thousand Oaks, California 91320

Sage Publications Ltd
6 Bonhill Street
London EC2A 4PU

Published by Tejeshwar Singh for Sage Publications India Pvt Ltd with the assistance of the Cultural Service of the Embassy of France.

Phototypeset at InoSoft Systems in 10 pt Cheltenham and printed at Chaman Enterprises, New Delhi.

Library of Congress Cataloging-in-Publication Data

Reading beyond the alphabet: innovations in lifelong literacy/editors, Brij Kothari, P.G. Vijaya Sherry Chand, Michael Norton.
    p. cm.
    Includes bibliographical references.
      1. Literacy. 2. Books and reading. I. Kothari, Brij. II. Chand, P.G. Vijaya Sherry. III. Norton, Michael, 1942–
LC149.R42   302.2'244—dc21   2003   2002190883

ISBN: 0–7619–9708–3 (US–PB)   81–7829–184–3 (India–PB)

Sage Production Team: Shweta Vachani, Neeru Handa and Santosh Rawat

Exmouth

ding Beyond the Alphabet

Uni

Subj

h

To illiterate Azul, early literate Bernadette, functionally-literate Mummy and literate Babuji (I mean Hindi literacy).
• Brij Kothari

To Sarvar
• P.G. Vijaya Sherry Chand

To ideas and innovation, which are the fuel of social change.
• Michael Norton

Contents

List of Abbreviations

BGVS   Bharat Gyan Vigyan Samiti
CE   Continuing Education
CIVA   Centre for Innovation in Voluntary Action
CM   Chief Minister
DSS   Door Step School
ESL   English as a Second Language
HLC   Home Library Centre
IPCL   Improved Pace and Content of Learning
IRMA   Institute of Rural Management
KMVS   Kutch Mahila Vikas Sangathan
MFP   Minor Forest Produce
MP   Madhya Pradesh
MTs   Master Trainers
NAEP   National Adult Education Programme
NFE   Non-formal Education
NLM   National Literacy Mission
PESA   Provisions of Panchayat Extensions to Scheduled Areas Act
PL   Post Literacy
PLC   Post Literacy Campaign
RPs   Resource Persons
SHG   Self-help Group
SLS   Same Language Subtitling
SRC   State Resource Centre
TLC   Total Literacy Campaign
TRIFED   Tribal Co-operative Marketing Federation of India, Ltd.
VTs   Volunteer Teachers

Acknowledgements

This book journey began with a fortuitous 10-minute meeting in Kutch, sufficient time for a national conference on literacy to be proposed and accepted in principle. Thereafter, it was all electronic, involving no face-to-face meeting with any member of the Steering Committee. The committee itself, comprising of Sekhar Raha (Rajiv Gandhi Foundation), Nirmal Kanti Bhattacharjee (National Book Trust), Urvashi Butalia (KALI for Women), Sushma Iyengar (Kutch Mahila Vikas Sangathan), and Jaya Sharma (Nirantar), was an e-creation. As co-ordinators of the conference, we are grateful to this committee for their inputs from a distance and showing up at the conference for a first formal meeting.

'Reading Beyond the Alphabet: A National Conference on Innovations in Post and Lifelong Literacy', was conducted by the Indian Institute of Management, Ahmedabad (Ravi J. Matthai Centre for Educational Innovation) and sponsored by the Centre for Innovation in Voluntary Action (CIVA), London, on 18 and 19 August 2000. Both these institutions deserve our deepest appreciation for encouraging this effort. So do the numerous participants for presenting papers on innovative efforts in literacy. Vimala Ramachandran and Anita Rampal merit a special mention for their thought-provoking keynote addresses; and the academic support community at IIMA for ensuring smooth functioning.

Innovation is the key to progress in solving problems—whether the subject being addressed is poverty alleviation, watershed management or creating a literate society. Disappointingly, however, national and state agencies working for literacy were conspicuous by their absence at the conference. As co-ordinators, perhaps we underestimated the distance between New Delhi and Ahmedabad or even Gujarat's capital, Gandhinagar and Ahmedabad (separated by a stone's throw). But if routine matters or matters routinely prevent policy makers from lending an ear to innovations emerging from civil society, then civil society must find ways to take innovations to their ears. This book is a step in that direction, hoping to borrow more than an ear.

PART I

INTRODUCTION

CHAPTER ONE

Literacy in India: A Tide of Rising Rates but Low Levels

Brij Kothari

'I can't read because I'm not literate. If I become literate, I may still not read. But that will be my choice.'

—Anonymous

This book is not about the importance of literacy. Jean Drèze and Amartya Sen have written eloquently and persuasively on the indispensability of basic education and literacy for economic and social development (Drèze and Sen, 1995) and, more recently, for development as freedom (Sen, 1999). The importance of literacy is its potential to enhance freedom and choice. Sen and Drèze's inspirational work in basic education has systematically highlighted India's poor record in terms of 'social preparedness', when compared to China, for example. Since 1968, as Drèze and Sen (1995: 121) have pointed out, there have been repeated calls by experts, committees and in national policy documents, for greater public expenditure on education, and a target of 6 per cent of GNP for education has been recommended. Yet, in reality, this figure has hovered around 3 per cent.[1] The available figures for 1985–87 and 1995–97 show that this number is holding steady at 3.2 per cent of GNP (UNDP, 2001). Furthermore, educational expenditure has another imbalance—'the relatively low share of elementary education in total education'. At around 50 per cent, this share is paltry in relation to the massive numbers of children and adults who may be considered to be in need of elementary education. Clearly, there is gross dissonance between commitment claims and commitment in practice for universal basic education (see also PROBE, 1999). From a market perspective, as Sen (1999: 42) puts it, 'The social backwardness of India, with its elitist concentration on higher education and massive negligence of school education, and its substantial neglect of basic health care, [has left the] country poorly prepared for a widely shared economic expansion.'[2]

This book is about innovations in lifelong literacy. What is meant by 'lifelong literacy'? The intention is not to get embroiled in a definitional quagmire. However, a few clarifications are in order. Lifelong literacy is a concept subsumed under lifelong learning. In a narrow sense, lifelong literacy is primarily concerned with the retention and improvement of basic reading, writing and numeracy skills throughout the course of life. In a broader sense, it is an inadequate term for which a more suitable candidate is lifelong learning. Yet, the book's focus is on 'lifelong literacy', primarily as a reaction to what is seen as a serious shortcoming of the national literacy movement, chiefly, the lack of progress in literacy beyond emergent skills. Thus, our aim is to glean innovations in lifelong learning that recognise the centrality of lifelong literacy in a variety of social development objectives, innovations that pivotally need and include the retention and further development of the 3Rs. This is not to say that innovations in lifelong learning that do not necessarily need literacy are not worthy of consideration. On the contrary, there are undoubtedly many such innovations with immense potential but, for want of a focus, will not form the subject of this book.

1. The lack of financial allocation for education is only a part of the problem. Even if the allocation does rise, important concerns regarding the use of these resources remain. However, the present situation of teacher salaries absorbing well over 90 per cent of the recurring expenditure (Drèze and Sen, 1995: 122) highlights the resource constraint.

2. Exponents of higher education often drag Amartya Sen's name to buttress their cause for greater funding and support in higher education. It should be amply clear from this quote that Professor Sen, whom we all like to appropriate for our causes (and I am no exception), primarily emphasised the need for basic education, including primary education and literacy.

The important place of literacy in India's challenge in basic education stems primarily from the negligence of primary education. In contrast, China effectively controlled their adult literacy problem through an extensive and equitable provision of good quality primary education (Drèze and Loh, 1995). While conceding slow progress, the fact, however, is that universal *quality* primary education has remained an elusive dream in independent India. One would like to be proven wrong, but this situation is not likely to change drastically in the near future for want of policy commitment. Unschooled, schooled, and dropped-out children will remain in need of considerable and lifelong literacy skill improvement, even if many of them may technically be enumerated as literate. Hence, the importance of lifelong literacy will remain for quite some time to come, even if all children in India receive primary education, bearing in mind present quality levels. Furthermore, there are an estimated 300 million or more people in the country already with skill levels that leave much room for improvement. While the national literacy movement has successfully generated scores of 'literate' people with neo-semi literacy skills, it has not been able to adequately address the persistent problem of low skill levels and steady skill erosion. There is, therefore, an urgent need to search for innovative and creative ways that have shown promise in pilot contexts and offer learnings for practitioners, planners and policy makers.

There are important considerations in the practice of lifelong literacy that need special attention, primarily because they tend not to be reflected prominently in the practice of mainstream literacy planning. The considerations relate to: (*i*) the literacy rate; (*ii*) literacy level, relapse and skill erosion; (*iii*) literacy development in phases; (*iv*) literacy and everyday life; (*v*) motivation for literacy; (*vi*) phonemic awareness; (*vii*) print exposure; (*viii*) media and literacy; and (*ix*) innovations and policy making. This introductory chapter is divided into 10 sections. The first nine sections discuss the considerations in lifelong literacy, as listed above. The final section provides an introduction to the 13 cases of innovation in lifelong literacy included in this book.

Literacy Rate

According to the 2001 census, India's literacy rate is 65.4 per cent in the 7+ age group, a leap of 13.8 percentage points during the 1991–2001 decade. The female literacy rate is 54.3 per cent and the male rate, 76.0 per cent. In comparative terms, the growth in the literacy rate in the last decade has been substantially better than any previous decade since

1951 (Table 1.1). The impressive upward trend has caused much hope. 'India could be expected to touch the sustainable threshold level of 75 % sometime between 2005 and 2006' (National Literacy Mission [NLM], 2000: 13). .

Table 1.1: Decadal literacy growth in India (7+ age group)

Year	Literacy percentage	Decadal growth	Non-literates (million)
1951	18.3	—	—
1961	28.3	10.0	249.40
1971	34.4	6.1	283.03
1981	43.5	9.1	305.31
1991	52.5	8.7	328.88
2001	65.4*	12.9	268.42†

Note: *2001 census; †Extrapolation in National Literacy Mission (2000).
Source: Reproduced from National Literacy Mission (2000).

While there is cause for optimism due to the rising rate, the rate by itself is only one window into the literacy scenario. Basu and Foster (1998) perceptively distinguish between two kinds of non-literates: (*i*) a 'proximate illiterate', i.e., a non-literate person living in a household with at least one literate person; and (*ii*) an 'isolate illiterate', i.e., a non-literate in whose household there is no literate person. Based on the 1981 census, they deduce that 43.3 per cent of the entire population of India (not just 7+ as is commonly reported in literacy rates) was literate, 31.7 per cent proximate illiterate and 25 per cent isolate illiterate. This means that around 44 per cent of the non-literate population at the time did not have any literate person within the household. For example, Sikkim and Meghalaya had the same literacy rate (42 per cent) but Sikkim was far better off with a lower isolate rate of 22.6 per cent as compared to Meghalaya's 29.3 per cent. In a follow-up paper, Basu et al. (1999) conclude that proximate illiterates do indeed benefit from intra-household externalities of the literate person's presence within the household, at least in terms of labour earnings. The intra-household benefits, in all likelihood, extend further to information access and other social benefits.

Important policy implications follow. Literacy programmes need to focus on isolate non-literate households more sharply than simply all non-literates. Dispersion of efforts is more effective than concentration. Thus, the involvement of five individuals from five different isolate households is far more purposeful than all five from the same household. Both approaches contribute equally to the literacy rate but one leads to greater social gains. Finally, within an isolate household it is probably more effective to secure a female member's participation.

Literacy Level, Relapse and Skill Erosion[3]

Another perspective on the literacy situation in India comes from a hard look at literacy levels. How literate are India's so-called 65.4 per cent literate people? In any 'literate' population, what percentage is neo, semi, functionally and irreversibly literate? The limitation of our census machinery to actually be able to record the literacy level of people is obvious. However, literacy policy has also not attempted to conduct sample surveys to gain insight into literacy levels. Qualitative accounts reveal, nevertheless, that the skill levels of a significant proportion of India's literates are very low and non-functional. In this respect, the survey of the Organisation for Economic Co-operation and Development (2000) measuring the literacy levels in developed countries in a comparative perspective shows us the way. Even in 14 of these 20 developed countries surveyed, it was found that 'at least 15 per cent of all adults have literacy skills at only the most rudimentary level, making it difficult for them to cope with the rising skill demands of the information age (p. xiii)'. One can well imagine the situation in India. Arguably, an obsession with increasing the literacy rate has prevailed over efforts to pro-blematise the literacy level. Consequently, pro-active efforts targeting the latter have suffered from policy neglect.

National progress in terms of the literacy rate needs to be qualified. Attention needs to be drawn to the reality that literacy skill maintenance and improvement among recent literates, what the NLM calls post-literacy, 'remains the single most difficult problem confronting the NLM, and the whole of the adult literacy programme' (National Literacy Mission, 1994b: 40). The NLM report goes on to cite an estimate that relapse in the earlier National Adult Education Programme (NAEP) was 40 per cent and suggests that the situation with the literacy campaigns in general in India may not be very different. There are two noteworthy issues here. Relapse into illiteracy and skill erosion are generally expected to be very high. Surprisingly, however, there are few rigorous and longitudinal studies commissioned or conducted on this crucial problem.

Literacy skill erosion or relapse is a much understudied phenomenon. Even the NLM's expert group's comments on 40 per cent relapse are based on what the group was 'informed'. The extent and nature of skill erosion and relapse, the process by which it happens, the conditions that prevent it and strategies to combat it are the stuff of frequent from the gut

---

3. Relapse here means a fall back into illiteracy. Skill erosion is the loss of skills that may or may not lead to relapse.

debates but rarely scientific study. The dearth of studies on skill erosion and relapse leave us little choice but to evaluate the limited evidence at our disposal.

Roy and Kapoor's (1975) study, although somewhat dated, is one of the few studies that has looked at skill erosion in the Indian context. Their primary conclusion was that skill erosion is definitely a concern for those who have attended less than four years of public school or achieved less than Grade III literacy training.[4] Children with only 1–2 years of schooling and adults with Grades I–II of literacy training experienced considerable skill erosion. Generally, literacy trainees experienced 40 per cent erosion of their skills as compared to 20 per cent among school leavers (this is based on percentage loss in test score). While one cannot generalise on the basis of the programme analysed by Roy and Kapoor, their comment hints at what one might expect to find in other literacy programmes: 'This rural literacy training is probably the most competent and effective training in India. The government pro-grammes are in general far less effective.' An interesting finding in their study confirms what may be obvious intuitively. Rural literacy trainees showed greater skill erosion than their urban counterparts, mainly due to the lack of print exposure in the environment with which to cement skills (an issue I take up later).

Abadzi (1994) reviews several country studies on retention of literacy skills among adults with the general conclusion that there are very few methodologically sound studies in this area and the few that exist paint a bleak picture. On average, 50 per cent adults who become 'literate' through programmes retain or improve their skills later. The success rate of the Total Literacy Campaign (TLC), nationally, is reported to be 62.4 per cent (National Literacy Mission, 1994a).[5] More recent figures are not very different. Chatterjee (1996) states that out of the 90 million non-literates enrolled, 53 million became literate, an achievement rate of nearly 59 per cent. These figures are considerably higher than the 30 per cent average success rate of programmes mentioned by Abadzi (1994). Based on Abadzi's earlier estimate of skill erosion, 70 per cent to 85 per cent

4. Unfortunately, the study does not clarify the meaning of different grades of literacy training, only stating that Grades I, II and III refer to the successive grades awarded on completion of prescribed courses within the literacy programme in which the study was conducted.

5. The success rate was measured on the basis of figures reported until March 1994, in National Literacy Mission (1994a). It is the ratio of the number of persons having completed Book III of the primers (20.34 million), hence, considered neo-literate at least, to the number of non-literates enrolled (32.62 million).

of all enrolled adults are at risk of skill decay. Since adult literacy programmes are only able to impart emergent literacy skills, the simple but important conclusion is that unless these skills are practised in everyday life, they are likely to erode. In a thought-provoking article, Rogers (1999) argues that adult literacy programmes should be judged not by success rates or numbers of people who became neo-literate, but by the use of their literacy skills.

Literacy in Phases

Arguably the most inspirational Indian experiment in literacy was conducted in Ernakulam district of Kerala in 1989, giving birth to the now famous Total Literacy Campaign (Athreya and Chunkath, 1996; Bordia and Kaul, 1992; Joseph, 1996 for an historical overview). Since then, policy making has been driven by a conceptualisation of literacy development as masses of people, first moving from non to neo to functional to irreversible literacy, in distinct phases. The National Literacy Mission, established in 1988, launched the TLC approach with the objective of taking 100 million non-literate people in the 15–35 age group (of the nation's more than 300 million non-literates at the time) to functional literacy by 1997 (Chatterjee, 1996). The TLC was administered throughout the country at the district level through the Zilla Saksharta Samitis (ZSS), specially created for this purpose.[6] The TLC had to be completed within a short period of 12–18 months, and consisted of five main phases: (*i*) environment building in a campaign mode; (*ii*) a door-to-door survey to identify and enumerate the target non-literates in the 15–35, but often 9–45 age group; (*iii*) identification and training of volunteer Resource Persons (RPs) in order to train Master Trainers (MTs), and MTs to train the Volunteer Teachers (VTs); (*iv*) literacy classes by VTs, usually at night, for roughly 30 learners per VT; use of literacy primers based on the Improved Pace and Content of Learning (IPCL) method; and finally; (*v*) external evaluation by an out-of-state agency.

The TLC model succeeded in creating a substantial number of neo-literates. But enabling and motivational factors to automate a neo-literate's transition to functional and irreversible literacy did not figure centrally in literacy planning. Post-literacy (PL), by which one actually means post-neo-literacy, seems to have been an afterthought emerging from a realisation of the limitations of the TLC mode. Non-literate adults

6. District literacy committee.

learn letter-sound associations reasonably fast but remain at early skill levels for much longer, as compared to children (Abadzi, 1994). Intense skill practice is even more critical for adults in the early phase of skill acquisition. Although PL and continuing education (CE) have now emerged as the new areas of emphasis, we missed a good opportunity during the 1990s to synergise emergent literacy skill development under TLC with simultaneous opportunities for skill practice, linked with everyday life. The crucial difference between PL and CE seems to be that the emphasis is on skill reinforcement in PL and shifts in CE to links with day-to-day activity. What may be called the golden decade of literacy growth in terms of neo-literacy, is also the decade of missed opportunity to capitalise on nascent literacy skills. The idea that we must first take the entire population of non-literates to neo-literacy before contemplating strategies for the entire neo-literate population's move to functional levels, is fundamentally flawed because of the long drought in literacy practice between the two phases, leading to skill erosion and relapse. This is not to imply that the TLC was a failure. In fact it was a resounding success from the point of view of raising awareness and interest in literacy at the grassroots, harnessing the spirit of volunteerism in society, and resulting in the enrolment of 130 million non-literate persons in the 9–35 age group. But the success was generally not consolidated by activating complementarities outside the learning centres with people's lives. There are some exceptions, however, such as Dumka district in Bihar where a concerted effort was made to link literacy with women's empowerment (Kothari et al., 1999). From a return on investment perspective, the lack of complementarities led to considerable wastage in terms of time, effort and financial resources. Building literacy's connection with everyday life is not just a good idea, it is essential for the sustenance of this ephemeral skill.

Literacy and Everyday Life

The NLM's PL initiative primarily targets neo-literates in the 9–35 age group who completed the basic literacy course under TLC and other Non-formal Education (NFE) programmes. Drop-outs in the TLC phase, NFE and primary schools are also included. Skill development is a major component of PL but activities linking it to development schemes in general are now beginning to be encouraged. This has come about after the realisation that an overemphasis on literacy skill development in isolation, without a use for emergent skills, was not attracting many neo-literates to PL programmes and not being able to sustain the interest of those who enrolled to begin with. There is a growing acceptance that in CE there is a need to build bridges between literacy and life (Figure 1.1).

Figure 1.1: National Literacy Mission's literacy model

Everyday Life
Women's empowerment
Education
Livelihoods
Microenterprise
Health
Rural development
Entertainment
Local knowledge
Culture
Conservation
Savings/Loans
Income generation
Basic skills
TLC
Skill reinforcement
PL
CE

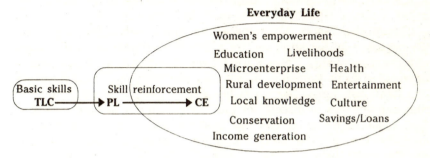

The important point of departure this book has with the NLM model is to move basic skill development and reinforcement into the arena of everyday life, without seeing these as occurring in a vacuum and in very distinct phases. Basic skill acquisition and improvement needs forging with the multitude of activities in everyday life mentioned illustratively in Figure 1.1 (and there are many others). In lifelong literacy, the development of basic skills, reinforcement and practice have strong links to everyday life (Figure 1.2).

Figure 1.2: Lifelong literacy model

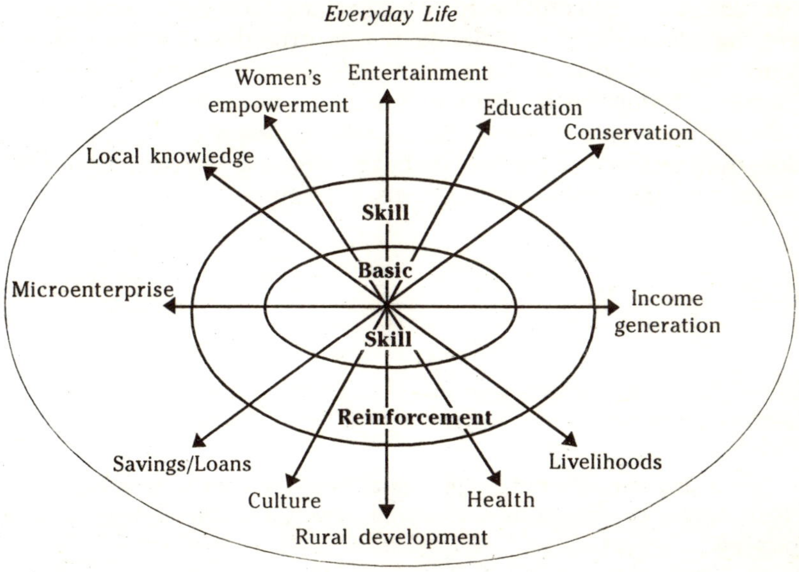

Everyday Life
Women's empowerment
Entertainment
Education
Conservation
Local knowledge
Skill
Basic
Microenterprise
Income generation
Skill
Reinforcement
Savings/Loans
Livelihoods
Culture
Health
Rural development

Lifelong literacy shares a similar orientation as the 'real literacies' approach (Rogers, 1999). The lifelong literacy model does not suggest that basic skill development cannot or should not develop within the TLC framework, just that the activities currently being planned under PL/CE were/are as relevant during the TLC as thereafter. TLC and PL are, in this conceptualisation, a part of lifelong literacy.[7]

The implications of this model is that linking literacy with everyday life becomes an essential part of a non-literate person's journey into literacy (e.g., Mishra 1994). If we are unable to form the links, then we have failed to find a use of literacy for that person. For most people, literate or non-literate, everyday life already includes literacy practices that one engages in directly or indirectly. The non-literate person requesting a neighbour to read a letter she/he has received is engaging in an indirect or mediated literacy practice as much as the neighbour who directly reads the letter. There are many other such examples of direct or indirect literacy practices—a person asking someone at the bus-stop where a waiting bus is going, who in turn reads the destination plate; a widow requesting another woman to fill out a form for her so that she can benefit from the Widow Pension Scheme.

In planning for literacy development, the basic skill development challenge is to use indirect literacy practices, already occurring, as starting points for literacy learning. Additionally, personal, familial, social developmental or life enrichment opportunities (including entertainment) that are valued but in which one's participation is hampered or denied because of non-literacy, are powerful points to anchor literacy learning into. For people with some basic skills (or even developing basic skills), one can creatively introduce new literacy-based empowerment, development and enrichment opportunities that could not or simply were not part of the non-literate person's lifeworld earlier. A creative introduction of literacy practices—hitherto unknown in the local environment, but, which people with all levels of literacy begin to value—can be of use to the literate but also have a powerful ripple effect in enthusing the non-literate towards literacy.

Motivation

Motivating adults to participate is one of the two main problems facing adult literacy programmes (Rogers, 1999). The other, according to Rogers,

---

7. Continuing literacy is not an appropriate substitute for 'lifelong literacy' because it implies 'continuity' from something which, it is being argued, cannot be separated.

is the inability of programmes to help the participants transfer their literacy skills outside the classroom/centre and into their daily lives. A primary hurdle facing the PL/CE initiatives is indeed motivating neo-literate people to enrol and attend programmes conceived at a macro level. The tendency has been to motivate people externally, for example, through media advertisements or exhortations by opinion leaders. There has been much less reflection on whether the programme and the implementation process are motivating. Literacy classes, libraries and resource centres have an intrinsic motivational value that may vary from place to place, but the implementation process can enhance these.

Thus, it is not simply a matter of opening centres/libraries and imploring people to use them. The problem, as it is often found, is that learners have other priorities. Especially those who may have acquired early literacy skills through the TLC but found few links between the skills and their own lives, cannot be persuaded easily or sustainably to participate in PL/CE programmes. This scenario is captured in the figures on enrolment and participation in PL centres (National Literacy Mission, 1994a). Out of the proposed number of neo-literates 61.4 per cent enrolled but only 31.5 per cent actually participated. These are official figures and the reality is grimmer. After visiting several PL campaigns, Matthew (1998) contends, 'Officially supplied statistics is hardly reflective of the field situation. Even on record, Post Literacy Campaigns (PLCs) have rarely managed to find more than a fourth of its TLC clientele participating regularly.' The argument is that the whipped frenzy of the TLC phase plus the novelty effect of 'literacy' as a desirable goal was shrivelled by the time PL came along. This occurred not just among the learners but volunteer teachers as well. People wanted very tangible benefits.

There is, thus, a wide gap in our understanding of a neo-literate person's motivations for engagement in literacy practices, whether these practices already exist in the local environment, are formalised as in classes/centres, semi-formalised as in a library, or simply introduced through the mass media. Gfeller (1997) found several motivational factors in a Zairian adult literacy programme. Of paramount importance are self-esteem and status gain within people's own societies. Another interesting benefit of literacy is direct access to the word of God through religious texts. Our own survey in rural villages of Rajkot district in Gujarat found that even though there is a near absence of print matter in households, the most commonly, if not the only, available texts besides textbooks are a rich variety of religious texts (Kothari et al., 2001). These include religious epics, stories of/by saints, prayer books and *bhajans*.[8] Besides the economic and social development focus, literacy programmes would do well to also understand the psychological underpinnings that drive or might drive people towards literacy and consciously build their action learning practices upon these. For example, if people's entertainment is enhanced as a consequence of literacy, the interest in acquiring and improving literacy skills usually becomes self-propelling.

Phonemic Awareness

Few will disagree that if the passage to literacy begins in adulthood, it is unacceptably late. Many will postulate that literacy learning must start in primary schooling. However, lifelong literacy requires that preparation for literacy (not alphabet teaching or formal instruction in reading) should start at birth (Leseman and de Jong, 1998). Clearly, pre-school learning has an important place in Indian thought, as exemplified by the legend of Abhimanyu. The translation of this thought into action is not always apparent. There is considerable evidence that pre-school learning is in reality not just a precursor to formal schooling but a foundational component of long-term educational development. As a general rule, the earlier in life is the investment in education, the greater is its leveraging power for pedagogic gains later on.

There are two areas of research with strong links to literacy that have enjoyed considerable scholarship in the West—phonemic awareness and print exposure. They have exerted tremendous influence on educational policy and debates, especially in North America. However, this voluminous research seems to have had a negligible influence on literacy policy makers and practitioners in India. While one understands the judiciousness of not adopting anything and everything from the West, there is also a need to seriously weigh the implications of strong research traditions elsewhere with a view to adapt them to Indian conditions. Phonemic awareness and print exposure scholarship offers us much text for thought in the context of lifelong literacy.

There is a general acceptance that the mental and cognitive processes involved in reading are essentially the same as in listening, except for the decoding skills necessary for reading (Gough et al., 1996). There is also substantial support for the idea that 'children's acquisition of literacy is akin to their acquisition of oral language' (Copeland et al., 1994: 26). In

---

8. *Bhajans* are songs, generally linked to religion or spirituality.

a landmark experimental study, Bradley and Bryant (1983: 419) concluded that 'Children who are backward in reading are strikingly insensitive to rhyme and alliteration.' This spawned a flurry of literature on, what has come to be known as, phonemic awareness, or 'the ability to perceive a spoken word as a sequence of individual sounds' (Lewkowicz, 1980: 686).[9] Alternatively defined, it is 'an understanding that speech is composed of individual sounds' (Snider, 1995: 443). Needless to say, it is beyond the scope of this introduction to delve into the prolific research on this topic; Snider (1995) provides a good introduction and overview.

The distilled conclusion of research in phonemic awareness is that it is a meta-linguistic skill that has a very strong correlation with later (or present) success in reading. Non-literate children who demonstrate strong phonemic awareness go on to become better readers than children with a similar background who are weak in phonemic awareness. If this is also true in the Indian context (and there is a need to verify because almost all phonemic awareness studies have been conducted in western contexts in languages that have a Roman script), then there is an urgent need to come up with innovative strategies to heighten the phonemic awareness of pre-school children across the country. Such inputs at a very early age can leverage the acquisition of literacy skills lifelong.

Snider (1995) provides a very practical and useful overview of a variety of techniques—rhyming, segmenting, phoneme substitution and blending—to teach phonemic awareness as a precursor to formal alphabetic and/or reading instruction (see also Copeland et al., 1994). Many of the techniques suggested are game-friendly, though they are structured and require some degree of facilitation. The scope to creatively localise these and integrate existing local practices that fall within the purview of phonemic awareness is tremendous. Yopp (1992) and Yopp and Yopp (2000) suggest, in addition, a series of approaches to phonemic awareness that act at a subconscious level. Carefully worded/selected songs, nursery rhymes, riddles, chants, poetry, story reading/listening and word-sound games form the core of these methods. The Indian context provides a vast treasure-trove of written and oral traditions that could be usefully tapped. For example, the memorisation and recitation of Sanskrit *shlokas*[10] may have a strong association with phonemic awareness given their penchant for rhyme, rhythm and musical orientation. Widely popular games like *Antakshari*[11] are another resource to build upon, as are a

---

9. Also known as phonological awareness.
10. Often in poetic couplets.
11. A game based on songs where the last syllable sung becomes the cue for the beginning of the next song.

range of folk, film, spiritual and religious songs. The crucial advantage of approaches that work implicitly is that they are amenable to a marriage with the electronic mass media. Only the media have the reach and power to spark and sustain processes of phonemic awareness development at the household level.

The important insight of the research in phonemic awareness is that it is not just developed through reading instruction, yet, potently fosters reading ability. The relevance of phonemic awareness for the pre-reading preparation of children, without recourse to print, necessarily, is not always intuitive. Of course, phonemic awareness and literacy skills are also substantially aided by direct or indirect exposure to print.

Print Exposure

Intuitively it is apparent that those who spend more time reading will also exhibit greater improvement in decoding skills and comprehension. Longitudinal research with children has established this clearly. Time spent in daily out-of-school reading explains improvement in reading comprehension (Cipielewsky and Stanovich, 1992), spelling, vocabulary, verbal fluency, word knowledge and general information (Cunningham and Stanovich, 1991). Among college students, it was found that print exposure is an independent contributor to the acquisition of content knowledge in a variety of domains (Stanovich and Cunningham, 1993).

To make an understatement, an average Indian's lifelong exposure to print is marginal as compared to an average person in a developed country. Print exposure is highest during the schooling year for those fortunate enough to go to school. For many people it is acutely low during the pre-school years and after schooling is completed. A lifelong deprivation of exposure to print outside the formal learning contexts, combined with low quality education in formal contexts, are primarily responsible for the existence of very low literacy levels in India. The PROBE (1999) report calculates that an average Indian adult has spent slightly over two years in school (1.8 for females and 2.9 for males; in China these are 3.8 and 6.1, respectively). Most school drop-outs occur during the first two years of schooling and more so in the first year. This pattern is found in Rajasthan (Vijaya Sherry Chand et al., 1998) and expectedly in other parts of India. Developing countries in Latin America too suffer from high drop-out during the first year of schooling (Liddell, 1998). Thus, if the reality is that many children still face the prospect of two years of low quality schooling (and many adults having already undergone this in the past), in a class where there may be 58 students to a teacher (Drèze and Sen, 1995: 117), the lifelong literacy challenge needs to build upon a very precarious skill set. Thus, complementarities between print exposure before schooling begins, during the schooling years (in and outside the classroom), and after one leaves schooling need careful planning.

There are two kinds of print exposure, which will be called incidental and mindful exposure. Incidental exposure occurs due to the existence of print in the environment, such as, billboards, movie posters, road signs, shop names, etc. Mindful exposure involves the conscious setting aside of time to engage in reading, say, newspaper, magazine and book. Both the literate and non-literate people experience incidental and mindful exposure, except their engagement is direct or indirect. As clarified earlier, one can directly or indirectly (with someone's help) read any text. Table 1.2 presents a matrix to categorise the likely reading responses (direct or indirect) of non-literate, neo-literate and literate persons, to incidental or mindful print exposure.

Table 1.2: **Likely reading response to incidental and mindful print exposure**

	Incidental print exposure	Mindful print exposure
Non-literate	I	I
Neo-literate	D, I	D, I
Literate	D	D

Note: I = indirect reading; D = direct reading.

To promote literacy, one needs to plan for incidental and mindful print exposure, somewhat differently for pre-school children, school children and adults.

For non-literate pre-school children, both print exposure forms assume importance from a phonemic perspective, but more so, the mindful kind. Mindful print exposure in their case would include parents, siblings or others reading habitually to very young children, whether they read, understand, watch the pictures or simply play along. Interactive story reading helps children acquire written language awareness, how print flows (e.g., left to right, top to bottom), vocabulary and concepts and an ability to identify letters and words or grapheme-phoneme correspondence (Kerr and Mason, 1994). A major gain is the attitudinal shaping towards books and reading as a fun-filled activity. In the West, the message of reading to pre-school children is all-pervasive. A parent can hardly escape this simple but powerful message, disseminated through media, pre-schools, libraries, schools and many other institutions.

The same message is absent even among the class of India that can actually afford books. In four rural villages of Rajkot, a survey to determine the presence of books for children in homes drew a near blank (Kothari et al., 2001). Not surprisingly, reading matter for the youth and adults, too, was in short supply. Due to the near absence of reading matter in households, many Indians do not experience incidental nor mindful print exposure forms at home. Culturally, book-buying has remained a low priority.

The message of reading to pre-reading children also has value for those who cannot afford books. In many poor households, there is at least one literate school-going child who can easily read stories from her/his textbooks to a younger pre-reading sibling. This idea, if reinforced through the school system and the mass media, may have a far-reaching impact. India is yet to tap the mass appeal of icons such as a Sachin Tendulkar or an Amitabh Bachhan in the service of reading, literacy and education. Icons themselves are yet to step into these roles. African-American basketball stars in the United States frequently appear on national television to lend their charisma to reading. Their goal is the infusion of reading practices in many disadvantaged inner-city African-American homes.

The cognitive and language development of adult non-literates are far too advanced for us to be concerned with the development of their phonemic awareness as a precursor to later reading development. Their strength is the language they know, their knowledge and motivations and uses they may have for literacy. As already discussed, understanding and building upon these while imparting decoding skills is necessary. Simultaneously, there is a need to improve print exposure in everyday life so that emergent skills are constantly challenged, used and satiated. Print-exposure for adult emergent literates and neo-literates may differ, not as much in content but in the packaging of the print so as to reinforce a range of skill levels. Print introduced into the environment needs to increase the frequency of direct engagement with print, for everyone and at all levels of literacy.

Book Floods have been attempted in developing countries to infuse school environments with quality books (Elley, 2000). These projects have mainly been on a small scale with a cluster of schools receiving a certain quantity of books. The books are divided among the schools and then rotated every so often. The Book Flood is thought to have resulted in improvement in writing, listening comprehension, and other language related skills. The limiting factors of Book Floods were primarily the high cost and the lack of cultural suitability of books. Books had to be imported because most of the projects were in countries that do not have an active children's publishing industry.

Media and Literacy

Work on literacy has generally been taken up by institutions involved in development. Literacy for developmental goals has wide acceptability. However, literacy as also a vehicle for personal life enrichment, including entertainment, is an idea that lies on the fringes of mainstream literacy planning. Yet, if one carefully examines the place of literacy in a literate person's everyday life, the personal enrichment and entertainment that literacy skills enable are anything but marginal. Without literacy skills, not only would we be deprived of information and knowledge that enables our careers and development goals, but our lives would also be devoid of novels, story books, comics, newspapers, and informative and *masala* magazines.[12] Stromquist's (1997) evaluation of a Freirean literacy programme for women' empowerment in Brazil found that literacy skills have an important place in reading film and fashion magazines, writing Christmas cards, and so on (reported in Rogers, 1999). The empowerment objective of literacy is not at odds with personal enrichment. Rather, both can be advanced more effectively via a confluence (Kothari, 2000). The mass media's ability to deliver information and entertainment makes them a powerful resource for lifelong literacy.

In the Indian context of over a billion people, the media's role in raising phonemic awareness and print exposure level is vital. Thus far, the mass media's function has mostly remained one of motivating people for literacy. For instance, despite the fact that there are over 300 million people who may loosely be classified as partially literate, there is probably not a single daily newspaper in any state (or for that matter in the Hindi belt comprising half the country's non and partially literate population), expressly written, designed and circulated among partially literate people. Since 1970, in Tanzania, the *Kisomo* (Literacy) page of the *Uhuru* national newspaper is written for neo-literates and appears regularly as the ninth page of the 12 page newspaper (Semali, 1993). The sporadic text that appears on television as a complement to the audiovisuals, probably gives more print exposure than the press in many rural homes in India.

The ubiquitous song-based programmes on television are a bottomless resource to build phonemic awareness and decoding skills upon. Radio, being an oral medium, can surely be used creatively to further phonemic awareness and even print decoding skills. For example, there could be a radio programme that reads the newspaper for neo-literates while people listen and simultaneously follow along on the paper. Semali

---

12. Spicy or gossip magazines.

(1993) used radio rather effectively for motivational purposes. Some ideas in this book might also trigger other possibilities for the use of the mass media, not just as tools for motivation, but also for engendering literacy practices.

Innovation and Policy Making

This book is a collection of cases to promote lifelong literacy, with a creative bent. Clearly, it is a small collection gleaned from a National Conference, titled, 'Reading Beyond the Alphabet: Innovations in Post and Lifelong Literacy', held at the Indian Institute of Management, Ahmedabad. Without a doubt, this collection is but a fraction of the creative ideas in this vast country. Although the existence of creativity is never in doubt, if there is a serious lacuna, it is in the active search, identification, support and promotion of creative ideas and innovation. Euphemistically speaking, the policy climate has not always been conducive to innovation. Many innovations succeed in taking root as pilot projects, despite the odds, but remain as 'neat' projects and ideas to be presented at conferences and written about in books. If at all they influence policy makers, it is usually after an inordinately long period of persistence in the face of several rounds of rejection. Given the extremely hierarchical nature of relationships within policy making, ideas in policy making circles likely emanate from or are distilled through a handful of experts and decision makers. Inbreeding of ideas has severe limitations unless there are in-built processes for actively seeking fresh thinking outside the small circle. Today, an idea or innovation born outside policy making circles faces an uphill task even to be heard, let alone be considered seriously. There are few processes whereby innovative ideas or projects can be sought through open competitions and screened by an independent body (independent of policy and innovator) and subsequently rejected or recommended for further consideration/support by policy making.

McLaughlin (1987) argues that the success and failure of policy-driven change does not depend as much on institutional mechanisms and central implementation issues as it does, ultimately, on the smallest unit—the individuals and actors who deliver and are affected by the change. The PL campaigns are a case in point where a centralised scheme did not resonate with the volunteers or the learners. Warwick et al. (1992) draw the following lessons from their analysis of the implementation of educational innovations: (*i*) projects need to explicitly consider culture in the design and implementation; (*ii*) innovations have to be sensitive to

the organisational context that they are or aim to be a part of; and
(*iii*) teachers are the instruments of change, i.e., an innovation cannot
take hold without their acceptance and participation.

The cases included in this book are examples of innovations that
have been implemented and found to provide useful lessons for the
direction of lifelong literacy in India. Because these are not just ideas
but practical attempts to address gaps in lifelong literacy, their success
and dilemmas are grounded in the practice of the 'smallest unit'. While
they have had to be culturally sensitive, they may or may not have given
adequate thought to the organisational climate to which they belong.
In a project mode, this issue may not have seemed to have a high priority.
Wherever instructors or co-ordinators of projects are at the helm of affairs,
their acceptance, naturally, had to be a constant process of negotiation.

Cases of Innovation in Lifelong Literacy

The contributors to this book are united in accepting that literacy is
much more than just the 3Rs. They also recognise the symbiotic relationship between the 3Rs and expansion of freedom, and personal and social
empowerment in different spheres of life. While none of the innovations
stop purely at the goal of imparting the 3Rs, they also do not eschew the
importance of strengthening the 3Rs. The innovations are united by the
links they forge between skill development and people's everyday lives.

The innovations loosely fall under the following categories: (*i*) empowerment and literacy; (*ii*) promotion of reading culture; (*iii*) reading
matter for early literates; (*iv*) publishing for rural areas; (*v*) libraries and
literacy, and finally; (*vi*) media and literacy. By 'loosely', it is meant that
a case may straddle more than one category. Therefore, categorisation
is based on the primary emphasis of the case.

Empowerment and Literacy

Three cases illustrate the relevance of literacy for empowerment. K.S.
Ram's case is one in which the everyday economic exploitation of tribals
in Bastar district of Chhattisgarh state became the entry point for post-
literacy instruction. The primary objective was not to emphasise literacy
skill reinforcement but to conscientise tribals to the petty exploitative
practices of middlemen. This led to the formation of self-help groups
that needed some functional literacy skills in order to function effectively. While one can debate Ram's thesis that literacy is meaningful only

if it is tied to livelihoods, one cannot deny that in poverty contexts, literacy's sustainability is assured if it does indeed contribute to economic progress.

Jaya Shrivastava's experience with adolescent girls in Delhi slums is a Freirean approach to literacy (Freire and Macedo, 1987). As basic literacy skills are imparted and words constructed, the idea of 'reading the world' through the word begins. Rich in women's testimonies, the case brings to the fore the enormous effort required to effect a deep change in women's understanding of their location in a patriarchal society. The case demonstrates that literacy learning conducted with a spirit of critical questioning can be empowering to women who experience a double disadvantage of poverty and patriarchy. Although many girls were empowered, the intensity of the programme also limited its reach.

Neo-literate women belonging to the Tiwa tribe in Assam are the primary stakeholders in the case by Jayanta Kumar Sarma, Biman Borah and Gitarani Bhattacharya. Through walks in their own habitats and communities, women gained new understandings through a series of observations, visualisation and mapping exercises. This ultimately resulted in community development activities, such as, the creation of a pond for fisheries. The crucial point made by this case is that literacy need not be thought only in terms of the 3Rs. Visual mapping is another form of literacy that is extremely effective in promoting an expression and understanding of a complex reality. If text is representational of thoughts, so are maps! Neo-literates (or even non-literates) who may lack confidence in their own ability to express their thoughts in text form, may well gain self-confidence through non-text but visualisable forms of expression, and an appreciation for the strengths and limitations of both.

Reading Matter for Early Literates

An isolated example of an effort to produce literature for neo-literates by a national institution comes to us from Sushama Merh-Ashraf. She unearthed a fascinating and little-known Gujarati drama from the colonial period for translation into Hindi literature for neo-literates. The drama itself is set in the context of a library where literacy classes are also held. The importance of the library as a community centre is thus established. Based on the Hindi translation, a Bengali version now exists. A practically unlimited supply of stories exists in every Indian language and subculture. Translations across languages can further enhance the existing richness. If there is anything that arrests the availability of literature for neo-literates, it is a commitment at the highest levels of decision making.

That which is not being achieved by national bodies on a scale that is required, is being attempted in modest but very effective ways by voluntary organisations. PITARA and Ujjas are two innovative efforts. Shalini Joshi recounts the story of PITARA, a 'simple but not simplistic' bi-monthly magazine in Hindi, expressly published for early literates. Informed by a feminist perspective, the articles provoke thinking around a range of issues, especially those that touch upon disadvantage and equity. A conscious effort is made to represent these issues in non-prescriptive and interesting ways. Entertainment, as a goal for neo-literates, finds a rare mention in this case. PITARA's struggles with the magazine's format, distribution and pricing convey that achieving sustainability in publications for early literates is by no means a straight-forward process. Where PITARA is centrally produced by a concerned group of urbanites, the next case provides a sharp contrast.

Preeti Soni's case on Ujjas breaks the boundaries of rural publishing. Ujjas is a Gujarati-Kutchi language newsletter, at present *entirely* created by rural women in Kutch. It is the voice of rural women's collectives, focusing on women's empowerment issues and activities undertaken by the collectives. The circulation of Ujjas is primarily among collective members but with time it has also been reaching key government officials. In rural publishing, Ujjas is indeed rare. It has not been created with the idea of specifically targeting partially literate people, although it is very cognisant that its readership is mostly neo- and even non-literate. Still evolving into newer forms, Ujjas continues to strengthen the women's collective movement in Kutch, at the same time contributing to literacy incidentally.

Promotion of Reading Culture and Publishing for Rural Areas

Most of the cases included in this book promote a reading culture. However, P. K. Sasidharan and S. Madasamy's experiences see reading culture as a pre-requisite for reading. Otherwise, there is no guarantee that the reading matter that is made available to neo-literates, for example, through libraries or other initiatives, will actually be read. The authors describe a variety of group read-aloud techniques that were used effectively to promote a reading culture and help launch a library movement. They break the deeply entrenched myth that one has to first turn a non-literate into a neo-literate before introducing books. Implied in their arguments is the contention that the TLC and PL phases must be merged. Prompted by the monotony of literacy primers, the second part of their case describes the development of innovative workbooks for PL, based on thought-provoking issues rooted in people's experience. The workbooks were designed to foster group discussion. Sasidharan and Madasamy draw attention to the fact that despite a plethora of literacy campaigns, relatively little effort has gone into the creation of texts for neo-literates.

Is there a demand for books in rural areas? Michael Norton's experience in Andhra Pradesh State posits that, indeed, there is a sizeable demand for appropriate and affordable books. However, the distribution network for rural book selling is poor or non-existent. Selling of books by rural agents on bicycles village to village has potential. In particular, the success of one such agent demonstrated that there is demand for books and it is possible to earn a decent commission. Yet, this optimism is tempered by the fact that the experience has not been repeated by many other book agents. Thus, there is a strong need for research and experimentation to understand distribution networks that work. Michael Norton offers several valuable suggestions to promote a reading culture, including some for the promotion of libraries and librarianship.

Libraries and Literacy

Sarah Kamala's contribution historically traces the development of the library movement from its birth in Andhra Pradesh to other parts of India. She contrasts the pre-independence commitment of policy to post-independence neglect and argues that centralised acquisition and management processes worked to the detriment of libraries. Her main purpose, however, is to suggest practical ways to revive the village library movement in rural areas.

In urban slums, Rajani Paranjpe speaks of the challenges of taking books to people's 'doorstep' in the slums of Mumbai and Pune. An understanding of distribution methods that worked with some measure of success emerged only after several experiments and a great deal of persistence. The learnings she offers relate to the need for targeting a library's readership, holding competitions and events around book reading, linking libraries to schools, the popularity of study centres, and other library-linked activities. Besides reiterating the shortage of books for children and neo-literates, she suggests that writing for them needs considerable simplification, the use of everyday vocabulary and the appropriate font and design considerations. Good local language dictionaries are found to be in short supply. A creative method is mentioned to keep track of the difficult vocabulary encountered by children in books. From a sustainability perspective, readers are generally reluctant to pay for reading and raising resources for the maintenance and acquisition of books is a concern.

The theme of libraries in slums continues in Saswati Roy's case from Kolkata. School drop-outs and neo-literates are the target of these libraries. Training of librarians, creation of library committees, book collections (donations), strengthening of the bond between the librarian and the community, awards and competitions for members, librarians and committee members, were included in the strategies used to promote the libraries. The success of these libraries is reflected in the rising membership and collections from it. Saswati Roy suggests that well-functioning libraries in urban slums can expect to charge Rs 2–3 per month as membership fees. The unavailability of books for neo-literates is reiterated.

Media and Literacy

The media's potential in lifelong literacy is argued by us (Brij Kothari, Joe Takeda, Ashok Joshi and Avinash Pandey). Same Language Subtitling (SLS) is proposed as a simple but effective way to keep neo-literates engaged in literacy practices through everyday television entertainment. The motivational constraint for neo-literates is overcome by integrating reading practice into song programmes. Reading, thus, becomes an automatic and enjoyable process. The strength of this idea is that it creates reading transactions on a mass scale at a fractional cost. The experimental study described found support for reading skill improvement through SLS.

D. Janardhana Reddy evaluates the effectiveness of a weekly newspaper for neo-literates that had been in existence for six years. It was started by the ZSS in Chittoor district of Andhra Pradesh at the beginning of the PL phase. Awareness of the newspaper among the neo-literate sample was high. Almost half the respondents even read the paper. Lack of time, poor circulation and inability to read were the primary reasons for not reading. Interestingly, over 60 per cent people needed 2–3 days to read the paper. Readers tended to attribute skill improvement and learning due to the newspaper. Suggestions relating to the format of newspapers are offered. The important role of newspapers for lifelong literacy is supported.

Bridging People's Math and Formal Numeracy

The only contribution that deals very directly with numeracy is Anita Rampal's chapter. She critiques the teaching of numeracy in adult literacy classes, arguing that it often imposes mindlessness approach with adequate care to relate them to people's lives. Going beyond a critique, she discusses several innovative strategies her group has experimented with. The hallmark of these strategies is that they consciously build upon what adults already know and do in everyday life while meeting their 'numerical' needs.

Innovation and creativity are the engines of progress. It will be clear from this book that innovations, although sparks at one level, do not easily turn into a blaze. If the fire still burns after the spark, it is because of the persistence and passion of the innovator. For practitioners of lifelong literacy, the book may provide new directions for thinking about their own projects. Academics and researchers will find in this book a variety of experiences deeply embedded in practice and providing a fertile ground for 'Grounded Theory' building. Policy makers, it is hoped, will not only detect the sparks in this collection of cases but also be moved to devise systems to tap these and other sparks in this not too small country. Most importantly, all these ideas come to naught if the multitude of non-literates and early literates do not at the end of the day feel that literacy has expanded their freedom.

References

Abadzi, Helen (1994). *What We Know about the Acquisition of Adult Literacy*, World Bank Discussion Paper 245. Washington, D.C.: World Bank.

Athreya, Venkatesh B. and **Sheela Rani Chunkath** (1996). *Literacy and Empowerment.* New Delhi: Sage Publications.

Basu, Kaushik and **James E. Foster** (1998). *On Measuring Literacy,* Policy Research Working Paper 1997. Washington, D.C.: World Bank.

Basu, Kaushik, Ambar Narayan and **Martin Ravallion** (1999). *Is Knowledge Shared within Households,* Policy Research Working Paper 2261. Washington, D.C.: World Bank.

Bordia, Anil and **Anita Kaul** (1992). 'Literacy Efforts in India', *Annals of the American Academy of Political and Social Science,* 520: 151–62.

Bradley, L. and **P.E. Bryant** (1983). 'Categorizing Sounds and Learning to Read— A Causal Connection', *Nature,* 301: 419–21.

Chatterjee, Bhaskar (1996). 'Strategies for Post Literacy in the Next Decade', *Indian Journal of Adult Education,* 57(1): 27–45.

Cipielewsky, Jim and **Keith E. Stanovich** (1992). 'Predicting Growth in Reading Ability from Children's Exposure to Print', *Journal of Experimental Child Psychology,* 54: 74–89.

Copeland, Kathleen, Pamela Windsor and **Jean Osborn** (1994). 'Phonemic Awareness: A Consideration of Research.' In Fran Lehr and Jean Osborn (eds),

Reading, Language, and Literacy: Instruction for the Twenty-First Century, pp. 25–44. Hillsdale, New Jersey: Lawrence Erlbaum Associates.

Cunningham, Anne E. and **Keith E. Stanovich** (1991). 'Tracking the Unique Effects of Print Exposure in Children: Associations with Vocabulary, General Knowledge, and Spelling', *Journal of Educational Psychology,* 83(2): 264–74.

Drèze, Jean and **Amartya Sen** (1995). *India: Economic Development and Social Opportunity.* Delhi: Oxford University Press.

Drèze, Jean and **Jackie Loh** (1995). 'Literacy in India and China', *Economic and Political Weekly,* 11 November: 2868–78.

Elley, Warwick B. (2000). 'The Potential of Book Floods for Raising Literacy Levels', *International Review of Education,* 46(3/4): 233–55.

Freire, Paulo and **Donald Macedo** (1987). *Literacy: Reading the Word and the World,* South Hadley, MA: Bergin and Garvey.

Gfeller, Elisabeth (1997). 'Why Should I Learn to Read? Motivations for Literacy Acquisition in a Rural Education Programme', *International Journal of Educational Development,* 17(1): 101–12.

Gough, Philip B., Wesley A. Hoover and **Cynthia L. Peterson** (1996). 'Some Observations on a Simple View of Reading.' In Cesare Cornoldi and Jane Oakhill (eds), *Reading Comprehension Difficulties: Processes and Intervention,* pp. 1–13. Mahwah, New Jersey: Lawrence Erlbaum Associates.

Joseph, P.J. (1996). 'The Total Literacy Project of Ernakulam: An Epoch-making Experiment in India', *Convergence,* 29(1): 10–19.

Kerr, Bonnie M. and **Jana M. Mason** (1994). 'Awakening Literacy Through Interactive Story Reading.' In Fran Lehr and Jean Osborn (eds), *Reading, Language, and Literacy: Instruction for the Twenty-First Century,* pp. 133–48. Hillsdale, New Jersey: Lawrence Erlbaum Associates.

Kothari, Brij (2000). 'Same Language Subtitling on Indian Television: Harnessing the Power of Popular Culture for Literacy.' In Karin Wilkins (ed.), *Redeveloping Communication for Social Change: Theory, Practice and Power,* pp. 135–46. New York: Rowman & Littlefield.

Kothari, Brij, Amita Chudgar and **Avinash Pandey** (2001). 'Feasibility Study of Multipurpose Community Telecentres in Rajkot, with a Focus on Education.' Commissioned by UNESCO, New Delhi. Indian Institute of Management, Ahmedabad. Unpublished report.

Kothari, Brij, P.G. Vijaya Sherry Chand and **Rajeev Sharma** (1999). 'When Literacy Campaigns Gave Birth to a Women's Movement', *Convergence,* 32(1–4): 94–106.

Leseman, Paul P.M. and **Peter F. de Jong** (1998). 'Home Literacy: Opportunity, Instruction, Cooperation and Social-Emotional Quality Predicting Early Reading Achievement', *Reading Research Quarterly,* 33(3): 294–318.

Lewkowicz, Nancy K. (1980). 'Phonemic Awareness Training: What to Teach and How to Teach it', *Journal of Educational Psychology,* 72(5): 686–700.

Liddell, Christine (1998). 'Conceptualising "Childhood" in Developing Countries', *Psychology and Developing Societies,* 10(1): 35–53.

Matthew, A. (1998). 'Sustaining Literacy in a Non-literacy Milieu: PLC Experiences Warrant Change in Policy and Perception', *Indian Journal of Adult Education,* 59(1): 16–31.

McLaughlin, Milbrey Wallin (1987). 'Learning from Experience: Lessons from Policy Implementation', *Educational Evaluation and Policy Analysis*, 9(2): 171–78.

Mishra, Renuka (1994). 'Concretizing Concepts: Continuing Education Strategies for Women', *Convergence*, 27(2–3): 126–35.

National Literacy Mission (1994a). *Annual Report 1993–94: Literacy and Post-literacy Campaigns in India.* New Delhi: Directorate of Adult Education.

——— (1994b). *Report of the Expert Group: Evaluation of Literacy Campaign in India.* New Delhi: Directorate of Adult Education.

——— (2000). *Literacy Rates: An Analysis Based on the NSSO Survey 1998.* New Delhi: Directorate of Adult Education. Also available at: <http://www.infoindia.net/nlm/nsso.htm>.

Organisation for Economic Co-operation and Development (2000). *Literacy in the Information Age: Final Report of the International Adult Literacy Survey.* Paris: OECD and Canada: Ministry of Industry.

PROBE (1999). *Public Report on Basic Education in India.* Delhi: Oxford University Press.

Rogers, Alan (1999). 'Improving the Quality of Adult Literacy, Programmes in Developing Countries: The "Real Literacies" Approach', *International Journal of Educational Development*, 19: 219–34.

Roy, Prodipto and **J.M. Kapoor** (1975). *The Retention of Literacy.* Delhi: The Macmillan Company.

Semali, Ladislaus M. (1993). 'The Communication Media in Postliteracy Education: New Dimensions of Literacy', *International Review of Education*, 39(3): 193–206.

Sen, Amartya (1999). *Development as Freedom.* New York: Anchor Books.

Snider, Vicki E. (1995). 'A Primer on Phonemic Awareness: What It Is, Why It's Important, and How to Teach It', *School Psychology Review*, 24(3): 443–55.

Stanovich, Keith E. and **Anne E. Cunningham** (1993). 'Where Does Knowledge Come From? Specific Associations Between Print Exposure and Information Acquisition', *Journal of Educational Psychology*, 85(2): 211–29.

Stromquist, Nelly P. (1997). *Literacy for Citizenship: Gender and Grassroots Dynamics in Brazil.* New York: SUNY press.

UNDP (2001). *Human Development Report.* New York: Oxford University Press.

Vijaya Sherry Chand, P.G., Rajeev Sharma, Brij Kothari, Parvinder Gupta and **Amarlal H. Kalro** (1998). 'A Review of Gender Issues in the Shiksha Karmi Project and an Assessment of the *Prehar Pathshalas.*' Commissioned by SIDA, Sweden. Indian Institute of Management, Ahmedabad. Unpublished report.

Warwick, Donald P., Fernando Reimers and **Noel McGinn** (1992). 'The Implementation of Educational Innovations: Lessons From Pakistan', *International Journal of Educational Development*, 12(4): 297–307.

Yopp, Hallie Kay (1992). 'Developing Phonemic Awareness in Young Children', *The Reading Teacher*, 45(9): 696–703.

Yopp, Hallie Kay and **Ruth Helen Yopp** (2000). 'Supporting Phonemic Awareness Development in the Classroom', *The Reading Teacher*, 54(2): 130–43.

PART II

EMPOWERMENT AND LITERACY

Chapter Two

Van Dhan:[1]
Literacy in Support of
Livelihoods in Bastar

K.S. Ram

Where is the Thirst for Literacy?

Literacy matters because life matters. This may sound like a platitude, but this basic truth is commonly overlooked by literacy programmes. Notwithstanding the considerable autonomy given to the Zilla Saksharta Samiti,[2] the literacy drive under it has tended to remain in government hands. Like most government-run programmes, this programme too has often become officer-driven and target-oriented. Under these influences, literacy is seen in isolation, becoming an end in itself. Block-level officials of the government are even known to pressurise people to become

---

1. Van Dhan can be translated as 'Wealth of the Forests'.
2. District literacy committee.

literate. Literacy is sought to be enforced, and this only proves to be counter-productive. A few people may become literate under such an approach, however, the risk of their sliding back into illiteracy remains a constant fear among the implementers of these programmes.

For sustainable literacy, it is not just important but critical that literacy become a felt-need—felt, that is, by the non-literates and not the implementers of programmes. The only guarantee for a literacy programme to succeed is when it is linked to economic activities. The programme should result in increased earnings and not just relate to occasional requirements like writing applications to the Tahsildar or other officials on one's own (which, in any case, people are able to do with the help of others). Until an integration of literacy with economic activity is established, the problem of neo-literates sliding back into illiteracy shall continue to be a concern. Literacy as an ornament cannot interest people, who are targets of literacy programmes, for too long. It will sustain and thrive if it is found to be applicable to everyday work for better income. The literacy worker will have to strive for an integrated socio-economic (more economic than socio) uplift of his/her target population.

Much of the failure of the literacy effort is akin to making unwilling horses drink water. One can force water down the horse's mouth but the possibility of its spitting it out remains. This is the threat of back-slide in the literacy programme, a threat which does not exist in the case of neo-literates who have become alive to the disadvantage (economic disadvantage, in particular) that illiteracy was causing them. The thirsty horses, so to speak! They welcome literacy programmes and work hard to become literate. Once the skills are acquired, literacy becomes a permanent part of their personality and life. The risk of their sliding back into illiteracy does not exist.

Post-literacy in Bastar

If there is a task for the post-literacy phase, it represents a certain failure of the initial literacy phase. If literacy programmes had linked literacy with livelihoods from the start, there would have been no need for a post-literacy programme. This was the line of thought we adopted in Bastar district of Madhya Pradesh (presently in Chhattisgarh state after the recent division of MP). The Total Literacy Campaign was launched here in 1995. Officially, 60,557 people were made literate. However, follow-up checking suggested that many were on the slide to illiteracy.

Many others had simply been labelled as having 'failed'. A new thrust was therefore planned in December 1998.

Our 'target group'—neo-literates, partial literates as well as non-literates—consisted of mostly adivasi forest dwellers. Having experienced a life of extreme poverty for years, cynicism was writ large on their faces, especially with regard to development programmes. Talking to them of literacy sounded like a joke. In fact they had coined a derogatory name for the literacy campaign, calling it *dokra padhayi* (literally, 'old person's schooling,' implying, an education for idle engagement with no practical application), a mention invariably followed by laughter. What was worse, the elders looked down upon all formal education as undesirable. Children who went to school were good for nothing, they averred. The 'educated' youth (X failed, mostly) had long stopped doing the traditional jobs at home, having 'risen above it all'. These young people waited in vain for a 'government job'. And while they waited, they whiled away their time dressing up and not doing much. This led many elders to feel that education is a corrupting acquisition! In this context, promoting literacy seemed futile. The need was to raise awareness of the importance of education. A demand and an urgency had to be created first. So we stopped emphasising literacy.

Awareness-raising for Van Dhan in Bastar

While the literacy team was thinking along these lines and brainstorming on ways to give a practical shape to the post-literacy objective of sustaining the gains from the earlier phase, a different programme was brewing in the district. This related to the procurement of Minor Forest Produce (MFP) in Bastar. We realised that the target group of the literacy (and post-literacy) programme was almost entirely among the tribal population engaged in the collection of MFP. They collected MFP from the forests all through the week and brought these in headloads to weekly roadside markets known locally as *haat bazaars*. Here the agents of the merchants—known locally as *koochiyas*—would buy these produces from the tribals for a trifle. This seemingly inconsequential business was not taken seriously by government authorities responsible for tribal development. Its economics were not studied closely.

One day the collector of Bastar witnessed a curious exchange. A sack of rough salt, marked 'unfit for human consumption' was being exchanged for an equal measure of precious oilseeds. When he learnt this was a common local practice, he decided to undertake some research into this trade. It was then found that in Bastar alone, MFP and the tribals' agro-produces represent a business of a whopping Rs 500 crore annually.[3] Seventy-five per cent of this business is controlled by just a dozen merchants operating through a network of around 500 *koochiyas*. Ninety-eight per cent of MFP and tribals' agro-produces are removed from the district in raw, unprocessed form. The tribals—owners of the produce—received less than 20 per cent of the terminal price. The balance 80 per cent was cornered by middlemen and merchants. The government had legislated the Provisions of Panchayats, Extension to Scheduled Areas, Act (PESA) in 1996 granting ownership rights over MFP to the tribals, but they were unaware of it. Here, there was scope for a major intervention that could result in substantial gains for the tribals. Illiteracy facilitated their exploitation. The ZSS clearly saw a task ahead of itself. Convergence of the literacy and MFP programmes was made easier by the fact that the district collector was in charge of both the ZSS and the new intervention in MFP that was being planned.

An intense programme of village-level meetings was planned. An estimated 1,000 meetings were held in one year! The tribals were informed of the pattern of MFP trade as it existed. They knew the *koochiyas* were doing brisk business but the magnitude of the siphoning was not understood well. The extent of exploitation was not always apparent to the tribals. Hence, special presentations and write-ups were prepared to raise

3. US$ 106 million.

the general awareness of the exploitative trade practices by the *koochiyas* (Box 2.1).[4]

Box 2.1: How big can small things be?!

When somebody tilts the balance and weighs 1.25 kg of your tamarind as 1 kg, you might think, *It's a small matter, why fight for that...*
Out of a gross weight of 5 kg, when somebody deducts 1 kg for the weight of an empty basket that weighs 250 gm, you might think, *It's a small matter, why fight for that...*
When somebody prices your tamarind at Rs 6 per kg against a fair price of Rs 6.25 per kg, you might think, *It's a small matter, why fight for that...*
When somebody calculates the price of 5 kg of tamarind priced at Rs 6 per kg as $5 \times 6 = 25$, and gives you Rs 25, you would not know the mischief and would not strive to know, thinking, *It's a small matter, why fight for that...*
But do you know the net result of these small matters? Can you guess how much has been looted? 52 per cent! Which means, if, at the end of the day, two trucks of tamarind have been transported out of your village, you have been paid for only one truck. One truckload of tamarind is a free-gift from you because you feel the matter involved is small and does not merit any attention.
Unless you become literate, can you guard yourself against such exploitation? If you do not send your child to school everyday, can she/he be safe from such exploitation when she/he grows up? Think it over. *Zara Sochiye!*

Data on several malpractices were gathered from the tribals themselves. For example, a flat deduction of 1 kg was made for the weight of an empty basket that weighs only 250 gm. The already suspect scales would be tilted to favour the *koochiya*. Unfair allowances were made against moisture loss. It was shown that these 'petty' cuts aggregated to an astonishing 50 per cent! To drive the point home, the people were asked to assess the number of trucks with tamarind that leave the market at the end of one *haat*. They would say something like 'two'. They were then told that this meant that the village had received payment from the *koochiyas* for only one truck. One truck had been robbed away! Such simple and comprehensible ways of explaining the situation helped

---

4. English version of a piece originally distributed in Hindi. It is one of a series of items under *Zara Sochiye* (think it over) for raising general awareness.

to stir people at the gatherings. People were then urged to imagine what this meant when *bazaar* after *bazaar*, season after season, truckloads were leaving with their produce but they were being paid for only half of those. A new awareness regarding the exploitation began to dawn with a perceptible urge to do something about it.

People were then informed of the new law granting them ownership rights over MFP and the power to manage their *haat*. In due course, they were advised to form self-help groups (SHGs) to eliminate the *koochiyas* and to deal in MFP themselves, thus guaranteeing fair trade terms. Dr V. Kurien of the Institute of Rural Management (IRMA) extended his expertise in guiding us. The Tribal Co-operative Marketing Federation of India, Ltd (TRIFED), a body promoted by the Ministry for Social Justice and Empowerment, was activated to buy from the SHGs the MFP procured by them.[5] TRIFED advanced money to the SHGs to operate in the market. *Koochiya*, if it was not already so, became a word synonymous with swindling and exploitation. SHGs mushroomed in the district. A movement of sorts gained currency as Imli Andolan (tamarind movement), owing its name to the fact that tamarind, an important produce of Bastar (35,000 TPA), was in season when the movement was growing. *Imli* later became a symbol for all tribal produces.

With the growing movement, the need for book-keeping and literacy skills emerged. In a manner of speaking, the Imli Andolan accorded respectability to the literacy mission in the district and Saksharta became an accepted programme. This acceptance was initially more in principle than in practice. However, such emotive acceptance represents a significant ice-breaking. It was soon obvious that the Imli Andolan was not an isolated intervention in trade. Between January and April 1999, literacy, Women's Thrift and Micro-credit SHGs, and Joint Forest Management converged into an omnibus of self-help development programmes.

In May 1999, at the instance of the Chief Minister (CM) of Madhya Pradesh (MP), Mr Digvijay Singh, a national seminar was organised at Jagdalpur.[6] In addition to the CMs of MP and Orissa, senior government officers including the chief secretary, principal secretaries, NGOs and subject experts from related fields participated in the deliberations. The experts unanimously applauded the central role given to literacy in the programme. Following the seminar, the Andolan was upgraded into a formal programme called Van Dhan.

---

5. TRIFED is presently under the new Ministry for Tribal Affairs.
6. Mr Digvijay Singh evinced a very keen interest in the Andolan and strongly supported it by declaring it a model for other tribal districts in the state.

Under this programme, the SHGs in the villages, promoted by the respective gram sabhas (in exercise of powers vested in them under PESA), act as procuring agents of TRIFED. TRIFED advances them money for this purpose,[7] which they use to buy the MFP flowing into the *bazaars* from the villagers. The villagers gain through fair trade terms. This, by itself, has helped people double their income. The SHG members receive a commission from TRIFED for the service, which constitutes their income. Around 8,000 tribals, mostly neo and partial literates, have found self-employment as SHG members. More employment opportunities are expected to be created in Phase II, where the emphasis is on value-addition activities.

Standard bye-laws were prepared for the SHGs. In return for a new source of income made available to them, they are expected to do something for their village. The most important of these relates to the spread of literacy. The SHG members engage in literacy classes themselves or help to organise them. The members also extend logistical support to literacy classes, e.g., providing kerosene for the lamps. The monetary value of the SHGs' support may be insignificant but, their support is very significant in terms of influencing the attitudes and opinions of fellow villagers towards literacy and education. If they fail to contribute to their village, they face the risk of losing their membership in the SHG, which implies a loss of their source of income.

Around 1,000 SHGs for MFP procurement and an equal number of Women's Thrift and Micro-credit SHGs have been formed in Bastar. The Government of MP has now overhauled its strategy for literacy and linked it to economic activities under the new programme called Padhana-Badhana Andolan. In Bastar this programme has received special acceptance. The basic points of the new approach are:

- *Linking literacy to an economic activity*: A literacy programme cannot be sustained in isolation. It must be linked to economic gains since literacy programmes in India concern the poorest segments of society. Literacy for its own sake is meaningless and, in all likelihood, will not be accepted by the people.
- *The Self-help group approach*: The rationale behind the SHG is that individuals are often found shying away from literacy because they feel there is something childish about it. A group helps them to overcome this shyness more easily. Furthermore, the SHG involves 'self-help', thus giving impetus to the process of learning.

7. Around US$ 32,000 was advanced, in all. Later, the SHGs were given bank loans under a Special Swarnjayanti Gram Swarozgar Yojana (SGSY) of the Ministry of Rural Development.

- *Self-selection of tutor*: Under the scheme, the tutor (*guruji*) is not imposed; the group selects its own *guruji*. This implies better acceptance, rapport, motivation and accountability on both sides.
- *Honorarium linked to success*: There is a token *guru dakshina* (honorarium) of Rs 100 per student, payable when the student becomes literate.
- *Calendar*: The programme operates according to a set calendar. The calendar relates to the teaching of the IPCL, Parts 1–3 books as well as tests relating to these. This lends discipline to the programme.

In Bastar, some additional points of strategy were practiced. These included:

- *Emphasis on writing*: Writing was emphasised from day one onwards. The ability to write thrills the non-literate person and is a great motivator for continued learning. The issue of neo-literates sliding back into illiteracy relates largely to their ceasing to write, not so much as ceasing to read. This is because literacy essentially is the assimilation of calligraphic symbols in isolation (as alphabet) and in combination (as words and sentences). Such assimilation through regular practice shifts in the course of time to the reflex-levels of our mind. This calls for regular exercise in the form of reading and writing. Writing in comparison to reading is more efficacious in this regard. Any strategy for lifelong literacy must emphasise regular writing. Regular reading will then take care of itself.
- *Group discussions*: Group discussion was an integral part of the class. Discussions relate to topics of local and current interest. The rationale behind this is that awareness is more important than mere literacy, and in fact, helps to inspire literacy. This leads to self-motivation.

Applied Literacy as a Strategy for Post-literacy

The neo-literate members of the Van Dhan SHGs have a hands-on post-literacy exercise every day, which is called applied literacy. SHG members have to regularly maintain simple records. First among these is a *purchi* (procurement slip). Every SHG is required to give to every villager bringing his/her produce for sale a *purchi* which carries the name of the villager, item brought, quantity, rate applied and the amount paid. The *purchi* register has a perforated original and a bound carbon copy. This provides the neo-literates a highly responsible opportunity to apply their

Literacy by Night in Bastar's Van Dhan

literacy and numeracy skills. Apart from the *purchi* register, there is a daily cash scroll register and a weekly abstract statement that the SHG submits to the CEO Janpad to obtain further cash for the following week. The *paridan purchi* (goods receipt), which TRIFED gives to the SHG, as also frequent circulars from the district, including a newsletter in Hindi called *Naya Bastar*, further engage the neo-literates.

Bastar's applied literacy approach has thus helped subsume literacy into a holistic effort at empowerment and development. It has, in this process, obliterated the technical distinctions between literacy and post-literacy learning. These merge into a continuous process of empowerment through the application of acquired skills. If a person feels empowered—socially and economically—through literacy, there can never be any fear of his/her sliding back into illiteracy. This is the guiding principle of the Bastar Approach and the gist of our experience.

Concluding Remarks

Koochiya Backlash

The *koochiyas* as well as their principals were naturally not very happy about the new initiative. Their reaction can be judged by the numerous headlines and stories planted in newspapers, such as: 'Undeclared Ban on the Fundamental Right to Trade', 'Hitler-shahi Unleased' and even, 'New Conspiracy to Exploit the Poor Tribals of Bastar'. Several memoranda were also sent to the government; there were *bandhs* (closure of all business activities); some tried to sow dissent among members of the apex committee guiding the programme; there was vandalism by hired hooligans in the collector's office; and demands to transfer the collector were floated as 'public' demands. The administration decided not to get provoked into doing something rash since this could snowball into a 'law and order' issue, distracting everybody's attention from the basic agenda. As a counter-offensive, an investigation was launched into the commercial tax evasion of leading traders and unearthing of large-scale irregularities, which had a good effect. Simultaneously, interactive sessions were organised in the rotary club, local colleges and tribal hostels. As public opinion began to form in favour of Van Dhan, those who stood to lose from it changed their strategy. There were a spate of questions in the legislative assembly. A writ petition was filed in the high court. The standing committee of Lok Sabha on labour and welfare visited Bastar for a field study and ended up recommending replication of the programme in all scheduled areas of the country!

Applying Literacy to Women's Micro-Credit SHGs

Around 3,000 (July 2001) SHGs consisting of women were formed for micro-savings and credit. Each SHG had about 20 members. Deposit mobilisation was very impressive—over Rs 30 lakh[8] was mobilised. The SHGs maintain a ledger and a register and also issue receipts for the money received. The credit aspect is yet to pick up. Literacy will be put to challenging applications when the SHGs start granting loans and will be required to compute the interest and undertake more involved book-keeping.

8. US$ 65,000.

Cascading Effect of Literacy Skills

Are there signs of literacy skills acquired in one domain extending to other contexts? It is perhaps too early to discuss this aspect in Bastar. However, it may be mentioned that literacy skills are part of the awareness and empowerment generated among neo-literates. Van Dhan in Bastar has had a perceptible and positive impact on forest protection and development. Backyard forestry has gone up very sharply. Bastar district was awarded the Vrikshamitra (friend of trees) award in January 2001 by the Ministry for Forests and Environment. The Government of India has chose Bastar for a new integrated horticulture development project. Another project for the plantation of *karanji*, a Tree-Borne Oil-seed (TBO), was also sanctioned through the tribal SHGs. Buoyed by these developments, a new thirst for progress is visible. The tribals have grasped the 'cash-value' of education and literacy.

To conclude, around 125,000 persons enrolled in literacy SHGs in Bastar, out of which around 83,000 persons emerged successful. Bastar recorded the most impressive growth in women's literacy in the state, according to the 2001 Census data. The incentive for those who emerge successful—in terms of the 3Rs—is that Phase II of Van Dhan is expected to create around 100,000 new job opportunities for self-help through the value addition activities for Non Timber Forest Produce (NTFP). This activity is still in its infancy, and for various reasons, is yet to take off in a big way. We earnestly hope that we shall never need any special post-literacy programme to sustain literacy skills.

CHAPTER THREE

Taleem Se Taqat: Educating Adolescent Girls in Delhi Slums— The Ankur Experience

Jaya Shrivastava

This chapter describes an educational initiative undertaken with adolescent girls living in the slums of Delhi, by Ankur, a non-governmental organisation. The initiative was aimed at building on certain basic literacy skills in order to move towards 'empowerment' of the learners. Though it was not specifically designed as a post-literacy activity, the lessons learned are applicable to any initiative that seeks to sustain basic literacy skills. The paper is based on organisational records maintained by various people.

Introduction

The programme for adolescent girls aged 13 to 19, the *Yuvati Karyakram*, was initiated in the early 1990s in six *bastis* of Delhi where Ankur was active: Jama Masjid, Anna Nagar, Gautam Puri, J.P. Basti, Nandnagari and Dakshinpuri. Some of the girls who joined the programme were school-pushouts; most had never been to school. They came from poor families. The male members were petty hawkers, vendors, construction labourers, rickshaw pullers, tailors, drivers, jewellery makers, embroidery workers, and part-time labourers. Women and girls were involved in pin-making, collar button-sewing, embroidery, *bindi*-pasting, paper box-making, and goat-rearing. Socially and religiously they belonged to different groups. Though those from Jama Masjid, J.P. Basti and Nandnagari were predominantly Muslims, within themselves there were cultural differences and differences of customs and language. Most people in J.P. Basti and Nandnagari were from Uttar Pradesh; some were from Rajasthan and Bihar. Gautampuri and Dakshinpuri had families from Rajasthan, Bihar, Haryana and Uttar Pradesh. People from Garhwal (Uttar Pradesh), Bihar, West Uttar Pradesh, Tamil Nadu and the Punjab lived in Anna Nagar.

Goals and Objectives

To Ankur, empowerment means the growing ability of learners to:

- learn and teach, listen and speak, express and articulate;
- acquire the skills of literacy and creative craft;
- question and search for answers where there are no easy answers;
- develop self-confidence and self-esteem;
- identify, and understand, familial and social struggles;
- realise that women everywhere face oppression in patriarchal society;
- become socially aware, analyse issues and intervene.

Ankur gives equal weightage to a woman's growth as a person and her role as a member of a group or *samooh*. Capacity-building as a *samooh-sadasya* means developing a caring attitude towards others, engaging in dialogue, having mutual respect and trust, participating in different activities and action programmes, sharing responsibilities within the group, searching for solutions together, taking collective decisions and generating a feeling of belongingness to the group.

Unfolding of the Programme

Structure

The Centres

The centres, based in the *bastis*, are the nucleus of the programme. They are run for three to four hours every day for four days in a week. Timings and places are decided according to the convenience of the learner-participants. The girls come to the centre for a period of one to two years. Two teachers, one for literacy and one for craft, work as a team with a group of 18 to 20 girls.

Project and Area Teams

A 'project team' consists of 12 teachers, 5 co-ordinators and a director. The 'area teams' are significant units in the chain of decentralised implementation. They consist of the area co-ordinator and all the teachers of a specific area, including those working with children and women. Daily planning and monitoring is done in this peer group.

Personnel

The co-ordinators have graduate or post-graduate degrees in social work or education. Two of the teachers are graduates; most have studied up to high school, and a few have finished middle or elementary school. All of them come from a socio-economic background similar to that of the learners. They have been with the organisation for 6 to 12 years.

Training of Teachers

Teachers in Ankur are not only teaching in the centres, they are also community workers and active participants in the evolution of the organisation and in the development of a holistic, feminist perspective that is central to the programme. They themselves went through a process of learning first so as to be able to address the demands of the programme as well as to deal with contradictions in their own lives. Their learning was facilitated through monthly and fortnightly meetings, individual inputs from the director or co-ordinators, individual or group studies, exposure to other organisations, participation in seminars, conferences, rallies and demonstrations, and structured workshops of two to eight days on specific issues. The themes covered included:

- Role of voluntary agencies, different organisational structures and roles.
- Democratic functioning, freedom and responsibility, and personal and professional life.
- Recording, reporting, planning, evaluation, curriculum, and creative methods of using activities for teaching.
- Functional literacy and education for social change, education policy and systems, principles of learning language and numbers, and choosing books.
- Evolving a primer, reviewing primers, and generating supplementary material.
- History of the women's movement, patriarchy, sexuality, *sati*—a historical context, women and law, women and religion, women and politics, and child marriage.
- Housing rights, religion and communalism, politics of health, new economic policy, large dams, the Bhopal gas tragedy, alcoholism, AIDS and HIV, and homosexuality.

The Learning Process

Centre

In the centre, girls are given the space they need. Individual and group confidentiality is respected. The pace of learning of every individual is taken care of. Co-operation rather than competitiveness, is the guiding principle.

Community

Regular interactions with families, sharing their joys and sorrows, and sharing Ankur's concerns and programmes, have helped build relationships. The learning, the problems, the dreams and the journeys of the girls have been regularly shared with their mothers through individual interactions and monthly 'meetings of mothers'.

Curriculum

Some of the salient features of Ankur's curriculum are:

- A learner-centred approach that ensures curriculum development according to age, interests, experiences, needs and pace of the learners.
- Subjects include language, arithmetic, general knowledge, and issues like gender, sexuality, patriarchy, communalism, housing rights and child labour.

- The basic concepts related to learning a language follow the 'experience → language' methodology, the word to letter approach, and the use of words with vowels right from the beginning.
- The curriculum is partly written and predetermined. New themes get incorporated as and when opportunities present themselves, for instance, 'plague', 'cholera' or 'eviction'.
- Creative role of the teachers in the development of the curriculum is very crucial. Experiences emerging during implementation become sources for material like newsletters, handbills, posters and booklets. The learners' articulations contribute to these in a significant way.
- Easily available—and waste—material, like pebbles, utensils, cardboard, matchboxes, are used for creating teaching aids.
- Physical and mental games, theatre, songs (be it folk or *filmi*, feminist or popular), pictures, activity sheets, questions, posters, newspaper clippings, and poems and stories—of their own lives, or women-oriented and open-ended stories—are important.

Approach to Literacy

The method is as important as the medium. Recognition of letters is coupled with discussions related to words. For instance, the word *chadar* (sheet) is used not only to create more words but also to generate discussions on the various dimensions of what the word stands for, like *burqa*, *ghoonghat* and *purdah*. *Ghar* (house) is used for recognition of letters, creation of new words and for discussions through questions like, 'How many types of houses are there?' 'Why do we live in *jhuggis*?' 'What is the right to proper housing?' In the sewing classes, names of garments and figures of measurements are used to strengthen literacy and numeracy.

Self-expression

Within 6 to 12 months the girls picked up rudimentary literacy and numeracy skills, but more importantly they started expressing their views in writing on issues like, 'my desires and my dreams', 'my body and my self', 'beauty pageants and commodification of women', 'patriarchy and self', and so on. The language was not grammatically correct, but connecting the written word to their own thoughts and feelings was a major feat for them. In their own words:

'We have written in and decorated our diaries. We make mistakes. But it feels great to say and write what we want.'

'We also made cotton stuffed toys and bags. People wanted to actually buy them. And we were thrilled.'

Theme-based Learning

Experiments in the use of standard textbooks or *Khilti Kaliyan* (a primer brought out by the Department of Adult Education), with supportive material (stories, statistics and songs) have their limitations. These primers, for instance, portray stereotyped images of women getting married and having children. Our own supplementary material consists of booklets like *Hamare Shareer ki Jaankari*, where the girls learn about their bodies and later their sexuality. But we had to drop the words from the supplementary material to go back to words in the primer. Hence, to enable these issues to be explored further, a theme-based open syllabus has been developed, with a clearer feminist perspective. A theme is chosen for each month, and all activities connected with literacy and awareness revolve around that theme. Over a period of time, a list of themes with feminist perspectives emerge. Some of the themes are, 'all about myself', 'my childhood', 'I am growing up', 'gender and feminism', 'friendship', 'sexuality', 'learning about my society and political environment', and 'government policies and our lives'.

Issues that touch the lives of girls are discussed to enable them to transcend their confined worlds. In one instance, an illiterate girl brought her boyfriend's letter to the class so that someone could read it to her. It became the take-off point for an exercise on 'love letters'. The girls were encouraged to explore the different types of letters one writes to loved ones—mothers, sisters, brothers and friends—not just those written by lovers of the opposite sex.

Exploring Different Themes

At times, local incidents are used to generate awareness. In two separate incidents in two areas, one-year-old infant girls were sexually assaulted. These cases were taken to the police and to a few non-governmental organisations. They formed the basis for discussions on the issue of rape, its larger context, the limitations of current laws, and what can be done. The girls wrote about their perceptions, participated in a *basti* meeting and a few of them went to Jaipur to participate in a rally in support of Bhanwari Devi. What they said was published in *Khidki*, an Ankur publication.

Material Used

A lot of supportive material is used to strengthen the learning process—publications like *Manushi, Sabla, Pitara, Hamare Kanoon, Child Sexual Abuse, Hamare Shareer ki Jaankari*, the *Chetna* series of stories, Ankur's own material like *Aawaas Adhikaar, Love and Harmony, Aurat aur Dharm, Taleem Se Taaqat, Safarnama, Mili Juli Batein, Shiksha ka Haq, Ravaiyya*, the Legal Literacy Kit, a child-birth calendar, news items from newspapers, TV advertisements and various posters and charts. Libraries in the Ankur centres give them access to the world of books. This has helped sustain their literacy levels and interest in learning.

Events

Melas

Melas and exhibitions in the *bastis* provide opportunities for recognition from family and community. The girls present what they have learnt in front of an audience consisting of their families, the community at large

Adolescent Girls Presenting a Skit on the Issue of Right to Basic Amenities in Anna Nagar Basti, ITO

and invited guests. The themes vary from 'Towards Empowerment' (their own journeys) to 'Id, Holi and Women's Day'. Their charts, posters, skits, puppetry and handicrafts convey the messages they want to put across.

Films, Exposure Trips and Workshops

Watching films like *Bandit Queen* leads to discussions on oppression and the strength of women, while *Maachis* leads to an understanding of militancy. Taking the girls out of their immediate environment to places inside and outside Delhi (historical places, museums or scenic spots) enriches their knowledge and awareness base and provides a space not otherwise available to them.

Structured Workshops

Workshops on gender, patriarchy, sexuality, commodification of women and the new economic policy, the education system, friendship, and self-reflection are held. No workshop is a one-time event. The plan for a follow-up is as important as the 'main event'. For instance, the discussions on a lesson in *Khilti Kaliyan* ('*Kamla ka Sapna*'), and 'the campaign on attitudes' (of adults towards children) were the backdrop for a workshop on 'friendship with boys', 'societal attitudes to girls', and 'our bodies and marriage'. The follow-up included, among other things, an activity around *sawaal peti* (question-box) where written answers to questions like, 'What does the baby eat inside the stomach?' and 'How does it come out?' were collected from everyone, while keeping their identities anonymous.

Rallies and Demonstrations

Participating in rallies and demonstrations is another activity that promotes the girls' understanding of socio-political issues. A particular issue is first taken up in the centres through handbills and news-clippings. Then the girls take part in action programmes on subjects like, 'women's day', 'plague', 'Narmada Bachao Andolan', 'Tehri Dam', 'beauty pageant', 'child labour', 'TV and advertisement' and 'communalism'.

Evaluation

Indicators to assess empowerment are not easily available. Over the years, Ankur has grappled with different concepts and has tried to define and describe them in simple terms. Benchmark information is collected through admission forms. Midstream assessments are a constant feature. In 1994 and 1997, planned evaluations were undertaken. The format had two sections. The learners filled in the first part, '*Mere Panne*

Meri Baat' and '*Maine Kya-Kya Seekha*'. The teachers filled in the second section. The areas of concern were:

- Vocabulary enhancement, language development and functional literacy.
- Skill enhancement in crafts, especially drafting, cutting and sewing.
- Evolution of a feminist perspective vis-à-vis an understanding of the women's situation and attempts at change in family environment.
- Development of learning processes and of a capacity to question, imagine and create.
- Development of general knowledge of different things like, time and division of time into days, weeks, months, the solar system, weather and climate.
- Flowering of a group-consciousness, reflected in relationships with others and participation in group activity.
- Development of a socio-political consciousness related to larger issues and participation in related action.

The Process

The information gathered is shared with the group, the individual and the area teams, and feedback is recorded. Some girls—in this case, Kalavati, Mehsar and Kusumlata—take the forms home to share the information with their parents. Others let the teachers share them with the mothers. A few are not very comfortable and do not want everything to be shared with the parents.

Some responses of learners and parents are revealing:

- I was glad my parents came to know of my dreams and my feelings (Shahnaz).
- We enjoyed listening to what was in the other forms, but were also embarrassed (Draupadi).
- After reading my form, I felt like studying more (Shaeena).
- Family members say I don't know anything. After reading my form, and hearing about the others, I have developed courage (Rimpi).
- All that I had learned was revived (Shahzaadi).
- I came to know my weaknesses and understand my behaviour (Raahat).
- I wish similar evaluations would take place in government schools (Sapna's mother).
- Saira has started talking too much at home (Saira's Abba).
- I am not going to let my sister go without schooling (Nasreen).

Towards Empowerment

Individual Growth

Through these processes, the girls have become more confident, assertive, expressive and in better command of their lives. Their ability to analyse, to make linkages between micro and macro situations and to look at themselves in a totally different light are reflected in the following statements.

Self-image

- I used to stay at home, for fear of Abbu. Slowly I have learned to go out on my own (Saira).
- Going out of the city of Delhi and the confines of society, we breathed fresh air, walked on new paths without fear and saw the vast blue sky (Shakeela).
- Whatever I am, I am. My face, my complexion, my body are mine. They are given by nature. They are my identity (Aamna).
- Why can't we do what we want, just as men do? (Rabiya).

The beauty of being 'my self' added a fresh assertiveness to their consciousness, reflected in this short poem written by Vimlesh who was illiterate when she joined.

Identity
Sita, Savitri, Draupadi, Anusuya,
Not one of them am I, Myself am I,
I am a woman, A human being,
Struggling with the problems of my times.

Assertion and Analysis

Meena was to get married at the age of 12. She took the family ration card to her father and told him, 'Now I know that girls should not get married before 18. In the ration card my age is shown as 12. So I'll go to the police and tell them.' Her father kept quiet after that.

Many of the girls have understood societal constraints, patriarchy and sexuality through analyses of their own situations. In their own words:

- Coming to the centre I have understood what a woman's life is— marriage at a young age, dowry, violence, rape and divorce. We have so many problems. I have started thinking about them and about my rights. I go to the International Women's Day rally every year.

- When I saw that there were so many like me, I did not feel alone.
- We keep hearing, 'You are a girl. Don't play on the street. Don't laugh so loudly, don't dress up and look beautiful, as boys will tease you.' Can't I look good for myself? Why aren't boys punished for teasing?
- Here I learnt that there is a world beyond the four walls of the home. If I had not come to the centre, I would have wasted my life cooking and cleaning.
- Unripe tomatoes taste bitter. Similarly, if I am married in my childhood I'll shrivel like the tomato plant.
- I know now that a girl is born because of the sperm of the man and not because of the woman. Still, why is the woman blamed?
- Rituals and customs have been made to keep us imprisoned within their confines. But some of them are joyous occasions when we dress up, sing and dance and come together. How do I feel free?

Dreams

They talked, wrote and drew pictures about their dreams and their re-alities. Their feelings and desires got the space to fly high, and yet they were aware of the ground-realities.

- I want to study but it is difficult. Education is expensive.
- I long to become a doctor and to treat people.
- I want to see my daughter driving a scooter.
- I want to become a police-inspector so that I can put a stop to eve-teasing.
- I would like my son to do housework. I would teach him 'girlish' ('*ladkipana*') sensibilities so that he does not indulge in eve-teasing.
- Why is it a sin to love? Even gods made love. What about Radha-Krishna?
- I would ensure that my daughter and son have the freedom to choose.
- It is not true that one spends more on a girl because of dowry. After all you need money to educate and settle your son also.

In recent workshops, proud mothers have talked about their daugh-ters with understanding and compassion:

- At times we thought our daughters were learning dirty things at the centre. Then in the meetings we realised it was useful knowledge. Our daughters can take care of themselves better. We could not give this information to them.
- In our workshops we became like our daughters, we played *kabaddi*, and talked and talked till late into the night. Back in our village, we used to play. In the *basti* we can't.

- When our daughters came back from Udaipur, they were mature persons. When we came back from Ghaziabad, they valued us more and did not mind our scolding as much. We have developed a more friendly relationship.
- The problem is you need money for schooling. The government should make arrangements so that poor people can have education. Otherwise our dreams of making our daughters pilots or police officers, lawyers or doctors are useless.

Group and Social Consciousness

Dakhila Abhiyan

The girls participated enthusiastically in campaigns on the 'attitudes of adults towards children' and 'school education and children'. In the 'admissions campaign' or '*dakhila abhiyan*', they were trained to get the children of the neighbourhood admitted to schools. They worked in small groups (of 10 to 20 members each), with the name-tags of their groups as identities, namely Nai Roshni in Jama Masjid, Ekta and Mahak in J.P. Basti, Mamta and Dosti in Dakshinpuri, Gulistan and Himmat in Gautampuri, Samjhauta and Nai Muskaan in Nandnagari, and Bageecha in Anna Nagar. They went to court to get affidavits made for children who did not have birth certificates. It was an opportunity for girls who had never been to formal schools to come in contact with formal schooling and get the opportunity to see a court and learn about its procedures directly. As Rubeena from Jama Masjid said, 'I had never imagined that I could have talked to the principal of the school where I had longed to go.'

Narmada, Communalism and Globalisation

The girls participated in larger concerns as well. Two groups collected donations for the Narmada Bachao Andolan and talked about migration at a public meeting. Many of them took part in demonstrations against communalism, and price-rise and new economic policies. Some understood the interdependence of various factors in today's eco-political system. Sixteen-year-old Kalawati read out her poem at a demonstration against beauty pageants.

New Economic Policy
What is our fault, that we are being punished?
We are told this is freedom. Are fashion-shows part of this freedom?

Fashion shows fascinate men. And we girls become victims of men.
We have scarcely money to feed ourselves.
Why do they tempt us with so much on the shelves?

Girls and Women Participating in 8th March Women's Day:
Rally on the Issue of Peace and Non-violence

Follow Up

'Achievements' apart, one needs to understand where the girls are today, how far and in what ways has their empowerment been sustained,
and how they cope with real life situations.

As individuals, they have used their experience in different ways, to
think through things, to take decisions, to build better and newer relationships, and to tread new paths. After leaving the Ankur centres, some
took professional courses in designing, tailoring and beauty culture,
where they sat with confidence with 'more educated', English-speaking
girls in the class. Suman went back to her village and wrote back to say
that she had started a literacy class.

The trajectory of Shakeela, who had developed as a leader of the Ekta
Samooh, took some bizarre turns. She worked for a while with a political
party. Then, she fell in love and married an already married man. Soon
she realised that his promises had been false. A rethinking followed.

Eventually, she was able to extract Rs 12,000 out of him before divorcing him. She took things in her stride and continues to hold her head high.

For some, difficult decisions have demanded all their strength. When Julie decided to marry a person outside her caste, there was stiff resistance. Her future mother-in-law said that she was welcome as a daughter but not as a daughter-in-law. Her elder brother-in-law refused to accept her. When he tried to throw her out of the house, she just sat on the bed and dared him to throw her out, knowing full well that traditionally an elder brother would not touch the wife of his younger brother. But when he was in hospital after an accident, she visited him regularly. As she put it, 'One cannot go on fighting all the time. I did what I wanted to, married the man I wanted to. But I also wanted love and peace in the family. Eventually I won them over with tact and affection.'

Sixteen-year-old Shakti did not want to get married but realised that a two-year delay would mean a heavier dowry. So she consented to marriage. But when her parents wanted to marry her into a traditional family in their native village, she put her foot down. With a lot of self-confidence, she argued that it would be difficult to cope with the constraints in the village. She wanted an atmosphere that was relatively familiar so that she could explore newer avenues. The counter argument could be that she might get a different kind of exposure in a village. Another one could be that she should not get married before the age of 18.

Arguments may go on and on, but the bottom line is that empowerment is not an absolute concept. Different individuals go through empowering experiences differently at different points of time. It is a journey every individual goes through in her own way, at her own pace, in her specific context, and her decisions are also the consequence of a gamut of factors best known only to her.

Conclusion

Challenges and Limitations

- Because of its intensity, the outreach of the programme is not very large. At a time, there are only 15 to 20 girls in a centre.
- Irregular attendance, due to illness, problems in the family, visits of relatives, travel to the home-village, affect the flow of learning.
- Assessing qualitative and attitudinal changes is a challenge. Despite meticulous work based on examples, we may risk missing out on the nuances that may be reflective of certain aspects of empowerment.

- Culling out examples and putting them into a conceptual framework for evaluation, at times leads to oversimplification.
- The energy and input required are of a high order, not easy to sustain over a long period. Rejuvenating courses for the teachers are necessary.
- Despite 'small steps' that may develop into 'long, new paths', larger economic, social and political forces are the reality of their lives. After a point, the struggles of these empowered girls become very severe.

Despite various limitations, the Ankur programme has empowered several hundred girls over the years. They are taking life as it comes, dreaming and struggling for a better world. While the micro-level experiences of an organisation like Ankur can provide ideas for similar programmes, one should guard against generalisation and the temptation to duplicate. Something that has succeeded in one situation may not succeed in another. A dimension of empowerment that was explored in a specific phase of life may be irrelevant in another.

Julie's strategy of asserting independence in Gautampuri may not be suitable for Asama in Jama Masjid. And what Asama is able to do now (going out without Abba's permission) was not possible a few years back. Each person is helped to explore possibilities keeping in mind her horizon. Learners, teachers and co-ordinators enter into dialogue, and discover, share and build together. No hard and fast 'ism' is thrust upon anyone.

However, certain fundamental principles inform all our programmes.

- An evolving perspective which has space for different points of view but is clear on the issue of justice, equity and peace for all.
- A programme meticulously detailed within the framework of this perspective which has flexibility to respond to change.
- A strategy which keeps individual weaknesses of different individuals in mind and tries to push the agenda further.
- Regular training for planners and implementers emphasising internalisation and full understanding.
- A general atmosphere of mutual love and respect.

The act of balancing organisational philosophy with the realities is not easy. But that is the challenge. Even to start a modest process of change within individuals, families and communities, one has to work hard to reach out to the core of human beings.

CHAPTER FOUR

Participatory Village Level Land-use Mapping: A Post-literacy Exercise[1]

Jayanta Kumar Sarma, Biman Borah and Gitarani Bhattacharya

The use of participatory land-use mapping exercises as a tool for post-literacy education is the focus of this chapter. An exercise carried out in 1998–99 in Assam, with a group of neo-literate women belonging to the Tiwa tribe, is described. The exercise aimed at improving the skills of observation, visualisation and quantification. It was also expected to result in better decision-making processes and to provide a platform for collective activity.

The women belonged to Dhalthapara village of Morigaon district of Assam. As part of the land-use mapping exercise, they undertook village

1. This study was carried out with the support of the Assam Mahila Samata Society, Morigaon. The authors wish to thank the State Project Director and members of the District Implementation Unit, AMSS, Morigaon, for their constant support and encouragement.

transect walks,[2] recorded their observations and evaluated the information gathered. They also prepared perception maps, cultural maps, home-space maps, homestead cluster maps and habitat maps. The maps provided the basis for deriving land-use patterns. The exercise did help women build on their literacy skills, more importantly, it provided a new understanding of their habitat and increased their self-confidence. The latter led to new group activities, like development of a community pond for fisheries.

Vision and Initiation

Literacy does not mean imparting skills for reading and writing alone. In its broadest sense, it implies the expansion of the horizons of people's knowledge in order to equip them with the ability to analyse and assess the situations in which they find themselves. Such reflection should develop courage and skills in people to change their situations. Development of literacy should be a dynamic process of learning in which participants gain access to meaningful information, engage in reflection, and act as a collective to transform the material and social conditions of their existence in some way. Therefore, in the context of the land-use mapping exercise, improving the quality of observation of the habitat—the physical as well as social aspects of the habitat—visualisation of the observed phenomenon, and analysis, were decided as the objectives for the post-literacy initiative. The principle of learning through doing—which provides opportunities for acquiring information and using it for decision-making—was felt to be a useful principle for organising the activities envisaged.

In Dhalthapara village, Morigaon district, 27 Tiwa tribal women had passed through the literacy phase. Dhalthapara is about 5 km from Morigaon, the district headquarters. The village has 69 families of Tiwas and the population size is about 550. Agriculture is the mainstay of the village economy. The *Assam Mahila Samata Society* (AMSS) started the Mahila Samakhya programme in Dhalthapara in 1997 with the objective of empowering women. In the process, a Mahila Sangha (women's group) was formed in the village. This group undertook the literacy venture and formed the Jagriti Kendra, a women's literacy centre, with the guidance of the District Implementation Unit of the AMSS. The first phase of the

---

2. A transect walk is a 'walk-and-observe' exercise, carried out along the cross-section of the village.

literacy programme saw the 27 women who participated in the land-use mapping exercise becoming literate.

Towards the end of their literacy education, the women began to express concern about their low levels of income and the problems associated with poverty. Arriving at a decision on what to do was not easy. After long discussions, the authors (who were also associated with the literacy phase) decided to introduce participatory land-use mapping as a tool to facilitate decision-making processes among the women.

It became clear very early on in the mapping exercise that the participants, who were very familiar with their village, did not have the rigorous perceptional skills needed to arrive at a logical visualisation of the features of the habitat. So, understanding the mental maps of the women and training the women for logical observation of the environment became important during the initial stages of the exercise.

Strategies and Methods

The basic approach followed in this exercise was the participatory approach, in which decisions are taken by the participants themselves, with outsiders playing the role of active facilitators. The stages in the exercise were: preparatory work, orientation, home-space mapping, household-cluster mapping, habitat mapping, land-use map preparation and information sharing.

Preparatory Work

Preparatory work comprised environment building and sensitisation, village transect walks, and collection of secondary information. The initial discussions centred around the habitat, the need for careful observation, preparation of maps, and the usefulness of maps. The facilitators initiated most of the discussions.

The transect walk is a useful exercise to develop the skills of habitat observation. In this walk, each and every road and track in the village is covered. In the process, important environmental objects are identified, and issues such as land-use patterns crop up. In the experiment under discussion, a perception map was first prepared by the participants; this was followed by a 'cultural landscape' which was prepared on the basis of the observations made during the transect walk. The different codes or symbols to be used for mapping were also finalised during this phase.

The secondary information collected (usually by the facilitators) included the cadestrial maps,[3] holdings numbers and list of holders from the local revenue department.

Orientation

In this phase, abstract visualisation and mapping techniques were introduced to the participants. Initially, a pre-designed code for mapping, finalised during the preparatory phase, was discussed with the participants. The participants were then trained in the use of such codes. The steps followed at the various stages of mapping were the following:

1. Framing the boundary through observation.
2. Plotting various features within the space framed by the specific boundary:

   - plotting housing features;
   - plotting water sources;
   - plotting vegetation, highlighting the special categories of vegetation; and
   - identifying specific uses of land.

3. After completing the plotting of features, observing the area once again with reference to the prepared diagram or sketch map.
4. Observing the diagram and identifying the features in the sketch that have potential to help in the group's development.

Home-Space Mapping

During this stage, every participant prepared a sketch map of her own home space or homestead, following the four steps introduced during the orientation stage. The name of the head of the household was also mentioned on the sketch.

Household-Cluster Mapping or Neighbourhood Mapping

The participants then prepared the household-cluster sketch or neighbourhood map by compiling the homestead or home-space sketches.

---

3. Cadestrial maps are revenue maps in which the holdings are indicated with their shapes and to scale.

This consolidated sketch was able to provide a picture of the neighbourhood environment, from which the participants were able to identify the features that could be tapped for their own benefit. In this phase, aspects of quantification were important. Some of the items which were considered were: facilities in the various households, kitchen garden facilities, households with betel-nut trees, households with bamboo, and households with access to water.

Habitat Mapping or Village Mapping

The next stage of consolidation saw the neighbourhood maps being converted into a total habitat map or village map. This map presented a holistic picture of the village to the participants, leading to a proper visualisation of the habitat and to the framing of a useful mental map.

Land-use Map Preparation

At this stage, the information in the maps that had been prepared was plotted in the cadestrial maps with reference to the name of the head of the household, holdings numbers and holders' list. This exercise resulted in the preliminary identification of land with potential for agricultural and non-agricultural use. Then, a series of group discussions generated information about the crops cultivated and about other areas that were considered important by the participants.

Information Strategy and Discussion

Each phase of the entire mapping exercise was followed by group discussions among the participants. Individual experiences were shared, and learning at the group level led to collective decision making. To cite an example, through the exercise described above, the women identified a pond within the village which actually belonged to the community. People had forgotten about this area and it was not being used properly. The women recovered the pond and initiated activities like weeding and digging, with the aim of making the pond usable for inland fisheries. In another instance, a plot of community land which had been usurped by an individual was identified and recovered. This plot is also being converted into a fishery pond. The women have approached the state's fisheries department and have undergone the necessary training.

Conclusion

Having gone through the land-use mapping exercise with women who had just become literate, we have realised that incorporation of mapping activities in the post-literacy phase expands the ability of newly-literate people to imagine and visualise their situation, and improve their decision making. An important aspect of our work was the opportunity created for the women to practice newly-learned writing and reading skills as a result of the need to record information systematically at each stage of the mapping exercise. One must, however, mention that the experiment was limited to just one village and to a very small group of women. Replication of the experiment with larger groups in many more areas should help identify other features, both positive and negative, of land-use mapping in relation to post-literacy education.

PART III

READING MATTER FOR EARLY LITERATES

CHAPTER FIVE

Preparing Reading Materials for Neo-literates: Some Ideas and Innovations

Sushama Merh-Ashraf[1]

The context and perceptions about the role and importance of literacy and continuing education have been changing rapidly in recent times at all levels—global, national, regional and local. On the one hand, these changes are being driven by ideas of eliminating poverty and creating a participative society, and the need to take into account concerns of human development in terms of equity, empowerment and justice. On the other hand, they are being significantly and fundamentally affected by the information technology and communications revolutions. I want to explore the development of literacy and continuing education within these unfolding changes, which are creating a need to redesign strategies for the format and content of materials developed for literacy and

1. I would like to specially thank Dr Varsha Das, Chief Editor and Joint Director, National Book Trust, New Delhi, for her continued guidance, discussions and enlightened suggestions.

continuing education, and for creating new delivery mechanisms for a 'learning society'. This will involve making use of the potential of multimedia, multi-channel digital technologies, and the coming together of learning through informal, non-formal and formal education in an overlapping delivery framework.

Lifelong Literacy and Continuing Education in Context

I will start by discussing some salient features of the ideas and policies that are emerging for meeting the challenges of lifelong literacy and continuing education, with a particular emphasis on the need to develop relevant resource materials for neo-literate readers. It is important to step beyond misplaced stereotypes and false assumptions about the relationships among literacy, orality, education and development, and to broaden the concept of appropriate 'reading' materials for neo-literates within a rapidly changing Indian society.

With knowledge and information synonymous with power (or should it be 'empowerment'?), the demand for more literacy is rapidly rising. In India, the crucial educational concern is the large gap between the small but powerful segment of literate 'information affluent' people (who have a monopoly over the tools of accessing information) and the much larger yet weak 'information poor'. The latter group is mostly made up of the non-literates (the so-called 'left-outs', 'excluded', 'drop-outs' and 'pushed outs', as in the case of women, *adivasis* [tribals] and other highly disadvantaged groups).

In recent years, literacy has come to be viewed as a social process which involves many individuals and occupational groups at many economic, social, cultural and political levels. This complex interaction has given rise to the concept of 'multiple literacies'. Thus, terms such as scientific literacy, visual literacy or computer literacy have come into vogue. Paradoxically, in the context of a rapidly changing society, advanced-level professionals (who need continuous upgradation of their skills), as well as the 'alphabetic' non-literates, come under the category of 'functional non-literates' (Kumar, 1999: 15).

The divide between literacy (ability to read and write) and orality (passing on information via the spoken word) correlates well with gender and social development. This divide has influenced public attitudes towards literacy and continuing education in India. The literates are labelled as the wise and knowledgeable, while the non-literates (who may possess oral skills and are articulate but poor) are tagged as 'primitive' and 'backward'. Though changes in perception have occurred in the past decade or so, deep-rooted stereotyped messages and mind-sets still dominate. Continuing education materials (both print and non-print media) which are being produced and used today reflect these (Finnegan, 1988; Hadoo, 1992; Kamber, 1992; Khubchandani, 1981; Pattanayak, 1990). Recent academic research in several disciplines and social movements across countries and cultures has brought to light the unfounded basis for this misconception about the relationship between literacy and orality.

The interaction between print and non-print electronic media is creating a convergence of the written and the oral. It is being recognised that features of 'oral' and 'written' combine symbiotically to form an osmotic framework that is reflected in multiple expressions of communication. This is equally true at the oral (spoken), the aural/audio (hearing), and the written and visual levels. Within these parameters, the meaning of literacy as limited to the alphabetic 3Rs no longer holds ground. India, with her advanced level of oral culture and literature, and a tradition of reciting and listening—in addition to reading and writing—represents one of the richest examples of a holistic relationship between the oral and the written (Daswani, 1999).

The distinction between literacy and orality is getting all the more complicated and blurred with the concept of 'secondary orality', which is rapidly gaining relevance due to the emergence of 'electronic orality' through radio, multi-channel television, mobile phones, the worldwide web and the exponential growth and convergence of these new technologies. The (re)technologising of the 'written word' within an electronic framework gives new meanings to written, oral, aural and visual forms of communication and is changing the very basis of the concept of literacy and lifelong learning (Kibby, 1999: 749).

All this has been accompanied by a growing perception of the importance of the productive role of women in the economy. Despite the multiple roles that women play in family and community development, gender stereotypes about women continue to exist in printed materials and media portrayal. So do biased perceptions about the standing of 'indigenous knowledge', which continues to be thought of as backward in terms of learning and education in the Indian context (Patel and Dighe, 1997). As has now been well documented, the 'literacy-development' link in India has failed. Kerala has failed to show any tangible and commensurate link between economic development of gender justice, on the one hand, and its high literacy status and tradition of a reading culture, on the other. In the Punjab, economic prosperity exists alongside high levels of atrocities, human rights violations and violence against women and the girl child! With the introduction of the panchayati raj system with its emphasis on grassroots level representation in local political structures, the voices of people and the visibility of women's quest for equality and justice can no longer be overlooked when producing materials for literacy and lifelong learning. At another level, the 'indigenous knowledge base' into which local 'folk experiences' are woven, cannot be disregarded.

A New Policy Framework for Lifelong Literacy and Continuing Education

In view of the need for changes in attitudes and practice, new international and national guidelines for lifelong literacy and continuing education in the 21st century have now been drawn up. At the international level, there is a major thrust to consolidate democratic processes and to recognise the value of diversity, with its variegated indigenous knowledge bases and cultures. The guidelines strongly advocate the right to lifelong learning for all. They categorically promote a policy of literacy and continuing education as part of 'mainstream' planned educational change, with the hope that this will lead to equality and empowerment, as against treating it as some sort of ad hoc remedial provision. The use of information technology (IT) in these processes is specifically emphasised at all levels and in all educational settings, especially with regard to materials and training (IAEA, 1997).

At the national level, the Ministry of Human Resource Development published its new guidelines for continuing education in April 2000 (NLM, 2000). These guidelines stress a need for providing a 'matrix' of educational 'outreach' programmes to meet the diverse needs of 'excluded' continuing education learners. It proposes a flexible 'multimedia' approach (which is open to various interpretations), which will recognise the complexities of different local situations. It calls for promoting a social environment in which knowledge and information are considered important determinants of human development. In addition, the guidelines suggest mechanisms for linkage and collaboration between continuing education centres (CECs), village education centres (VECs) and nodal continuing education centres (NCECs) to strengthen local infrastructure for literacy and learning, with libraries playing a central role. The need to develop a 'seamless' strategy of systematically planned education and training programmes at the grassroots level, which is supported by well-designed learning materials, is specifically stressed (NLM, 2000).

The Importance of Libraries and Reading Rooms

With literacy rates in India improving (Mukarji, 2000), the new guidelines for continuing education propose a much wider role for libraries and reading rooms in furthering continuing education goals. The major thrust is on encouraging reading and learning amongst adults. However, the library is also visualised as a 'community information window', with the additional provision of multimedia and distance education facilities which will also make it a 'community education centre'. The new guidelines suggest that continuing education materials should integrate the functional and vocational components of knowledge and promote multiple literacy skills, while keeping in view genuine needs of readers and learners. Interesting formats of presentation—fiction, stories, drama, cartoons, poems—supplemented with audio and visual IT support materials are suggested, with the aim of encouraging problem solving in imaginative ways.

A cautionary note is underlined in the new guidelines—'not to use difficult governmental pamphlets', but to prepare easy, creative, informative and attractively presented material in local dialects, making use of IT techniques and involving the local community and local functionaries to the greatest possible extent. This multifaceted concept of the village library is important. But the availability of good books with relevant subject matter and topics, which not only interest the readers but also reinforce educational and lifelong literacy goals will remain a critical success factor.

Lala Patel-Ki-Laibary: Adapting a Gujarati Play into Hindi for Neo-literates

The year 1990 was declared the International Year of Literacy by the UN, and this acted as a catalyst for a number of studies and activities in the area of literacy and lifelong education all over the world. With an experience in adult and continuing education in India of over two decades, I had the opportunity to work in close collaboration with the National Book Trust (NBT) on two major projects during the 1990s. The first involved reviewing and evaluating selected books written by eminent writers in Gujarati for recommendation to libraries under the national 'Operation Black Board' programme. The second involved preparing reading materials for neo-literates and semi-literates under the *Navsakshar*

Sahitya Mala series (neo-literate literature), with the aim of encouraging the retention of literacy skills and advancing knowledge, especially among rural audiences. A secondary aim was to emphasise the multi-dimensional role that libraries could play for neo-literate people (Thanvi, 1992).

During the same period, I also attempted to define the parameters of a 'post-colonial paradigm' for lifelong education in India (Merh-Ashraf, 1996–97b). I examined the 'orality–literacy interface' in depth within a historical perspective in order to establish the reciprocity of these two factors in the processes of communication, education and learning. The inferences and conclusions from this study provided good insight into issues of 'inequality' and 'exclusion', and the divide between formal and non-formal education that existed in India at that time. This not only assisted in developing criteria for assessing materials developed for post-literacy and continuing education over the previous four decades, but also helped suggest strategies for the future.

Following up these efforts in 1993–94 (and stepping out of the 'colonial British India' framework), I undertook a detailed study of the public library co-operative movement during the early decades of the 20th century in the state of Baroda in Gujarat under Maharaja Sayajirao Gaekwad III. My aim was to ascertain the progress made through Baroda's policy of 'mass education' and promoting a reading and learning culture through public co-operative libraries. The study showed the wide spread of the infrastructure of public co-operative libraries in those times, which reached out to the taluka and village levels and which were accessible to everyone. During that period, the social changes taking place were not only accompanied by a wave of political awareness in the wake of the freedom movement, but were also being imperceptibly affected by industrial and scientific developments in the country.

I began reviewing Gujarati literary works from a period when a number of progressive writers were writing profusely on socially relevant themes in a style that was people-oriented. Many of these writings reflected the fervour created by the spirit of the times inspired by Mahatma Gandhi; this fervour was engulfing the entire mass of people in rural and urban areas. Much of the writing depicted the changing rural situation brought about by the scientific and industrial developments knocking at the doors of modern India! Both these strands were combined in the educational reform policies of the Gaekwad State of Baroda.

I then conceived of the idea of experimenting with adaptations of Gujarati writings from this period which had contemporary educational relevance. I felt that interesting and relevant reading materials could be developed for neo-literates through translating and adapting such writings within the 'post-colonial framework' for lifelong literacy and learning being proposed for the future. I selected a particularly interesting Gujarati drama *Lala Patel-Ni-Laibary* by the well-known Gujarati writer, Ramanlal Vasantlal Desai, for translation into Hindi and adaptation as a story for neo-literates (Desai, 1938). The National Book Trust supported this work.

The Author Interviewing Grassroots' Women of Women's Collective (KMVS, Kutch, Bhuj) Recording Their Perceptions about IT

The drama interestingly has the opening of a library in a village in Gujarat as its central theme. Lala Patel, the 'non-literate' *mukhiya* of the village is a highly respected elder, who gives up his post and goes back to farming. Most of the transactions that were resolved orally in *chaupals* (home courtyards) earlier, were now shifting to written modes of communication in the 'modern' set up in the village, where the younger generation was entering schools and colleges, and literate 'sahebs' were working in offices. Lala Patel felt inadequate to perform effectively in his role as *mukhiya*. So he decided to relinquish his post to make way for a literate *mukhiya* to be appointed in his place. In this context, the drama unfolds using an oral-dialogue genre which is interspersed with narrative to bring the story alive. The story can briefly be described in the following way (Merh-Ashraf, 1999):

There is a written *farman* (directive) from the local government office of the village for opening a *granthalaya* (library) in the village. This information is put in writing on the notice board of the office, and is also circulated orally through the new *mukhiya* to the village people. All villagers, men and women are asked to gather at the *chaupal* to discuss the issue democratically and take any necessary action. Though there is a new 'literate' *mukhiya*, the people of the village, including the new *mukhiya*, take advice from Lala Patel on crucial matters relating to the well-being of the village. Hence, the village people insist that Lala Patel be present at the *chaupal* meeting. They request the government officer to invite Lala Patel and agree to give their consent for opening a library in the village only after consulting Lala Patel on the matter. Lala Patel is summoned to the meeting. But he has many reservations about the idea of a 'modern' library being set up in the village. He expresses his fear thus: 'It will spoil the village youth and will adversely affect young girls. They will look down upon manual farm and fieldwork and "waste" their time in futile intellectual activities. They will become like the desk clerk in the office, with a pencil stuck in his ears, wearing thick formidable glasses!'

After repeated requests from the villagers, including the young people, Lala Patel comes to the meeting. After hearing the different views and the younger generation's enthusiasm for the library, he gives his approval for a library in the village. Everyone is very happy and excited. The matter is put to a vote. People present in the meeting are asked to sign a document to register their consent. The literate amongst them put their signatures, while the non-literate, including Lala Patel, put down their thumb impressions. The drama relates the entire process of arranging the library premises on the basis of modern norms of cataloguing and coding books, overseeing its management and appointing a *granthpal* (librarian), who 'comes from the city'. As the library begins to function as a learning and information centre, people start coming, leaving their fears and apprehensions behind. Women also start making use of the library through the 'reading sessions' when the librarian reads aloud for the non-literate visitors. Soon a literacy class is opened in the library for adults. Discussion sessions are held; men and women, young and old, farmers and artisans, all begin to gather at the library, truly making it a learning and social centre. Lala Patel and many of the elders, who were fearful of the corrupting influence of a library culture, are proved wrong. Children, students and other literate people start teaching the non-literates to read and write. They are able to read news and information on topics like health and have informed discussions on the Swaraj Movement against the British. Books are available in the library on new agricultural technologies which provide farmers the information to help them improve their livelihoods.

The librarian, Keshavbhai, becomes very friendly with Lala Patel. He tries to learn the art of farming and cultivation from Lala Patel at the latter's farm. While this is going on, the librarian trains Lala Patel in the procedures of managing and maintaining a library. In a couple of years Lala Patel is able to read newspapers and simple books, and also acquires basic skills needed to manage the village library.

In due course, Lala Patel encourages his school-going daughter to organise literacy 'night classes' for women in their houses with the help of literate village youth. He is a transformed person now—an 'empowered literate' with skills in library management! In turn, he has introduced the *granthpal* to the basics of agricultural know-how to enable him to perform as a farmer, if ever the need arose.

One day, the librarian, who is suspected of 'anti-British activity', is removed from his job and asked to leave the village. The entire village is shocked at the tragedy of losing their *granthpal*. They are deeply concerned and worried about their *'laibary'*. They refuse to let the librarian go. But Lala Patel knows that Keshavbhai will have to go. With a young person's fervour, he stands up among the village people and says, 'I will not let the "laibary" close. I will look after it and put in my resources. I will request my rich friends from the village to contribute, while each one of you will give your services in cash or kind.' He adds, 'I was a farmer. Our *granthpalbhai* has trained me to look after the "laibary". I shall manage and run it as before.' The librarian and the people are deeply moved. The librarian says, 'I came from the city as a *"Granthpal"*—a *"kitab babu"*, as you call me. I have learnt the art of cultivation and agriculture from Lala Patel. I have some land in my village. I shall return to my village and till that land to become a farmer like Lala Patel,' he adds with some humour. The story ends with Lala Patel, initially an 'illiterate' farmer, becoming the 'literate' librarian of the village *'laibary'*, and the educated librarian resolving to become a farmer, both having learnt new skills from each other and having transformed their roles.

This is the story in brief. The sophisticated drama format in one language, Gujarati, is adapted into a simple story form in another language, Hindi, which is specifically aimed at Hindi speaking neo-literates. The 'oral' component of the dialogue and conversations, the colloquial lexicon and humour are maintained by using an equivalent appropriate vocabulary in Hindi to maintain the grip and spirit of the story. Throughout the story, the technical and the participatory features of the library as a learning centre are highlighted. Diverse educational and vocational activities are included in the narrative to bring in the oral and interactive aspects of communication amongst the various characters.

Reading, discussion and practical sessions show the broader role that the library can play as a community centre. Experiences are shared and crucial development issues are discussed in a democratic environment. Men, women and children gather for recreation, forgetting their age, class, gender and caste differences. They exchange books and share information. They read to each other, reflecting upon national and local issues, sometimes through heated debate, and sometimes through humorous discussions. Through these processes, a rural society is shown transforming itself. The desire for learning begins to influence people, and all the changes are shown as being brought about by the opening of a library in the village.

This drama provides ideal subject matter to sensitise people to the concept of a library as one crucial component of a programme of continuing education and social development. It also allows experimentation with the interface between oral and written genres, highlighting the significance of both for creating good educational material. It weaves within a story various issues that touch the lives of village people. With the opening of a library, the people try to resolve these issues democratically, in an environment of reading, writing, listening and discussion, on a continuous basis. Some of the situations are interestingly illustrated in the book. The format of the book is based on norms for visual and textual presentation as prescribed by the NBT guidelines for neo-literates. The simplicity and colloquial nature of the language used by the people is maintained. For instance, the village people pronounce 'library' as *'laibary'*, and that is the way the word is written, reflecting people's own colloquial lexicon and 'grassroots literacy'. Similarly *'granthpal'* is referred to as *'kitab babu'* by villagers, who address him by his name *'Keshavbhai'* as well.

Adapting a literary drama form from one language into a simple story form in another language for neo-literates is not an easy task. It involves not only a sensitivity to literary nuances in both languages, but also a good grasp of the interests and needs of Hindi speaking readers at the grassroots. In the present case, the style and vocabulary chosen were drawn from field discussions that I carried out with Hindi-speaking neo-literates. The Gujarati vocabulary, names and linguistic slang had to be changed to create a Hindi-speaking environment and situation for the story. I must admit that the drama format was much more interesting, but it was too long with songs and other prop elements that are required for performance. Two reprint editions of the book have come out since its first publication in 1996. The Hindi version has been translated into Bengali, which was published in 1998. The book has been used at the field level with adult learners. It is displayed at various book exhibitions and fairs organised by the NBT and other educational institutions, especially in rural areas.

Alongside printed materials such as this example, formats such as audiovisual, multimedia, theatre, television, distance education self-learning materials, should be tried while developing materials for life-long literacy and continuing education. I have now translated another Gujarati play, *Ek Tak*, by the same writer into Hindi for semi-literates. It is titled *Ek Avsar*. It was given to a school in Delhi to be performed on stage as it dealt with environmental and gender issues in a lyrical and musical form.

Reading Material with a Difference: The Impact of New Technology on Literacy and Learning

I would now like to link the above experiences and ideas with 'outreach educational possibilities' that information technology (IT) and interactive networking promise. These include access and support systems that are acquiring importance on two major fronts, the 'human' and the 'technological'. The IT revolution is creating new opportunities for developing 'reading' material and providing continuing education. On the 'human front', human development issues of equality, gender justice, empowerment and human rights need to be addressed if progress is to be made in meeting the needs of the disadvantaged. On the 'technological front', IT can create new linkages among people working together. This has implications for material production and for organising distribution to a wider readership on affordable terms. In this section, I will outline some ideas developed from working on a field project in Gujarat with a multimedia distance education framework which was undertaken in collaboration with the Distance Education Council (DEC) of the Indira Gandhi National Open University (IGNOU).

It is important that educational material for lifelong literacy be future-oriented, incorporate a creative vision, and provide a voice and visibility to the disadvantaged. Research and innovative attempts to generate alternative learning strategies and techniques need to underline the consistent and sustainable practice of 'partnership', where substantial amount of 'unlearning' becomes obligatory to remove the accumulating deadwood of old-fashioned and no longer appropriate mind-sets.

It should be recognised that the concept of a 'library' is drastically changing all over the world. This is all the more true in India where plurality of needs and programmes and the devolution of decision making to the panchayat level show a need for multiple roles for a library—as an 'information kiosk' (rather than a centre for book borrowing) and as a broad-based centre for continuing, lifelong and vocational education.

Distance communication technologies, ranging from terrestrial and satellite and now to wireless and mobile phones will revolutionise the concept of learning and reading from a linear process to a non-linear multimedia process. The convergence of print and non-print formats for providing resource materials (as packages and kits), combined with multi-channel transmission technology, is making it possible to reach out to learners in even the remotest places. Electronic materials are now being rapidly developed all over the world, not only for the formally educated literates, but also for the 'excluded' non-literates, the remotely distanced and the physically challenged (including the blind). Efforts to 'reach the unreached' are fast making this possible even in a country such as India with its vast size but limited financial resources.

The concept of 'reading' itself is changing with information becoming available in 'multimedia', 'multi-channel' forms! We do 'read' pictures and facial expressions, and not just written words, don't we? It is note-worthy that the 'learning society' agenda for the new millennium rightly stresses a need to develop greater synergy between the existing media and the new information technologies, reinforcing their role for the delivery of lifelong literacy and education (CONFINTEA, 1997).

There have been a number of developments in the area of using IT for educational purposes in India, not to mention the advances made in countries such as Canada in developing multi-institution partnerships and using telecommunications and distance education networks (Masco, 1994). In recent years, projects have been initiated in India to spread and strengthen IT-infrastructure for rural development. The interactivity of the new media presages a fundamental shift away from the 'top-down' approach. For example, the concept of a 'wired village' is being tried in Warana village in Maharashtra, which has one of the best-integrated co-operative systems in all of India. A successful 'electronic information, education, and social services system' has started operating in the vil-lage and is beginning to bring equal benefits to all (Gupta, 2000; Ramakrishnan, 2000; Vijayaditya, 2000).

Other similar attempts include health care, ancillary paramedic train-ing, tele-education and communication in commercial and agricultural ventures, to name a few (Reddy and Grave, 2000). Similarly, about 600 IT-based multipurpose centres for training, service and production have been initiated at the village level in many states by the Department of Education and the Department of Science and Technology, where mate-rials are being prepared in local languages and there is provision for rural electronics entrepreneurship development (Choubey, 2000).

A certificate programme was launched in July 2000 by IGNOU for development practitioners on 'Empowering Women Self-Help Groups'. The print and non-print material is devised not only to be legible and of interest to the non and semi-literate women, but the content and approach reflect women's crucial role in social transformation. Concepts such as 'empowerment' and 'autonomy' in decision making, especially on legal and economic matters, are defined in action-based terms. A panchayati raj project for elected members, a Commonwealth of Learning Literacy project, courses on human rights, disaster management, health care and other courses are indicative of a trend to reach out to the 'excluded' through distance education. An example from the Ministry of Health and Family Welfare, Government of India is the 'In-service Programme for Auxiliary Nurses and Mid-wives & Field Health Workers'. These are all attempts towards integrating non-formal education with mainstream educational reform (Bhatia, 2000).

'IT' Intervention for Women's Empowerment

Experiments being carried out at the Indian Institute of Management in Ahmedabad (IIMA) are worth special mention. One interesting piece of work is being undertaken by Brij Kothari on the concept of 'same language subtitling' of songs in films to promote literacy, so that film-goers can read the words as the song is sung (Kothari 1998; Kothari and

Takeda, 2000). He asserts that since Indian society is more a 'reciting society' than a 'reading society', in the context of literacy, attaining significance beyond alphabetism, reinforcing literacy skills and promoting reading habits through the use of same language subtitling of film and popular folk songs on TV will facilitate language learning and literacy. The experiment has been successfully field tested, and can easily be taken up on a large scale for films and television. In a society where films have an enormous significance, this could have an enormous impact at very low cost. A similar approach is informing work in other cultures and countries, such as Canada and Australia with their IT-outreach educational programmes for the natives, immigrants and the aborigines (Merh-Ashraf, 1996–97a). Another innovative venture at IIMA, promoted by Anil K. Gupta, is an attempt to share information among grassroots innovators through a multimedia database, a 'Shodh Yatra', the Honey Bee Network, and 'Lok Sarvani', a newsletter initiative specifically designed to overcome barriers of language, literacy and localism. The 'Swatah Shodh Pranali' (self-discovery method) being advocated in this venture seems to be one of the cardinal principles for preparing material for lifelong literacy and continuing education using participatory techniques.

These attempts underline the role that IT can play in helping to empower the 'knowledge rich but economically poor'. More importantly, IT has the potential to align key actors in civil society to combat alienation and fragmentation, to overcome the difficulties in accessing knowledge and sharing ideas and experiences, and to make it easier for grassroots activists to come together and collaborate. The Honey Bee philosophy shows how IT can reduce transaction costs and produce institutional mechanisms for exchanging ideas and innovations so as to be better able to deal with the various challenges for social and community development (Gupta, Kothari and Patel, 2000). Material preparation will be given new support as a result of the IT revolution, and this reinforces the need to alter the 'reading material paradigm' towards equality and justice, on the one hand, and towards quality and integrity, on the other. It will also be important to find ways of establishing partnerships between the state, the corporate sector and the civil society, if the full potential of IT is to be realised.

Conclusion

In this chapter, I have focused on the changing perspectives in the preparation of reading materials for neo-literates. The rapid development of information and communications technologies is extending the concepts of 'reading' and 'reading material', which now must consider combining print and non-print media to become multimedia and the use of non-linear modes of reading and learning. I have also highlighted the idea of innovation in adapting and translating literary writings, and underlined the significance of the library and reading room as a community based centre for continuing education and lifelong learning. The example of *Lala-Patel-Ki-Laibary* illustrates how these ideas can be taken forward. What I try to stress is a possible direction towards more imaginative, more interesting and more innovative approaches to preparing reading and learning materials for neo-literates which communicate more effectively and have a greater impact. To achieve this, I visualise a partnership between the state, the corporate sector and civil society that would cover the entire 'assembly line' of preparing reading and learning materials for continuing education and lifelong learning for the 'excluded'. Such a partnership should also consider the educational, technological, technical, communications and economic aspects which enable conditions under which 'alphabetism' is no longer seen as a limiting factor to becoming functionally (and media) literate.

References

Bhatia, B.S. (2000). 'Satcom for Extension Training.' In Subhash C. Bhatnagar and Robert Schware (eds), *Information and Communication Technology in Development,* pp. 151–62. New Delhi: Sage Publications.

Choubey, Santosh (2000). 'Multipurpose Electronics and Computer Centres: Promoting IT Centred Maintenance and Employment in Rural Areas.' In Subhash C. Bhatnagar and Robert Schware (eds), *Information and Communication Technology in Development,* pp. 187–92. New Delhi: Sage Publications.

CONFINTEA (1997). *Adult Education: The Hamburg Declaration—Agenda for the Future,* Fifth International Conference on Adult Education, UNESCO Institute of Education, Hamburg, Germany.

Daswani, C.J. (1999). 'Born to Learn.' In *Towards Life Long Learning,* State Resource Centre, Jamia Millia, on behalf of National Literacy Mission, Ministry of Human Resource Development, Government of India, New Delhi, and UNESCO.

Desai, Ramanlal V. (1938). 'Lala Patel-Ni-Laibary.' In *Pari-Ane-Rajkumar, A Collection of Plays,* by Ramanlal V. Desai. Bombay: R. R. Sheth & Co.

Finnegan, Ruth (1988). *Literacy and Orality: Studies in the Technology of Communication.* Basil Blackwell: New York.

Gupta, Anil K., Brij Kothari and **Kirit Patel** (2000). 'Knowledge Network for Recognizing, Respecting and Rewarding Grassroots Innovation.' In Subhash C. Bhatnagar and Robert Schware (eds), *Information and Communication Technology in Development,* pp. 115–31. New Delhi: Sage Publications.

Gupta, Raj (2000). 'Inmarsat Experience in Village Telephony.' In Subhash C. Bhatnagar and Robert Schware (eds), *Information and Communication Technology in Development,* pp. 141–48. New Delhi: Sage Publications.

Hadoo, Jawaharlal (1992). Oral Literature in Indian Tradition: Folk Categories and Modern Indian Societies. Mimeographed paper presented at the seminar on *Oral Tradition, Written Word and Communication Systems,* India International Centre, New Delhi.

IAEA (Indian Adult Education Association) (1997). Adult Learning: A Key for the 21st Century. Special issue of the *Indian Journal of Adult Education,* 58(3), on the Fifth International Conference on Adult Education.

Kamber, Chandrashekhar (1992). Oral Tradition and Indian Literature. Mimeographed paper presented at the seminar on *Oral Tradition, Written Word and Communication Systems,* India International Centre, New Delhi.

Khubchandani, L.M. (1981). *Language, Education, and Social Justice.* Pune: Centre for Communication Studies.

Kibby, Marjorie (1999). 'Web Weavers: The Gender Implications of the (re)technologising of the World.' In *Proceedings of the International Conference on Winds of Change—Women and the Culture of Universities,* University of Technology, Sydney, Australia.

Kothari, Brij (1998). Film Songs as Continuing Education: Same Language Subtitling for Literacy. *Economic and Political Weekly,* 33(39): 2507–10.

Kothari, Brij and **Joe Takeda** (2000). 'Same Language Subtitling for Literacy: Small Change for Colossal Gains.' In Subhash C. Bhatnagar and Robert Schware (eds), *Information and Communication Technology in Development,* pp. 176–86. New Delhi: Sage Publications.

Krishna Kumar, K.K. (1999). 'Towards Life Long Learning.' In *Towards Life Long Learning,* State Resource Centre, Jamia Millia, on behalf of National Literacy Mission, Ministry of Human Resource Development, Government of India, New Delhi, and UNESCO.

Masco, Vincent (1994). 'Telecommunications for a Democratic Public Sphere: The Case of Canada.' In Slavko Splichel, Andreiev Calabrese and Colin Sparks (eds), *Information Society and Civil Society,* pp. 307–49, Indiana University Press: West Lafayette.

Merh-Ashraf, Sushama (1996–97a). *A Study of Adult Functional Literacy and Further Education for Women's Empowerment through Telecommunications and Electronic Mass Media,* Final Report. New Delhi: Shastri Indo-Canadian Institute (For Gender and Development Fellowship Project). Mimeo.

———— (1996–97b). 'Literacy Discourse in the Indian Context.' In *Adult Education in India: Search for a Paradigm.* Shimla: Indian Institute of Advanced Study. Mimeo.

———— (1999). *Lala Patel Ki 'Laibary'—Reading Material for Neo-Literates.* New Delhi: National Book Trust. (Adaptation of R.V. Desai's Gujarati play into Hindi.)

Mukarji, Apratim (2000). India Catching Up on Literacy Rate, *Hindustan Times* (Delhi edition), 17 April.

NLM (National Literacy Mission) (2000). *Scheme of Continuing Education for Neo-Literates.* New Delhi: Directorate of Adult Education, Ministry of Human Resource Development, Government of India.

Patel, Ila and **Anita Dighe** (1997). Gender Issues in Literacy Education, Working Paper 108, Institute of Rural Management, Anand.

Pattanayak, D.P. (1990). 'Orality and Literacy: An Indian Perspective', *Indian Journal of Adult Education,* 51(4): 14–20.

Ramakrishnan (2000). 'Application of Information Technology for Rural Postal System.' In Subhash C. Bhatnagar and Robert Schware (eds), *Information and Communication Technology in Development,* pp. 105–12. New Delhi: Sage Publications.

Reddy, N.K. and **Mike Grave** (2000). 'Electronic Support for Rural Healthcare Workers.' In Subhash C. Bhatnagar and Robert Schware (eds), *Information and Communication Technology in Development,* pp. 35–49. New Delhi: Sage Publications.

Thanvi, R. (1992). *Preparing Reading Materials for Neo-Literates,* a report (translated into English from the original Hindi 'Navshaksharon ke liye Pathan Samagri: Ek Report', by Sushama Merh-Ashraf), for National Book Trust, New Delhi. Mimeo.

Vijayaditya, N. (2000). 'A Wired Village: The Warana Experiment'. In Subhash C. Bhatnagar and Robert Schware (eds), *Information and Communication Technology in Development,* pp. 132–40. New Delhi: Sage Publications.

CHAPTER SIX

Pitara: A Simply Written News and Features Magazine for Readers with Low Levels of Literacy

Shalini Joshi

Pitara is a bi-monthly news and features magazine published in Hindi by Nirantar, a resource group based in New Delhi working in the area of women and education. Our activities include creating gender-sensitive information, publications, training, documentation and action research. *Pitara* was launched in 1994 to provide appropriate reading material for people with low levels of literacy. There is a dearth of such material and the material that does exist tends to be dull and didactic in content and written in a language and style which is not sufficiently simple. With readers in rural areas, who have little or no access to entertainment or information, we felt that such a publication would meet a real need.

The target readership of *Pitara* is neo-literate and semi-literate readers, including both men and women. It contains a variety of material—current affairs, stories, articles relating to development, the law and the environment. *Pitara's* working principle is to be 'simple but not simplistic', a principle it applies to complex issues too. It seeks to be informative as well as entertaining. A gender perspective informs the entire content. The magazine often incorporates issues that relate to disadvantaged sections of society, including tribals, 'backward' castes and other minority groups.

The magazine is sent out to individual subscribers and distributed through Total Literacy Campaigns, non-governmental organisations, women's groups and development agencies all over the Hindi-speaking belt, and also in some non-Hindi speaking states.

The Need to Sustain Literacy

Much has been done by Total Literacy Campaigns, NGOs, women's programmes and others to help millions across India to achieve literacy. This has involved organising literacy camps, setting up literacy centres, and creating forums for the dissemination of information.

However, newly learned literacy skills are very fragile. In the absence of a reading culture and without continuing access to 'appropriate reading material', these skills instead of being consolidated can be lost quite easily. The same is the case for semi-literates, for instance, those who have dropped out of school after the fifth standard. Here too, lack of 'practice' in reading and writing over time can easily lead to the loss of literacy skills.

To sustain literacy, building on what has been achieved through the Total Literacy Campaigns and what has been learned in school, it is important that appropriate reading material be published and distributed, material which is specifically produced for neo-literate and semi-literate readers.

It is just as crucial to understand what is meant by 'appropriate reading material'. The language and style of most mainstream newspapers, magazines and other literature is far too difficult; it uses complex vocabularies which are way beyond the scope of a neo-literate reader. But also, the material that is specially created for this readership is usually exceedingly dull and preaches worthy messages which are deemed necessary (by us) for the poor (them) to help them improve their lives.

There is also a tendency to tell readers about the way things 'should' be. Cleanliness, hygiene, family planning and vaccination are often the subject matter of such publications. The image of rural people as being ignorant, dirty and lazy is often reinforced. Women's issues are seldom discussed, and women are almost always portrayed within the stereotyped context of performing household tasks or being part of the scenery instead of central to the plot itself.

Compare this material to what 'we', the educated, like to read. We are literally spoiled for choice. Far more information is available than we can possibly read. We are curious to hear about news from the wider world and about current events. And we read for entertainment—novels, romance, thrillers, science fiction, etc. We regard access to enjoyable and useful reading matter as an inalienable right.

Why then should readers in rural areas have such a limited range of reading material available to them? Why is 'their' need different from 'ours'? Why is their right to literacy and education not complemented by an equally important right to regular access to enjoyable and informative reading material?

The inadequacy of our perception of what rural readers need came across clearly at a workshop that we conducted with the fieldworkers of a south Bihar NGO. All participants were asked to tell us what sort of written material they like to read. They were then asked to describe what they imagined village-level readers would like to read. Both sets of responses were noted. The disparity is striking.

The NGO workers wanted to read about:

- current affairs including political news;
- love stories, folk stories, religious stories;
- legal information;
- new, interesting, unusual information;
- jokes and comics;
- sports news; and
- film magazines.

Their views of what a village-level audience would like to read included:

- issues related to women, such as dowry and rape;
- information related to health, including diseases and cures; and
- social issues and inspiring examples of change.

Why do we imagine that their needs do not include entertaining reading matter such as jokes and comics, sports features and film magazines?

The Format and Content of *Pitara*

The divide between what readers want and what is provided to them, and the underlying notions of 'doing good' and 'bettering people's lives', reflects in most of the little reading material published for neo-literate and semi-literate readers. In an attempt to redress this situation, Nirantar started producing *Pitara* as a monthly news and features magazine in 1994. However, the need to get feedback and develop a dissemination strategy eventually led us to turn it into a bi-monthly.

Why the name *Pitara*? We were keen to select a name that reflected variety and the range of issues that the magazine would cover, and which would also communicate a sense of creativity and fun. We hit upon *Pitara*, traditionally a chest or basket containing a variety of interesting things.

From a News and Features Service to a Magazine

For the first year, *Pitara* was a news and features service. It consisted of items written on separate pages which were then clipped together. The idea was that organisations could then adapt and use all or some sections as resource material for their own work at the local level simply by selecting and using the pages they needed.

From the feedback we gathered that *Pitara* was mostly being used as direct reading material. This was because using *Pitara* as resource material and adapting it to meet local needs clearly required additional effort. There was also a sanctity that people gave to the package, and the idea of unclipping the pages and using them separately was unpalatable. Therefore, we changed to a magazine format, which continues till the present day.

Pitara's Content: Bridging the Gap between 'Us' and 'Them'

The content of *Pitara* seeks to challenge prevailing attitudes and perceptions of the reading habits and information needs of people who have low levels of education. While neo-literate and semi-literate readers do require material which helps them achieve a better quality of life and reflects their own situation and experiences, there is no reason why they should not or cannot read about things and events which are new to them, which give them a range of different information, and which are not always 'serious'. Each issue of *Pitara* tries to strike a balance between complex, information-heavy items and lighter stories, and aims to introduce new ideas. *Pitara*'s content includes:

Current Affairs

Pitara covers topical national, and sometimes international, news items. News items try to be unbiased, presenting both sides of any argument and raising questions at the end for readers who are able to relate to issues outside their immediate concern. For example, readers in rural Haryana could immediately relate to an article on the suicides committed by cotton farmers in Andhra Pradesh. Crop failure due to an overdose of pesticides was the cause, which they understood. But the article also raised larger issues about the development policies being pursued by the state.

Women at a Continuing Education Centre in Mandi District, Reading the Article on 'Dolly Cloning' in Pitara

An article on the issue of cloning written after Dolly, the first sheep to be cloned, led to a discussion amongst a group of women workers in Kutch, Gujarat. There was a heated debate on the issue of 'nature' versus 'nurture', and the advantages and disadvantages of science tampering with human genetics.

Stories

Pitara includes different types of stories in every issue. Some are serious and address issues related to gender, communalism, or development. The stories themselves try to raise questions for the readers, hopefully, without being moralistic or message-loaded.

Another category is 'meaningful' yet light stories. 'Roti Banaye Jat' is an example of such a story. It talks about a man who wants to prove to his wife that her work at home means nothing. So he takes over at home one day, while she goes to the fields to do the work that he is responsible for. He obviously has his hands full at home—cooking, cleaning, seeing to the children, etc. He is terribly late, of course, but he is determined to impress his wife by cooking her a really tasty dal. So after a day of frazzled nerves, he finally runs to her with great pride offering the food he has cooked. She is indeed thrilled, but cannot stop laughing when she sees her husband. He is perplexed and demands an explanation for her laughter. She replies: *'dal to theek hai jatji, par neeche to dekho.'* He was so inundated with work that he forgot to wear his dhoti before going out. This hilarious story has time and again served to communicate the message of how women's work at home is not valued.

Humorous stories make up the third category, and these are meant purely for entertainment.

Women's Issues

Unlike certain niche magazines, *Pitara* is not a magazine solely for women. Some items, however, specifically address the needs of women, in recognition of the fact that there are issues that are of immediate concern to them.

A women's special issue was brought out to mark the occasion of International Women's Day in March 2000. In it, we focused on the more recent concerns of the women's movement. Some of these issues were explored through profiles of 'ordinary' women. These included single women, victims of sexual harassment at the workplace, survivors of child sexual abuse and women living in situations of political conflict.

Culture and Lifestyles

There is a natural desire in us to know about how others live, work, what they wear and eat, and what their cultures are like. Articles on other societies and countries in *Pitara* expose different cultures and ways of living. These items have helped in breaking the notion of 'this is the way things have to be', thereby facilitating a process of questioning life, as we know it.

For example, an article on Eskimos caused much excitement and wonder in a literacy centre for women and girls in Banda. Learners were asked whether they thought that the Eskimos were better off than them. An animated debate followed. Learners compared and contrasted various aspects of the Eskimos' lives with their own: *'they take only two hours to build a home'*; *'they do not have any jatis (castes)'*; *'they kill animals'*; *'they choose their own spouse'*.

Understanding Everyday Phenomena

Some articles also provide explanations for 'mundane' everyday things. These are things and make us curious and make us seek answers—Why do fireflies glow? Why do we feel sleepy after eating? What causes day and night?

In a recently workshop held with a group of facilitators of literacy centres on the use of our material, the question 'why does milk boil on heating' raised the curiosity of the participants. A guessed reply was that 'there must be germs in the milk which just have to get out once it's heated, and therefore milk boils'. All of them admitted that though they've often wondered about several such ordinary things, they haven't been able to find answers to all of them. Then they read the article with great interest.

Development Issues

We also provide information on development issues—issues that relate to health, the Panchayati Raj, agriculture, livelihoods, etc. These articles raise questions on the very nature of development and government policies. Even here, the content is not always within the realm of the familiar. For example, an article on forest fires in Indonesia talked about issues related to small farmers and how the government was unresponsive to their needs. Women, who were part of a literacy programme in Delhi, responded with concern and anger to this item.

Entertainment

In order to address the need for entertaining material, jokes, riddles and short humorous pieces are regularly included. The idea behind this is that reading should be fun. Humour for humour's sake! Jokes are always popular, and very often they are read out even during training sessions in order to provide a break and to lighten the atmosphere.

Survey and Feedback

In 1999, Nirantar undertook a survey of readers in two districts (Bilaspur in Madhya Pradesh and Udaipur in Rajasthan) who had been receiving and reading *Pitara* for more than two years. Some of the findings were:

- Readers considered *Pitara* to be informative and interesting. Most readers thought that *Pitara* gave authentic and unbiased news.
- Readers enjoyed reading the humorous stories, and liked articles on other lifestyles and cultures. They also felt that employment issues, sports news, local news and religious issues should also find place in the magazine.
- Readers wanted *Pitara* to be more interactive and many of them were interested in writing for the magazine.
- Most readers felt that *Pitara* was a 'complete magazine', and it was exactly what they wanted.

Some Comments from Readers Received as Feedback

'*Pitara* is my only link with the outside world.'—Raj Kumar Gupta, an inmate in Nasik Central Jail.

'Sometimes when I read an issue related to women in *Pitara*, I feel that the article is representing me and my world.'—Suneeta, a grassroots activist in Ranikhet district, Uttaranchal.

'*Pitara* is different from all other magazines. I look forward to receiving it every time.'—Mohammad Haroon, a journalist in Karvi, Uttar Pradesh.

'I feel that the writers don't impose their views on the readers in *Pitara*. Instead they raise questions that make readers think on their own. Gender issues are dealt with sensitively in *Pitara*. These issues address both female as well as male readers of the magazine.'—Vasudha, a student of Delhi University after reading one issue of *Pitara*.

'I enjoyed reading about computers and its use in *Pitara*. However, there are people in my village who have not even seen a television screen. How do you expect them to understand this article?'—Milani, a 28-year-old domestic worker in Delhi who reads *Pitara* regularly.

'I and my wife do not have any children. We read the article on test-tube babies in *Pitara*. We too would like to go in for this process in order to have children'—Bhairon Singh, a reader in a village in Udaipur district of Rajasthan.

A 60-year-old Neo-literate Woman Reading Pitara *to Other Women*

Pitara's Style: Creative and Interesting

Material that talks down to people is boring and will hardly ever be read. In *Pitara,* we make an effort to write in a way that is alive and respects readers, but, at the same time, is simple and informative.

Development issues never get written in an essay style; they are generally built around an event, an incident, or even a story which forms the focus of the article. Dilemmas and contradictions are discussed in the stories and case studies. Rather than presenting the issues in black and white, we give them shades of grey.

Thus, while writing about Flavia Agnes, a lawyer who experienced domestic violence, the article discussed her dilemmas, her negotiations with her husband, her fears of 'destroying her family' as part of her struggle, instead of presenting it as a success story of a woman who had overcome violence in her life.

Stories dealing with serious social issues will often have open endings. 'Naam' is a simple story about a woman who is unable to give her name to the man who is compiling the electoral roll. She is embarrassed and her family and neighbours are unable to help her as she is only referred to by her husband's, father's or children's names. Ultimately, while visiting the village where she was born, her friend calls out her name. The story does not make any kind of explicit statement at the end, but it forces the reader to think. This story has been used by several trainers during gender training to initiate discussion on the identity of a woman.

We try to avoid using explicit definitions when new terms and new concepts are introduced. Instead we weave the definition of the word or the idea around a sentence. For example, while referring to the waiting room of the railway station, which not all will be familiar with, we wrote '*Wah railway station ke vishram grih mein agli train ka intezaar kar rahi thi.*' For an item on whales, we had to first establish that just like there is a world on land, there is also an entire world of living creatures which exists under water.

In writing for this particular constituency, we constantly need to question the concepts and contexts which may be familiar to us but may not be understood by the reader. Most of the jargon of development work needs to be avoided.

Pitara's Language: Writing Simply, Not Simplistically

We try to write in the way we speak—this is an important working principle of *Pitara*. We attempt to avoid formal and difficult words. Pure Hindi is not the language of self-expression and communication in most 'Hindi speaking states'. Mainstream Hindi is also an iconic symbol of power and the powerful. While a wide range of reading material in Hindi is available, it is usually written in a style that is incomprehensible and intimidating.

Having realised through feedback the limitations of material that requires a reasonable level of literacy, we created and field tested much simpler material aimed at those at the initial stages of literacy. We used a larger type size, shorter sentences, simpler words and almost no conjoints. One needs to recognise that the situations in which neo-literates read will vary. Sometimes readers will have to negotiate the material on their own, and sometimes they might get assistance from those who have better reading skills.

Keeping in mind the levels of comprehension of our readers, sentences in *Pitara* are kept short and brief. Each sentence will not be more than 13 to 14 words (8 to 10 for those at the initial level of literacy). Each page will not contain more than 250 to 270 words (170 to 200 for those at the initial level). Simplifying the language, yet not simplifying the content, and not talking down to people or thinking of them as children—this is the challenge.

Pitara's Design—Making the Magazine Attractive to Readers

We try not to include illustrations that may look absolutely unfamiliar or very urban or culturally very different—or worse, child-like—to the reader. We often use photographs to illustrate a point. Readers are not able to relate to diagrams of particular parts of the body, which leaves them wondering whether the person shown is physically challenged. The use of bubbles to show thoughts or speech makes readers wonder why there is a cloud above the person's head.

We try to use lots of illustrations and photographs. Apart from providing visual relief by breaking up the text on the page, placing the illustration or photo next to the text it relates to, makes things much clearer to the reader.

Catchy titles generate interest. For example, an article on the benefit of iodised salt was entitled '*swad bhi, sehat bhi*'. Readers told us that this title aroused their curiosity. To avoid any possible confusion or maintain clarity, for serious development articles and news items, we usually use a straightforward title. We use a subtitle where the title is not straightforward. We signpost what is important. The cover of the magazine shows the main feature and lists three other interesting articles. This is done to give readers a flavour of the items in *Pitara*.

The type size of the magazine is larger than usual. For readers who have to struggle with each word, comprehension becomes even more difficult if the words are hard to read. We have not adopted the usual practice of setting the text in more than one column. Columns imply a style of reading that only the more literate are familiar with. Feedback has shown us that neo-literates have a problem with not knowing where to read next when they reach the bottom line of a column.

How *Pitara* is Distributed

Initially, *Pitara* was sent to Total Literacy Campaigns and NGOs working with neo-literates. From the feedback we received, we discovered that neo-literates were not the only readers. A number of letters were sent to us by semi-literate and even literate people who had read or heard of *Pitara*. The magazine crossed the urban-rural boundary, and is being read in semi-urban areas and in big cities. During a visit to Bhopal, we met journalists, doctors and government employees who are avid *Pitara* readers.

During the study that we conducted in Bilaspur and Udaipur districts, we realised that the magazine was shared not only within the family, but also within the whole village. *Pitara* was being read not just by the individual subscriber, but by a large number of people, often before it reached the subscriber.

> Mohanmati, an 85-year-old woman in Gadgodi village of Bilaspur district is a *Pitara* subscriber. Her daughter's father-in-law, who is the local postman, is the first person to read Mohanmati's copy of *Pitara*. He then passes it on to his daughter-in-law. After she has read it, she gives it to her husband, and he to his brother. Only then does Mohanmati get to see her copy.

Pitara is used by activists and volunteers of Total Literacy Campaigns and NGOs as material that can be used for generating discussions at village meetings. Activists read it for themselves. The magazine helps them get a balanced perspective and upgrade their skills. An activist working with a grassroots organisation got so inspired by an article on nurses riding mopeds in villages that she herself started learning to ride a moped.

Items from *Pitara* are used as training resource material. In particular, items on health and panchayati raj have proved valuable as resource material for issue-based training and discussions. Stories on women's issues have been used in gender training to initiate a discussion.

Pitara is used at literacy camps and workshops conducted by NGOs working with neo-literates. For example, Aastha, based in Udaipur, enlarges articles from *Pitara* which it uses as reading material at its literacy camps.

Several local broadsheets and newsletters adapt and use items from *Pitara* in their own publications. Lighter items as well as more serious development items are used in this way. A few regional non-Hindi broadsheets translate our material for their own use. *Akshara Thunga*, a broadsheet in Kannada, uses items from *Pitara* in almost every issue.

Reaching Out to Readers

Pitara was distributed free of cost for its first three years. The initial print run was 1,000 copies. With a growing readership and more and more demand coming in from organisations, gradually the print run increased to almost 20,000. This continued until August 1997, the year in which we sent out letters to our readers requesting that they pay an annual subscription.

Pricing the Magazine

Pricing *Pitara* was something that we had been wanting to do for quite some time. There were several reasons for this:

- We did not want our readers to take *Pitara* 'for granted'. Several organisations had placed bulk orders for *Pitara*. Whilst we sent copies to them, we were not very sure how they were being used, whether they were being used at all. If they had to pay, we felt that this would indicate that they really liked and wanted to read *Pitara*.
- *Pitara* was accessible to most individual readers either through a Total Literacy Campaign or through an NGO functioning in their area. One of our objectives behind bringing out *Pitara* was to make this kind of reading material accessible to the maximum number of people. However, to reach out to individuals outside these networks was a big challenge. One way we felt that we could achieve this was through paid sales from some sort of retail outlet.

- We also felt we needed to make *Pitara* financially self-sustaining in the long run. We had obtained funding from donor organisations and from the government, but we did not want to be dependent on external funding for too long. We realised that subscriptions would not cover the entire cost, yet they could contribute something.

We sent letters to our readers asking for a nominal annual subscription. The subscription rate was initially set at Rs 15 but was increased to Rs 30 in 2000. For bulk orders, the rate was slightly lower. We also realised that in an environment where there was no culture of buying something to read, we needed to 'create a demand' for reading material. In order to do this and also to enthuse people about *Pitara*, we organised cultural programmes (*jathas*) around *Pitara* in some villages in Gurgaon, Haryana. Whole villages turned up to see plays, skits and songs whose themes were related to the items in *Pitara*. This certainly created interest, but was expensive in terms of the human and financial resources involved.

So we tried another experiment. We recruited individuals as promoters or 'agents' of *Pitara*. In some areas of Delhi, Gurgaon and Uttar Pradesh, we identified small shopkeepers, magazine and tea stall owners, grassroots workers and others who were interested in acting in this capacity. The sales through this approach were not very encouraging because the profit margin that we offered our agents was not high enough (as compared with other magazines), and we found it difficult to monitor the performance of all the agents we had recruited.

We also tried distributing *Pitara* through the Central News Agency in Delhi. However, this only reached out to people who already had access to a lot of other reading material, and who were based in cities and towns. For a newly literate person the idea of approaching a magazine stall or a book shop in order to 'buy' reading material would be alien.

To try to improve our distribution, we sought the help of an expert in rural marketing to review the introduction of paid subscriptions and to suggest more effective ways of reaching out to the maximum number of people. The study was conducted in two districts of Madhya Pradesh (which included a Total Literacy Campaign district) and Rajasthan (where we selected a district where several NGOs were active). The main recommendations of the independent consultant were:

- To include a readers' page in each issue of *Pitara*, which would contain stories or articles sent in by the readers.
- To have contests or competitions, which would encourage readers to write for *Pitara*. This would also provide a forum to readers to share their experiences with others and send in news from their area.

- To network with government officials at the state level for distributing *Pitara* through their networks.
- To ask activists of field-based NGOs to become promoters of *Pitara*.

To take forward this last recommendation, a system of agents and supervisors was set up in Tilonia district of Rajasthan with the help of a local NGO. The three agents whom we had identified included a student, a newspaper vendor and an NGO activist. Out of the three, only the NGO activist was really committed to the idea of promoting *Pitara*.

After experimenting with how to organise this method of distribution, we have now arrived at a mechanism which we think is both effective and replicable for marketing a publication like *Pitara*.

NGO activists, volunteers and other field-level workers will become agents of *Pitara*. These are people who are committed, who understand the value of a magazine like *Pitara* and our concern of reaching out to readers who are deprived of reading material, and for whom profit is not the major concern. They will take annual subscriptions from potential readers (in contrast to selling individual copies). After keeping a commission of 10 per cent, they will send the remaining money along with the address of the reader to Nirantar. We will then correspond directly with the reader.

Up until August 1998, when copies were being distributed free, the print run of *Pitara* was 20,000, and the number of copies actually distributed was approximately 17,000. When we asked for subscriptions for the first time (in August 1998), the print run dropped to around 4,000. At present we are printing 8,200 copies, and the number of copies being distributed is 8,000. The number of organisations subscribing to *Pitara* is 5,500 (this includes both distribution through NGOs and Total Literacy Campaigns). The number of individual subscribers is 2,500.

We are continuing to look for mechanisms for increasing our distribution. We are also making efforts to develop links with other organisations that bring out materials for people with low levels of education. A first initiative of stocking each others' publications has been taken by three organisations—Eklavya, Bharat Gyan Vigyan Samiti and Nirantar.

The *Mahila Dakiya* Experience: Producing Reading Material Locally

Being a centrally researched and written publication, *Pitara* definitely has a wider outreach than material that is produced locally. However, material produced locally serves another purpose—making local news, local issues and local information available to local people. The experience of bringing out such material can also be an enriching and empowering one for the group involved, as is clear from the example of *Mahila Dakiya*, a newspaper produced by a group of neo-literate and semi-literate women in Uttar Pradesh.

Nirantar wanted to find other ways of creating news sheets for neo-literates. We wanted to create a prototype for a broadsheet newspaper. Some members of Nirantar were placed at the National Institute of Adult Education (NIAE) at that time. They started to explore ways of doing this.

We wanted to develop a way of working that actually involved neo-literates and semi-literates in both the writing and the production processes. This, we hoped, would ultimately transfer skills and lead to the setting up of a decentralised production unit. This effort resulted in the creation of what is an entirely locally produced broadsheet, *Mahila Dakiya.*

Like *Pitara*, *Mahila Dakiya* was also conceived of at a stage when there was little being published for women who had just become literate. Not only was there a need for material that could sustain their literacy skills, but also for material that would provide them with information and be able to create a forum so that they could share their experiences and ideas.

Both Nirantar and Mahila Samakhya (a government programme based in Banda for the education and empowerment of women) felt that if women needed material which was responsive to their needs, then they should be part of creating the publication themselves, and in their own language. This entailed running training workshops in order to facilitate the transfer of skills to the women who would edit and produce the publication, who were mostly neo-literate and semi-literate.

Over the years, *Mahila Dakiya* has become a weapon to report and comment upon topical issues and matters arising outside the Mahila Samakhya programme. The newspaper includes lighter, humorous items such as jokes; articles on other cultures; local news; and information on government schemes, whilst keeping its main focus on women's issues.

The process of bringing out *Mahila Dakiya* regularly has been a continuous learning process for the team. The newspaper has given the team members recognition and respect not only within the community, but also by the administration, for providing information that is true and unbiased. The *Mahila Dakiya* team was chosen for the Chameli Devi Award for outstanding women journalists in 1996, the first time that this was given to a group of rural women.

The experiences of women have been covered in *Mahila Dakiya*, which includes issues of gender, caste and class. While we cannot say that these incidents have changed social structures and perceptions, they have definitely brought them to the centrestage as issues for discussion in the community.

Over time *Mahila Dakiya* has gained the image of being a watchdog in relation to these issues. Information on government funds, local incidents of harassment and other such matters have been published in the paper, and this has made the community recognise the potential of the *Mahila Dakiya* as an effective tool for reporting and highlighting these issues.

This has resulted in a flood of letters from readers who are seeking some form of redress for their grievances. Feedback from the community has proved beyond doubt that *Mahila Dakiya* caters to every section of the rural audience, that it knows the pulse of the villagers, and that its form, style and language are all highly appreciated.

The experience of bringing out *Mahila Dakiya* has been an enriching one for all concerned. It has provided many insights into what interests women, what they are interested in reading, what issues they give priority to, and the matters of visual literacy.

Whilst the experience was empowering for the group concerned, it has remained a very localised experience. In the macro context, the reach of such individual initiatives by themselves have their limitations unless they are replicated widely. Training groups to bring out local material would be a crucial factor since there is a danger of locally produced material being poorly written and produced, and therefore, being considered of low or little value. And there is the question of who can sustain this kind of an initiative. Many grassroots groups may be interested in producing a community newspaper, but they do not always have the time or the human resources to carry the idea forward.

This approach contrasts with publishing centrally researched and written material. The content and reach of such material will definitely be far wider, and it will be far better produced. But it is not an either/or situation in terms of centrally/locally produced materials. Both have value and both can be relevant and interesting to readers.

Some Challenges Facing *Pitara*

With the experience we have gained so far, we can begin to assess the impact we are making and how we can improve what we are doing. The following are some of the factors that have emerged and which appear to us to be important:

Creating a Demand for Books and Reading

One of the objectives in bringing out *Pitara* was to reach out to as many readers as possible with limited or newly acquired literacy skills and low levels of formal education. A number of strategies were adopted to do this. However, there is not, at the moment, a reading culture amongst such people, certainly not for reading books or magazines. A contributory factor might be that there is not much available for them to read. But there is a still a need to create a demand for reading material.

The Problem of Pricing

Asking for subscriptions from readers with very low incomes, who are not part of the book/magazine/newspaper reading culture, is an enormous challenge. Our interactions with readers in the past have shown that buying something to read, no matter what its price, is something that figures extremely low or not at all in their list of priorities.

When we started to price *Pitara* and letters requesting subscriptions were sent out, many organisations either did not respond at all or substantially reduced the number of copies of the magazine that they now had to pay for. Our print run at this stage came down drastically. We are now trying to redress this in several ways, including sending out letters to heads of organisations and discussing the potential of *Pitara* with organisations doing grassroots work. Despite this, the print run still remains far lower than what it was.

Another issue with pricing is the extent to which the need to sell copies will begin to influence editorial policy. Would this lead to the inclusion of more 'sensational' issues simply to increase circulation? Whilst it is important to give readers what they want or need, this should not mean compromising the objectives of the publication.

Difficulties in Marketing

Our experiments with marketing *Pitara* through other channels have not been very encouraging. One question, to which we are struggling to find a solution, is how alternative media can successfully tap mainstream channels of distribution. While it may be beyond the capacity of any organisation on its own to do this, a number of organisations together might collaborate to set up a central distribution system for all their publications. There is a need for organisations to create a forum for discussing such issues and finding some answers.

Long-term Sustainability

The issue of becoming independent of donor support and sustainable in the long term is crucial. Our funding has been erratic and our dependence on government funding has meant long waits for renewal of the grant, with the potential danger of some degree of censorship over what the magazine contains. Given this situation, we have found it extremely hard to keep bringing out the magazine regularly and on schedule. We know that subscriptions by themselves will not cover the costs of publishing and distributing *Pitara* (see Box 6.1). How then can we make it independent of any large-scale funding?

Box 6.1: Current income and where it comes from		
Total annual income is Rs 14,62,324 from the following sources:		
UNDP	*Department of Education*	*Subscriptions*
6,19,350	7,79,760	63,214
42.35%	53.32%	4.32%

Getting Systematic Feedback from Readers

Feedback is not merely of academic interest to us. The information we get back from our readers enables us to understand them and their needs better, and to modify *Pitara* accordingly. This is essential if *Pitara* is to succeed. We also need to validate our assumptions about writing for people with low levels of literacy and education. And if we can make valid generalisations, then this will be of value to others engaged in the process of bringing out material for these readers.

In the past, we have sought feedback in several ways. In feedback sessions, we have asked readers to read the magazine whilst we take note of where they are stopping to see what they find difficult and what they are comfortable with. We have also asked readers to rank items that they liked in a particular issue. We have divided participants into small groups and asked them to read and explain to others the meaning of a particular article. In the study we conducted in 1999, we designed a questionnaire which asked readers to note what they liked and disliked about *Pitara*, and what suggestions they could make for improving it.

There is a danger that readers will only tell us what they think we want to hear. We have found it difficult to evoke spontaneous responses, and we now feel that there is a need to develop simple and non-threatening feedback mechanisms. We would also like to use our findings in our advocacy with the government.

With this feedback from our readers and learning from our experience as we go along, Nirantar should be able to respond creatively to these challenges. Publishing a magazine like *Pitara* is aimed at readers with low levels of literacy, will never be easy; but it can play a really important part in sustaining literacy by providing interesting reading material in an accessible form.

CHAPTER SEVEN

Finding Light (*Ujjas*) in the Space between Literacy and Communication

Preeti Soni

This is the voice of *Ujjas*, the magazine we produce in Kutch. Three sample editorials written during the last five years are provided here:

1995: How has this happened? The foundation of human society is man and woman, yes? The man becomes literate, and the woman is left illiterate! What kind of behaviour is this—by society, by our mothers and our fathers? Our society is a lie, and is responsible for this state of affairs. A daughter's right to education is equal to that of a son. Then why are we, as mothers, also denying them this right? Why are we women also ruining the lives of our young girls? Come on! Let us, together, change the lives of our daughters, and begin educating them.

1996: All of us got together, and formed a Sangathan, right? At the village level, we formed mahila mandals. All the mahila mandals together formed taluka sangathans. In the mandals we are working towards our development—and we work together on issues of our health, education, credit, crafts, etc. The mandals have also nominated group leaders—'agewans'. They ensure that we all stay on track. From amongst these 'agewans', we have formed block-level samitis of our sangathans. We thus take the responsibility for our development. Supporting us are the 'shaher' (city women) from the organization. They support us in our difficulties, and they enable us to work with all women. Now, let us look at what happens sometimes. The 'agewan' gets one set of information and guidance from our taluka samiti members. Then the city women come and give her another set of guidance. Her own mahila mandal members want her to work according to their guidelines. Who should she listen to? Who should she not listen to? Oh dear! The poor thing is really confused. And what is the cause of all this? The lack of coordination between the samiti women and the 'city' members of the organization! They need to coordinate their messages better! This is what I think!

1997: Long ago, we were ruled by the 'Angrez' (the English). After great difficulty, we became independent from their rule. Many people paid with their blood for this independence. This year, we are supposed to be completing 50 years of our independence from 'angrez' rule. The whole country is rejoicing this 50th anniversary. But wait a moment. Just think! We have become independent as Indians, but have we become independent as human beings? Earlier, the fight was for independence from foreign rule. Now we and our own society are responsible. But, we have all become selfish. In our villages we do not get regular employment, we do not get our full wages, we do not have enough to eat, we do not get education. Perhaps, the whole country is like this. How then can we be called independent? Put your hand on your heart, and say honestly: 'Have we really gained independence?'

> '...and that is why we sing.
> We have chosen this path of struggle,
> So that human eyes are not clouded by tears,
> So that the fading light of dusk does not confuse,
> So that the night does not bring fear,
> So that no one's days are unhappy,
> So that no one snatches someone else's 'roti' for their own happiness,
> That is why we sing...'

... and that is why we write.

Brief Background of KMVS and *Ujjas*

Kutch Mahila Vikas Sangathan (KMVS) is a collective of rural women's groups from six blocks of Kutch district in Gujarat—Abdasa, Nakhatrana and Pachcham region in north-west Kutch on the border with Pakistan; Mundra Taluka in south Kutch; and the eastern region of Kutch called Vagad. The objective of our Sangathan is to help women understand the causes of poverty and become confident as decision makers. By doing this, they can exert greater control over the development process, they can become empowered members of their community, their village and their home, and they can provide the leadership for community action.

The Sangathan is primarily engaged in addressing issues of domestic violence, providing education, meeting the information needs of women and girls, giving access to credit and markets for craft producers, dealing with ecological degradation and the impact of drought on agriculture and animal husbandry, meeting women's health needs, and making the government health system more accountable.

KMVS has sponsored and supported four block-level federations of mahila mandals, called 'taluka mahila sangathans'. One of these, the Mundra Taluka Mahila Sangathan, which works primarily on issues of domestic violence, runs the Ujjas Mahiti Kendra, which publishes and prints a monthly newsletter called *Ujjas*. Its readership is the membership of the Sangathan.

The objective of *Ujjas* is to make useful and relevant reading material accessible to neo-literate rural women in simple Gujarati, to document and share experiences of the Sangathan members across the six blocks through the newsletter, and give voice to the collective expression of the Sangathan through the written word. *Ujjas* is conceived, compiled, edited, handwritten and silkscreen-printed by rural women who are members of the Sangathan, and reaches out to 2,500 readers every month.

The Birth of *Ujjas* (April 1993 to June 1995)

In 1993, 20 members of the Pachcham Sangathan—a region with 100 per cent illiteracy amongst women—showed a desire to acquire literacy skills after three years of discussing the issue. Two 40-day literacy camps were organised by KMVS. By the time the camp ended, most of the women had acquired some basic functional literacy skills. But they also raised an important question: 'how can we retain and sustain our new found skills?'.

Whilst most of the women were already involved in managing their mahila mandals' activities, they did not think that this by itself would help them retain their literacy skills. After much discussion, they came up with a solution. They would write a regular letter reporting the Sangathan activities for all the other members of the Sangathan. Gradually, the idea of publishing a newsletter emerged, which neo-literate women would write and send out themselves. The readers would primarily be women who had begun to take a leadership role in their mahila mandal. The idea was that neo-literates would get regular reading material and that the newsletter would become a medium of sharing information and ideas for the Sangathan. They felt that the literacy camp had brought a new light to their lives. They described the camp as having spread *ujjas*, and they promptly named their newsletter *Ujjas*.

Gradually, women from the other Sangathans began to feel that they wanted to participate in the making of *Ujjas*—after all, they argued, 'even women without literacy skills, but who had knowledge and understanding, could provide inputs and stories!'

In order to accommodate all the Sangathan's representatives and taking into account the long distances between each taluka (Kutch is the second largest district in all of India), *Ujjas* was started at the KMVS office in Bhuj. However, within a year the Sangathan members of Mundra taluka, which had a higher number of neo-literates (some with prior literacy skills and some acquired through the Sangathan camps), began to play a more active role in the making of *Ujjas*.

In many ways, the birth of *Ujjas* and the experience of its formative years provided the Sangathan with a more holistic understanding of 'education'. The setting up of *Ujjas* was accompanied by a surge of social action and training within the Sangathan. This enabled members to understand themselves and the society they were living in. Education became more clearly defined as something which combined knowledge and the exchange of information and experience, and the acquisition of new skills, with literacy being of particular importance.

The main responsibility for ensuring that *Ujjas* was brought out regularly at this stage lay with the KMVS staff, while the Sangathan members actually produced the newsletter. The newsletter was of two pages and 300 copies were printed. During the first two years, *Ujjas* helped foster a strong sense of ownership amongst the Sangathan's growing leadership, and it encouraged women to acknowledge their need for literacy and information. The problems encountered in this period were mainly a lack of systems, and irregularity in publication—often a month would be skipped.

The Next Stage of *Ujjas* (July 1995 to March 1999)

After a year and a half of writing the newsletter, and using a photocopier to produce the copies, Mundra Sangathan offered to learn printing skills in order to cut copying costs. KMVS facilitated a screen-printing training course for a team of Mundra women, who set up a one-table screen-printing unit. The publication of the newsletter then shifted to Mundra Mahila Sangathan.

For a few months, women from the other talukas would get together in Mundra to bring out the monthly newsletter. This became increasingly difficult as the distances were more than 100 km. So Mundra Mahila Sangathan became the main publisher of the newsletter.

At this stage, though the readers were primarily members of the mahila mandals, they also comprised sarpanches, mahila panchayat members, government officers, voluntary organisations and local citizens. The objective during this phase was to share and disseminate information in a simple manner, to inform opinion and provide a perspective on issues, to develop the Ujjas Information Centre, and to ensure that *Ujjas* was published every month. All the activities, editing, reporting, printing and posting copies to readers was undertaken by a team of seven to eight women from Mundra Sangathan working for 15 to 20 days every month with guidance from the KMVS education team. The number of readers increased during these four years from 300 to 2,000. At the same time, the newsletter was extended to eight pages.

During this period, the focus of the entire Sangathan was on skills training and information, with *Ujjas* becoming the focal point of its activity by 1998. The overall focus on adult literacy began to wane once the first generation of Sangathan leaders became literate. The identity of the Mundra Sangathan, and to some extent, of the KMVS as a whole, began to be established through *Ujjas*. The readership shifted from being women only to including young men as well. The main difficulty faced was the constant turnover in the *Ujjas* editorial team, which meant constant training and re-training. In 1998, *Ujjas* also faced its first litigation case. It was accused of defamation by a village community because of an article about the rampant alcoholism in the village and a report on the village's harassment of its mahila sarpanch who was trying to fight this alcoholism.

The Current Phase (April 1999 to December 2000)

The publication continues to be published by Mundra Sangathan. The readers remain the same as in the previous period, but there has been an increase in the mahila mandal membership. There is now a team of 12 rural reporters who go out and find the news, bringing in stories both from the villages and the readers, researching and writing special reports, and producing illustrations.

The Ujjas *Editorial Team at Work*

The objective during this phase has been to make *Ujjas* a completely self-financed publication through subscriptions, with exceptions being made in cases where the women cannot afford to pay. The price is Rs 3 per copy, and this covers all the costs of production and distribution. It is aiming to achieve a 100 per cent subscription rate with its rural readership. Subscription drives have already been started in the villages. By 2003, *Ujjas* aims to be fully self-sufficient. As of now, the revenue from the screen-printing unit ensures that administrative costs are completely covered, but not the publication costs, which have been funded partially through grants.

With the gradual growth in the membership of the Sangathans, there was an accompanying increase in the readership of *Ujjas*, perhaps not in proportion with the membership, given the very low literacy levels in all the Sangathan areas. But the Sangathan members soon felt that their voice needed to be heard, not only by other women in the villages, but also by the world 'outside'. Copies of *Ujjas* have started going to some of the key government officers, district officials, local politicians, and other voluntary organizations, and local citizens, especially those who are in some way associated with the Sangathan, such as sarpanches, and more recently, to all the mahila sarpanches of the district. The readership now stands at 2,500. *Ujjas* has been newly designed with 16 pages to accommodate the growing amount of news and information. The current objective is to increase the readership even further.

This increase in readership, both within the Sangathan and outside, provided a clearer feedback to *Ujjas* and also increased the expectations of the readers. The rural women readers wanted all kinds of information—stories, health information, political news, happenings in the world outside and Sangathan news. Clearly, they did not only want articles inspiring them to take action on development issues! And with the outside readers, the Sangathan and KMVS both realised that for the first time people in Kutch began to genuinely understand what this organisation was all about.

The *Ujjas* team began to realise the potency of information sharing. They began to perceive the newsletter not only as reading material for neo-literates, but as an important medium of communication. What may be obvious to us was only gradually recognised by the Sangathan members. This resulted in them doing more than just collecting Sangathan information. They began to read other literature and news so that they could reproduce articles or features in *Ujjas*. Two women became particularly good at reading, comprehending, simplifying what they had read, adding their perspective, and writing it for *Ujjas*. KMVS and the Sangathan members also began to realise that *Ujjas* had become a documenter of Sangathan activities and history over the years. Reading the 12 issues published each year, it was easy to reconstruct the progress of the Sangathan.

Ujjas is in the process of going through some changes itself. It is developing from a newsletter into a magazine which will be largely printed with only the editorial in handwritten form, which is always written in the local dialect, Kutchi, albeit using a Gujarati script, while the rest of *Ujjas* is written in very simple Gujarati.

From *Ujjas* to the Ujjas Information Centre

It was through the medium of publishing and disseminating the newsletter that the *Ujjas* team began to feel the inadequacy of the newsletter to reach out to all within the Sangathan. Surveys undertaken by KMVS in 1996 and 1998 showed that although *Ujjas* had interested even the men of the villages to become readers, and had contributed to an increased demand for reading material (in some villages people had started buying the Kutch daily newspaper *Kutch Mitra* after regularly reading

Ujjas), illiterate women had to depend on someone in the village to read out to them, or remain outside the world of *Ujjas*. Scores of women within the Sangathan and outside felt that they would like something on audio-tape too.

The *Ujjas* team began to think of themselves as an information centre, and not just as newsletter publishers. The idea of communicating through radio began to be discussed. As a pre-test, the *Ujjas* team broadcast a trial programme on radio. Following that, as an experiment, KMVS produced a tape which contained a radio drama and a section covering literacy teaching through the audiotape. While the experimental tape demonstrated that literacy could be taught through audio with a primer, if the material was well designed and accompanied by contact sessions, it was also clear that the drama and literacy components did not go well together, each detracted from the other.

Through the trials, the pre-testing and the feedback it received, the *Ujjas* team decided that they would extend their activities to radio broadcasting, but only after KMVS had helped set up the systems and train the reporters to handle the medium. It was also decided that in the first year, Ujjas Radio, which functions from Bhuj, would attempt to build a listenership through a docu-drama, which would also provide a motivation for literacy. And after a year of working with the medium of radio, only then would the teaching of literacy with a primer be taken up. And that is how in 1999 the Sangathan was able to develop a year-long radio programme called '*Kunjal Panje Kutch Ji*' (the Sarus Crane of our Kutch), which airs the many issues surrounding mahila sarpanches and Panchayati Raj in a dramatised form. All 53 episodes of this weekly radio serial are situated in an imaginative village also called Ujjas.

An effort is now being made to create a synergy between the newsletter and the radio programme.

Key Issues Emerging from the *Ujjas* Experience

I want to share a few of the key issues relating to *Ujjas* that have raised much discussion and debate within the Sangathan. There are many more dilemmas and questions that have been generated through our work with rural women, including issues of their empowerment, of creating a curriculum for adolescent girls, promoting and sustaining adult literacy and developing a community managed information centre. I will restrict this discussion to *Ujjas*, which constitutes just one part of our overall education for empowerment work.

Is *Ujjas* Providing Information or Meeting Literacy Needs?

Ujjas started as a post-literacy initiative. It was clear that where basic literacy skills exist, a newsletter such as *Ujjas* could go a long way towards stimulating a desire for knowledge and information. It was only later that it became evident that it can also stimulate an environment of information sharing within the community, when the time becomes ripe for doing concentrated literacy work.

The Sangathans supported by KMVS are now demanding knowledge and information, but this is happening only after 10 years of effort. *Ujjas* has definitely contributed to this demand. Often when someone asked the active members of the Sangathan what their most primary need was—expecting them to say health care, clean water, etc.—they would invariably get the answer 'information' (*mahiti*). However, in the past couple of years, there has been a growing acknowledgement that while information, knowledge and training could build the capacity of the women, literacy was critical because this made them feel more 'able'.

This is also a reflection of how the Sangathan has been developing. In its earlier years, the Sangathan members were trying to build their credibility amongst the community. They were under constant pressure to show that their moving out from their 'families' and 'homes' and into the public arena had actually benefited the community. The most visible way in which this could be expressed by Sangathan members to the community at large was through a furious exchange of information. Members began to be seen as the most credible sources of information about government programmes, health matters, loans and much more.

Once the scale of the development programmes increased, needs have shifted to more 'on the ground' abilities, when the commitment to literacy is finally increasing within the Sangathan.

Who Does *Ujjas* Represent?

While the Sangathan takes pride in the fact that the *Ujjas* is managed and edited entirely by a team of neo-literate women, there is a continuing debate on the question of whether the editorial team of *Ujjas* is a representative voice of the Sangathan as a whole, or whether *Ujjas* is only an expression of a few empowered women, who provide a role model to readers as to what they could do, if they too emulated Kamlaben, Radhaben, Dhanuba and the other women in the team.

A second question has arisen—what if *Ujjas* had been written, edited and published by, let us say, KMVS staff? How would it have been different? And would they represent the Sangathan less?

Radhaben, Ujjas' *Staff Artist*

The answers to these questions may not be quite as simple as it appears. The editorial team of *Ujjas*, whilst being a part of the larger collective, are more likely to think, speak and reflect like the other women in the villages. But they do not always do so. They identify more with *Ujjas* than with the larger Sangathan, and there are times when they need to represent all their readers, not necessarily only their women compatriots in the villages. They may sometimes slip into 'talking down' to the readers, as they have greater knowledge and experience. They may sometimes take a stand on an issue, through which they might gain greater credibility in the outside world. This underscores the fact that having a community-controlled media, which is truly community controlled and becomes a real representative voice for the community, does not happen automatically. This has to be developed through education by developing a proactive readership in this case, and by having an external support facilitator.

Should We Be Communicating in Kutchi or Gujarati?

The Kutchi dialect does not have a script, but is a dialect which is spoken all over the rural areas of Kutch, much more than Gujarati is. Over the past 15 years or so, Gujarati has become the language which is understood by most, though not always spoken.

The Sangathan had to make the difficult decision as to what the language of *Ujjas* should be. While most favoured Kutchi, they were also faced with the fact that Kutchi when written in the Gujarati script is extremely difficult for a neo-literate to read, as the phonetic structure of the language is quite different. The same problem has also been faced in developing the curriculum for women and girls in the learning centres.

Although it was not seen as the perfect solution to a knotty problem, it was finally agreed by everyone that all forms of community expression and any creative expression—be this through songs, poetry, proverbs, stories—and the *Ujjas* editorial should be in Kutchi. It was also felt that self-expression in Kutchi should be encouraged and enriched within the Sangathan, at the same time, the communication and teaching processes should be made much more personalised.

However, it was also felt that learning Gujarati was equally important. If this was ignored, it would only isolate and marginalise women further from the mainstream. Thus, news stories, interviews and features are all written in Gujarati. Similarly, in the radio programme, the 30-minute weekly programme consists of a drama in Kutchi and a 5-minute news report from other villages in Gujarati, although sometimes even that is in Kutchi.

The many positive responses on the 'Kutchi bhasha' of the programme from the listeners has affirmed the primacy of Kutchi in the social, cultural and political lives of people, especially women. However, KMVS still needs to create a better methodology for teaching literacy in Kutchi and Gujarati. Currently, we tend to tilt towards Gujarati because of the Gujarati alphabet.

How Can Information Create Change?

The true power and strength of a newsletter such as *Ujjas* perhaps comes from the fact that it is only one of many development activities that the Sangathans undertake. Whilst, on the one hand, *Ujjas* plays the role of a watchdog, critiquing government policies, attitudes and performance, it is immediately questioned by its readers on what the Mundra Sangathan is doing about these same issues, on the other.

We believe that the publication of *Ujjas* by a collective, which is also involved in social action on the ground, has led to a fairly good understanding of the line separating freedom and licence, on the one hand, and rights and responsibilities, on the other. They realise that they are not only expressing their views (though they do much of that, and quite rightly too!), but they can back up these views with action.

Their public stand on an issue gives them credibility and this then increases the scope for action. On the editing table, putting their views into print gives them a more confident edge. This has made us believe that people's organisations should have some form of medium of communication under their direct control. Of course, this idea is not new, the best example being the freedom struggle. But we have somehow lost this link between writing and action as an integral part of creating a movement. The idea has got replaced by a whole lot of newsletters produced by NGOs and professional development workers, which do not carry the same edge, though they might be more informative.

I would like to share an example here. The Mundra Sangathan last year launched an anti-alcoholism campaign, which soon spread into other blocks. But what was interesting to the Sangathan was that readers of *Ujjas* and listeners of Ujjas Radio were inviting Sangathan members to come and support them to launch their own campaign which had been inspired by reading or hearing about what others were doing. The point here is that the transformative capacity of the community is increased when the community itself controls the media. Shouldn't our efforts be directed towards helping many more of these hands-on initiatives to emerge all over the country?

PART IV

PROMOTION OF READING CULTURE AND PUBLISHING FOR RURAL AREAS

Fostering a Reading Culture and an Experiment with Workbooks in Post-literacy Education

P.K. Sasidharan and S. Madasamy

The mass literacy campaigns of the 1990s have created a new bond between people and books. Underlying this bond is a dialogue between two cultures, that of the 'learned' and of the 'learning'. The massive participation of women, the emergence of leadership among the rural youth, the evolution of a new literature for neo-literates, and the recognition of the potential of the neo-literates themselves to become 'neo-creators', are some of the developments which characterise this dialogue. However, in the absence of efforts to maintain the dialogue, the positive changes that have been witnessed are likely to disappear.

Reading Culture

One of the interventions that should be part of these efforts is an appropriate strategy to foster a reading culture so as to create a continuously learning society. In other words, how can a book 'reach' the reader—the neo-literate—or how will it communicate with him or her? This communication is of prime importance. Not even the best-furnished village library will serve any purpose in the absence of such communication.

There is no guarantee that the availability of books—or good literacy levels among the neo-literates—will automatically result in neo-literates taking to reading in a big way. In any case, to the neo-literate, books belong to a different, higher, realm. The impression we gathered from our experience in Virudhunagar District, Tamil Nadu was that our broadsheet called *Vaasal* was more popular than the books themselves, at least initially. *Vaasal*, meaning 'entrance', was the first ever neo-literate newspaper to be brought out by a campaign. Consisting of two pages of regular newspaper size, it presented on the first page regional, national and international (whenever the occasion demanded) news. The second page was devoted to stories and experiences of neo-literates. The language, the style and the content were carefully vetted in order to ensure that they would facilitate reading. Further, *Vaasal* was well-illustrated and in multicolour. The number of readers of *Vaasal* who chose to respond through letters rose to around 7,000. This was inspiring. But the situation regarding books was of concern. The campaign had provided for books with great expectations—the post-literacy proposal was accompanied by three neo-literate books and the prototype of the broadsheet *Vaasal*. But interest in books was low. The task was, therefore, to generate strategies to create higher levels of interest in books. The discussion that follows is derived from our experience while co-ordinating the Literacy Campaign in Virudhunagar District (erstwhile Kamarajar district) between 1991 and 1995. The initial interventions resulted in a library movement, Jan Vachan Andolan, in 1996, which was brought under the auspices of the Bharat Gyan Vigyan Samiti (BGVS).

Reading Aloud in Groups

While introducing books to the masses, the initial emphasis was on the age-old tradition of 'the listening culture'. However, integration into a cultural format was ensured. This resulted in a breakthrough at a time when the availability of some 26 books for neo-literates had not promoted reading to the extent expected. The manner in which the 'listening culture' was introduced is interesting. A girl volunteer was observed reading out a folktale, *Nalla Thangal*, in a clear, loud tone to a rapt audience of women in a post-literacy circle. This exercise was then repeated elsewhere, and it kept the neo-literates spellbound. The impact of the book on neo-literates was too significant for us to have left it at that. The book 'reached' them and could communicate with the listeners. While silent reading is a personal experience, reading aloud in a group turns it into a social event. Realising the potential of loud reading in a group, we made the introduction of a book an integral part of a two-hour transaction in post-literacy circles. Appropriate stories were chosen; the reading itself was followed by a participatory discussion based on concrete questions on the material. This inspired further interest in books. Having tasted the joy of books, the listeners could themselves go back to the books.

Types of Reading

Later, many ways of reading were developed.

- We can read a book from beginning to end without interruption, without ever trying to explain anything in the middle. It is reading, pure and simple, in the natural intonation of the language concerned. The impact depends on the quality of the voice and the fluency and the clarity with which the book is read out.
- Then there is reading with simultaneous visualisation. Even as a person is reading, two or three persons will be visualising simultaneously the portions being read.
- There is yet another method—joint reading. That is to say, two or three persons will share the reading of a book. By prior agreement each marks his or her portions. Then, when the book is read out, the listeners find out that there are two or three persons taking turns to read. A variation of this method is when one person reads standing before the audience, while the second reader remains among the audience and reads from his or her seat, thus springing a surprise on the audience.
- Yet another form of reading is reading alternating with narration. This means that one portion is read out while the following portion is narrated. This process is repeated till the book is finished.
- And finally, one can read just parts, asking the listeners to go to the books for the unread portions.

While experimenting with such methods of reading, it was necessary to remind the neo-literates periodically that the books were waiting to be read by them, and that the joy of reading was something they should look forward to. The book must not be far from their consciousness.

Another strategy to help neo-literates have access to the book is dramatisation or rendering it in skit form. A team of about six people can achieve both reading and dramatisation, if a campaign is planned well.

Library Movement: A Campaign

The reading strategies helped initiate a library movement, a campaign that aimed at strengthening or establishing village libraries for neo-literates and inspiring people to read. In May 1995, 45 teams trekked through 450 villages in the district in five days, carrying loads of books. Dividing a day and part of the night between two villages, each team talked to neo-literates and other villagers about strengthening the libraries. The teams donated books to the libraries, persuaded people to collect books for the libraries, and read out books to gatherings of neo-literates. They also sold books that had been specially produced by BGVS Resource Centre, Madurai and the Tamil Nadu Science Forum for neo-literates. The teams would take the books to the audience after the reading and the dramatisation. They also went from door to door showing people the books and asking them to buy. The book sales experiment (which sold some 65,000 copies in five days) exploded the myth that rural folk would not buy books. The success of the sales is further testimony to the efficacy of the strategies used for taking books to people. In fact, people asked for books by title or content.

The Prerequisites

What is needed for such a strategic effort? Availability of suitable neo-literacy books, availability of personnel and a structure for implementation, and adequate training to the personnel, are the three key elements.

Neo-literacy Books

Though there have been many campaigns, very few have tried to produce books for neo-literates. These campaigns had the potential to put to use creativity in the field, but most failed to do so. The Virudhunagar District Proposal, as mentioned earlier, incorporated neo-literacy books right at the planning stage. This campaign made use of the tales, songs

Taking Books to the People: Many Ways

and riddles contributed by the neo-literates themselves. In effect, the neo-literates were the authors, with the campaign functionaries giving a suitable shape to the reading material, so that it could meet the requirements of the print medium. By the time the library movement developed, the District campaign had come out with 40 titles in addition to six 'workbooks'. The BGVS Resource Centre, Madurai, also published about 40 titles for neo-literates. The BGVS books were priced between Rs 1.50 and Rs 2 per copy, since affordability of the books was a concern.

Structure and Training

A structure and a team are needed to carry out the activities. In the districts the co-ordinators for panchayats can easily organise training in book reading for the circle guide and a few others. Some good and clear voices have to be identified to do the reading. The next requirement is training in the various types of reading. One very important requirement is that the readers should be well versed with the books they are going to introduce. A casual approach will be disastrous. Similarly, in dramatisation, the team members have to be conscious of the supremacy of the book. They usually have a tendency to bring to the fore their acting talents, which may undermine the book. It is the book that is the hero and the message about reading the book should go home to the audience. That is, dramatisation and other cultural presentations should not become ends in themselves.

The BGVS built on these core ideas and developed a People's Reading Movement (Jan Vachan Andolan) in 1996. It could draw many other Indian states into it. How the movement develops in the future is to be seen.

Problems

As in any other work related to literacy, sustainability is a pivotal issue. Demotivation will set in because of apathy and lack of appreciation for the idea on the part of the campaign managers like the chairpersons of the Zilla Saksharata Samitis. Or, some of the workers may try to take away the books from the people just to deposit them back at the ZSS Headquarters because the accountant general's office might question the ZSS chairpersons as to why the books were not recovered.

One need not wait for the illiterates to turn into neo-literates before introducing books—one can start even in the total literacy phase. This will relieve the monotony and break the tyranny of the primer. If introduced to books and broadsheets at this early stage, the learner will be in a better position to read when the minimum required skill is achieved. A book (and broadsheets and newspapers) must go to the literacy centre or the post-literacy circle frequently, if not regularly. This means that there need not always be a big campaign to take books to people.

All this leads us to the question: 'What is the place of books in a literacy campaign?' Noone familiar with the literacy campaigns can have escaped the monotony of the primers. A look at the very first primer would show that it is teacher-centred and not learner-focused. It suffers from the problem of 'high load'; there is no touch of humour anywhere. Consequently, it does not give the learners an opportunity to taste success. A study undertaken by Saraswathy (1999) in Pudukottai district, Tamil Nadu, corroborates and complements these observations.

Having become aware of these negative characteristics of the primers, we tried to redeem the situation in the Virudhunagar district Arivoli Iyakkam (the TL campaign of the erstwhile Kamarajar district) during the TL phase itself through strategies other than developing new and diversified material. This included intensive, regular training for improving the skills of the volunteers and the promotion of greater two-way communication between the volunteers and the learner-groups in the specific context of sharing folk heritage. Such a process contributed to reducing drop out among both volunteers and learners. However, when the campaign moved into the PL phase, a determination to develop a variety of materials took hold. This was helped by the fact that the interaction between volunteers and learners had brought in folk songs, riddles, puzzles, epigrammatic and picturesque speech,[1] and stories—all in written form.

In this part of the chapter, we wish to focus on the 'workbooks' we produced during the PL campaign. The pedagogical doubt about the propriety of workbooks in PL, which might assail some, did not occur to us. Even if it had occurred, we would not have been deterred by any technicalities. The only goal was to involve the neo-literates more in the process of reading, writing, thinking and responding. The assumption was that the circle guide or volunteer should not dominate the scene but be part of the group of learners. Together, they would create knowledge.

It has to be observed here that with each workbook the objectives also evolved further. The following explanation illustrates the point. The first workbook was a mix of exercises demanding oral and written responses. Besides, there was scope for drawing. There was a combination of fun, challenges and values incorporated into it. All the same, it took too long to complete the workbook. From here, the series progressed through a development of witty riddles to a process of conscientisation and decision making and freeing oneself from fear through collective contemplation and discussion. In addition to these workbooks, there was a workbook for a specific group, namely, the neo-literate workers in the match factories. Each of the six workbooks that were produced has an internal pattern of progression—from the simple to the complex or from the concrete to the abstract. But it must be admitted that the series

---

1. In Tamil this is called *solavadai*. It is different from a proverb in that it does not try to moralise; instead, it offers a sharp comment, which may be witty, sarcastic or pathetic. For example, in Hindi, there is the one about the cat going to Kasi after killing 99 rats. Often it is alliterative. A few examples: *Elumpillatha naakku enkittum pesum* (The fickle tongue that it is, it would wag this way or that with ease). *Vengala poottai odaichu velakkumaru kalavandanam* (Heard this?...breaking the bronze lock he has stolen just the broom). This is a sarcastic expression of incredulity or a comment on big efforts that produce small outcomes.

is incomplete as we could not attain the goal of 10 we had thought of. The workbooks that were developed are as follows:

1. *Arivoli* Exercise Book
2. *Ettikku Potti* (A Battle of Wits)
3. *Yarukku Ethu Thevai* (Who Needs What?)
4. *Kalvi Namakku Kalkandu* (Learning is a Joy)
5. *Oru Mudivu Eduppom* (Let us Decide Now)
6. *Achathil Irundhu Viduthalai* (Freedom from Fear)

A brief sketch of the contents and the format in which they are presented is provided below. All the workbooks are illustrated. The third workbook has only pictorial representations as the core content.

Arivoli Exercise Book: PL Workbook 1

This first workbook had 36 exercises spread over 40 pages. The exercises were interesting and demand oral and written responses. They also involved some drawing. However, there was a feeling that smaller workbooks, given at intervals of one or two months, would ensure greater involvement of learners and be less forbidding.

Ettikku Potti (A Battle of Wits): PL Workbook 2

Ettikku Potti consisted of 20 pages and was sent to the learners in the post-literacy circles. They were retrieved from the learners after they had done the exercises. After ascertaining the performance, some specimens were retained at the Block *Arivoli* Office and the District *Arivoli* Office, and the rest were returned to the learners.

Ettikku Potti means stiff competition, or as implied here, a battle of wits. The actors, a grandfather and a grandmother, are engaged in a fierce battle of wits, but they use only riddles. When the grandfather throws a riddle, the grandmother provides the answer with another riddle. Both lead to the same thing. The learner has to find out the answers and write them down in the boxes given for this purpose. After that, the learners have to go a step further and write down, to the extent possible, words that are associated with the answers.

For example, the grandfather throws the, following challenge: 'The hen with a single leg has a tummy-full of eggs. What is it?' The grandma counters it with: 'The one in a red saree has a tummy-full of kids.' The answer is 'red chilli'. The learners would then write down associated words like hot, masala, cook, water, chutney and tears. The grandmother tries to puzzle the grandfather with, 'Just in eight days a harvest, that too, without any bullocks and plough.' The grandpa's answer: 'A flower, born in water and having no roots in the soil, liked by men and women, but never worn by maidens in their hair. The answer is 'uppu' (salt). The word 'poo' which is how the last syllable of 'uppu' is pronounced, means flower in Tamil. The learners may very well go on to write down a large number of words connected with the answer—sea, workers, food, taste. We can even introduce the Dandi March, Gandhiji, freedom, and so on.

Yarukku Ethu Thevai (Who Needs What?): PL Workbook 3

Next in the series was *Yarukku Ethu Thevai*, a workbook with the theme of man's individual and community needs. This was a workbook which had illustrations that the neo-literates had to observe, recognise, interpret and explain in written form. The answers would then lead to discussions. For example, Exercise No. 4 represents a bus stop with a few people waiting eagerly. Exercise No. 10 shows a bride and a priest all ready to solemnise the marriage. All that is needed is the bridegroom. Exercise No. 20 shows a family on the pavement. Their need is obvious. Exercises 53 and 54 depict a family and a village, respectively. What are their needs? Thus, the neo-literates proceed from the simple and immediate individual needs to the larger and ⸀nore community-oriented needs, and write them down.

Kalvi Namakku Kalkandu (Learning is a Joy): PL Workbook 4, A Workbook for the Learners in the Match Factories

Virudhunagar district has a large number of match factories which employ a number of youth. We had a large number of learners from the match factories. Taking into consideration the environment with which they are familiar and in which they work, we prepared a special workbook capable of kindling their interest and involvement. Most of the exercises were oriented towards objects the match factory workers were handling. The words they regularly heard or uttered, the health hazards they were exposed to, and the educational opportunities that they were losing, figured in the workbook. The numerical part also reflected their financial activities. The workbook reached learners in match factories in Sattur, Sivakasi, Srivilliputhur, Vembakottai, Virudhunagar and many other places.

Broadsheet and Workbook

Oru Mudivu Eduppom (Let Us Decide Now): PL Workbook 5

The theme of *Oru Mudivu Eduppom* was decision making. The exercise were presented through the offer of a number of options in a given situation. The neo-literates were to consider all these options and arrive at a decision after weighing the pros and the cons of each. The exercise was done in groups. As an example, the simplest exercise is cited below.

Exercise: A child stricken with diarrhoea is represented.
Options:

- Father says, 'Need not do anything. She will be all right in two days.'
- Grandma says, 'Take her to the sorcerer and have some chanting done.'
- Mother says, 'Let us take her to a doctor.'

Another exercise deals with women contesting panchayat elections. The options are:

- Women should not enter public life. Their reputation may suffer. There will be problems.

• They must contest elections. They have reserved wards. They are capable of good management and administration.

Achathil Irundhu Viduthalai (Freedom from Fear): PL Workbook 6

This was in the format of episodes in the life of Sumathi, a young girl who grows up with her mother after her father has deserted them. The workbook presents different situations in her life when the girl stands dazed not knowing how to face them or what to do. It covers a variety of experiences like, getting beaten up by the teacher at school, becoming a target of eve-teasing, marriage to her relative (a drunkard) against her will, sadness at the death of her mother and her husband, and being approached by a young man of her liking with the offer of remarriage. On all these occasions, Sumathi is diffident and scared. The neo-literates were asked to advise Sumathi and give her courage and confidence. Their suggestions were written in the space provided for the purpose.

Who Devised the Workbooks?

The conceptualisation of these workbooks came from the BGVS activists who were co-ordinating the campaign. They also did the final editing and fine-tuning. But volunteers and panchayat level co-ordinators were involved in providing the concepts, the concrete exercises, and the various episodes and situations. All the workbooks acknowledge their contribution. A look at Workbook 5 shows that 43 village level co-ordinators contributed to the formulation of the exercises contained in it. It must be mentioned here that the co-ordinators were not graduates; most of them were just school graduates. But they lived among the neo-literates, worked with them and attended regular training sessions.

How Did the Workbooks Work?

The workbooks were for transaction in groups in the PL circles. The circle guide or the panchayat co-ordinator would read out the situations and facilitate the discussion. He or she was not supposed to impose an idea or suggestion on the neo-literates but was expected to elicit their ideas or opinions. That alone would give the neo-literate person the opportunity to speak out on her own. However, invariably, the group would finally ask the initiator as to what he/she thought of the situation. The facilitator would then offer an opinion. Often, the learners revised their earlier stand if they found that their opinion had been different from the really acceptable one.

For Workbook 2, the neo-literate circle was broken into smaller groups of four or five to facilitate group transactions. In the case of workbooks 5 and 6, in many villages, the presented situations were reinforced through role plays and dramatisation along with reading, before discussions started.

The impact of these workbooks was great, especially in breaking the culture of silence. Exercise No. 9 in 'Let us Decide Now' presents a husband who regularly beats up his wife. Unable to bear it any more, the wife goes to her parents. What should she do now? One option is to go back and fall at her husband's feet. Another is to go to court and ask for alimony. Yet another option is to remain with her parents and forget about the marriage. In a PL circle in Vembakottai block, this particular episode generated a lot of heat. A young woman was vehemently speaking in favour of the court solution when her own husband arrived on the scene. He could not believe what was happening and asked his wife whether she would go to court if something similar happened to her. She asserted that she would. The husband could not bear this and slapped his wife in front of the entire group. But the group rose as one to reprimand the husband and bring him to his senses.

During a visit to a remote village called Laida in Sambalpur district of Orissa, we had an opportunity to try out some of these exercises from our workbooks. This was done by taking them beyond the barriers of two languages, Tamil and English. Exercise No. 11 in *Arivoli* Exercise Book has the theme of 'Right Pairs'. Examples: Field and (crop or weed); Marriage and (dowry or love); Thirst and (alcohol or buttermilk). While interacting with a group of learners in the village on the right pair—thirst–alcohol or thirst–buttermilk—the learners, most of whom were women, came out in favour of buttermilk. Every one was talking against alcohol. An elderly woman learner then turned to an equally elderly man and began to scold him for drinking alcohol regularly. The woman was vociferous. The poor man, surprised at the onslaught, admitted that drinking was not good but also added that he only drank a little (not very little). This incensed the woman and she did not let him go until he had made a solemn promise not to drink again.

This interaction indicates how discussion responses get translated into action. And, in the case of 'Freedom from Fear', wonderful things happened in some villages. One situation the protagonist Sumathi faces is the compulsion to abort. When it becomes known that the child would be born in the month of *Aadi* (July–August), the mother-in-law, who is superstitious, wishes to have the foetus aborted since she believes the child would bring harm to the family. Sumathi does not agree but is too timid to argue. The learners in Anuppankulam village in Sivakasi, when asked to give confidence to Sumathi, came out with advice like, 'It is life, we should not take it'; 'After all, I am willing to bear the child and will meet the consequences, if any.' The learners believed that if polite suggestions did not convince the elder woman, then Sumathi should not hesitate to dare the mother-in-law. They said, 'Appadiyaanaa mamiyare oru kai parthida vendiyathu than' (If it comes to that, let it be a fight to the finish. No buckling under.). A general sentiment still persists in many villages against widow remarriage. Aware of this, we chose to present the widowed Sumathi before the neo-literates with Sankar, the man of her liking, wearing wedding garlands. When this episode was presented to learners' groups, in some villages women made auspicious cries of blessing; in some they made a gift of money to the married couple; and in others old men sang wedding songs to bless the couple.

Some Observations

Yet, some observations and self-criticism cannot be out of place.

- Workbook 1 was good and interesting but lengthy. Shorter workbooks were more powerful.
- Workbook 2 animated the neo-literates, making them laugh and write.
- In the case of Workbook 3, we saw neo-literates concentrating on writing. We had expected them to enter into a discussion on the illustrated situations. But probably the joy of discovery led them to concentrate on writing.
- In the other discussion-based workbooks, discussion took place effectively but writing did not occur to a considerable extent.
- Workbook 6 became an essential and powerful tool during the 'library movement' undertaken in the district in May 1995. So writing was almost neglected.
- In the case of a few exercises, the perception of the designers was found to be unrealistic. For instance, in Workbook 5, in a particular situation, the parents of a young girl are faced with the problem of choosing one bridegroom from among four men, each man having some plus points and some shortcomings. When this exercise was placed before the neo-literate group in a village, pat came the frank

P.K. Sasidharan and S. Madasamy

and blunt reply from a woman, 'Where on earth do so many young men queue up to marry one girl?'

- In the case of Workbook 6, some of our co-ordinators were of the opinion that neo-literates would not approve of the remarriage of the widowed Sumathi. From what was stated earlier, we can see that this fear was unrealistic.
- If the panchayat co-ordinators, who are so close to the reality of the villagers, can themselves suffer from imperfect perceptions and cause imperfection in material production, how faulty, imperfect and inappropriate can the materials produced by distant State Resource Centres (SRCs) be? Such SRCs are large in number. For instance, the PL Primer prepared by the SRC for Pudukottai deals with relevant women's issues like status of women, child marriage and dowry, but the presentation is so drab and lifeless that no learner will ever feel like getting involved in the situations.

Challenges or Threats

External and internal interference can bring the scope of such workbooks to nought, at least for some time. The Virudhunagar campaign had to suffer owing to the apathy of the campaign manager and the animosity of another functionary whose biggest complaint was that the campaign was publishing books, which many other districts were not doing! There are at least two things that should be done in order to minimise the impact of such blindness and apathy. One, in the case of government-sponsored campaigns, sensitise the bureaucratic structure to the special life and nature of literacy campaigns. The bureaucrats should be offered orientation programmes. Of course, this can happen only if the concerned government sincerely wishes the campaign to be carried out in its real spirit. Those who consider it to be just one of many schemes will achieve little. This is not to say that the entire bureaucracy is to blame. In fact, Virudhunagar had a district magistrate who conducted literacy classes himself and two other bureaucrats who took great interest in the production of good material for the learners.[2] Second, where

---

2. Mr K. Gnanadesikan, IAS, took literacy classes regularly in a village called Kooraikundu. Mr V. Gunalan, IAS, realised that there was a demand for books among neo-literates and initiated material production. Mr K.N. Venkataraman, IAS, inspired the production of books in large numbers. In fact, the resource group could not rise to his expectations. This sort of involvement inspired the district team.

there are good organisations specialising in materials and training but suffering from lack of resources, assistance will have to be offered. An illustrative case is that of the BGVS Resource Centre which wanted to provide a hundred books to neo-literates on 'Know Your Land: Tamil Nadu'. It approached many institutions without much success.

The BGVS Resource Centre, Madurai, now believes that it can address the issue of designing workbooks that would make people discuss as well as write down their discussions. It is our dream to have workbooks that integrate both discussion and writing. We also hope to produce adequate reading material for children and women. Already the women in self-help groups like *Malar* and *Thuligal* are using the broadsheet and books brought out by the BGVS Resource Centre, Madurai and TNSF. This is an encouraging sign for the future.

Reference

Saraswathy,L.S. (1999). 'Understanding the Process of Learning in the Context of Total Literacy Campaign and its Links to Basic Education: Pudukottai District, Tamil Nadu State.' A Study Report.

CHAPTER NINE

Bringing Books to People

Michael Norton

This is a description of a rural publishing initiative which was started in 1997 by the Centre for Innovation in Voluntary Action (CIVA) in Andhra Pradesh. Our experience suggests that: (*a*) there is a demand for books in rural areas that are both appropriate and affordable, but such books are not generally available; (*b*) there are opportunities for producing factual books that give people information, advice and an understanding of their rights, and that such books can enhance people's livelihoods and support development; but (*c*) a great deal of new thinking and experimentation is needed if we are to improve people's access to books and create a reading culture.

Challenges and Opportunities of Publishing in Rural Areas

Some two-thirds of India's population live in rural areas. This population can be considered a discrete target for publishers, where information can be provided to meet their particular information needs as well as for entertainment. This is not yet seen as an attractive market by most publishers, who see little opportunity for publishing or making a commercial return. Most prefer to concentrate on publishing for rural middle classes in English and the main Indian languages.

But we believe that this is an important market, and that if it is possible to publish successfully for this readership, then this will enable books to be brought into the centre of people's lives. Although the numbers of potential readers is large, this is not an easy market to publish for, for the following reasons:

- *Low levels of literacy*: But literacy will continue to remain low unless attractive and interesting books are published which people will want to read. This 'chicken and egg' situation is one of the key challenges. Any right to literacy must be accompanied by a right to access to books. Good books need to be published to create an interest in reading and build the desire for books.
- *Availability*: There are no well-established mechanisms for book distribution in rural areas. In most villages and smaller towns there are books on sale. Any successful rural publishing activity has to be accompanied by greater efforts to get books distributed into India's villages and into readers' hands.
- *Affordability*: People in rural areas are often extremely poor, so books have to be really cheap if publishing is to succeed. Publishing in India is relatively cheap (which is simply not the case in Africa). But can books be published cheaply enough? Our view is that this is possible, and also that people are prepared to pay slightly higher prices for books that are of particular interest or value to them.

If these problems can be overcome, there are many Indian languages where the number of speakers is large enough to sustain a viable publishing operation. For example, there are over 80 million Telugu speakers, which is a far larger population than exists for most European and African languages.

There are specific information needs for this market, which publishers could usefully address, and there are two opportunities for supporting these efforts.

1. *The literacy agenda*: Building on the Total Literacy Campaigns, the network of continuing education centres and other community libraries provides a potential outlet for the books that are published for this market. The new strategy for the National Literacy Mission launched in 1999 (NLM, 1999) sets out a role for NGOs and

private publishers. For suitable titles in Telugu, this could mean sales of up to 25,000 copies.

2. *The development agenda*: Many NGOs and international agencies such as the UN system have communication needs with their target audiences. But more importantly, they also have money which can be used to support the development or distribution of publications. They usually lack publishing expertise, and much of the educational material they have been producing has been expensively designed, poorly edited and of little practical use. So the successful publishing of information can assist them with their advocacy strategies and development work.

Genesis of an Idea

CIVA is a UK-based NGO which has been working in India since 1995. Our main projects in India are Books for Change, which is a specialist publisher and distributor of books and training materials for the development sector based in Bangalore; the NFI Innovations Fund which makes small grants for innovations in health, community development and the promotion of voluntarism, which is a partnership with the National Foundation for India and Oxfam India; and our village publishing work in Andhra Pradesh.

Our interest in village publishing was sparked by a talk entitled 'Low Cost Publishing for the Millions' at the 1995 Zimbabwe International Book Fair given by the late Asang Machwe, Managing Director of New Age International Limited, a leading Delhi publisher. He was also co-founder with the Rajiv Gandhi Foundation of a village library programme which at that time had established over 500 village libraries in eight states.

Asang Machwe was our partner in setting up Books for Change, although after his early death in 1996, we brought in ActionAid India. Books for Change publishes mostly in English and Hindi, but we wanted to explore ways of reaching out to rural masses with limited literacy skills with appropriate literature. This would build on publishing work that New Age had been doing in Andhra Pradesh where they had published books on sericulture and oilseeds for farmers. Our idea was:

• To publish factual books for rural people giving them information on their rights, the opportunities available to them for improving their lives and ideas for enhancing their livelihoods. These would be small, affordable publications, written in simple language with plenty of illustrations.

- To work in partnership with NGOs and other development agencies who were working with poor people on these issues, who had the technical expertise in the areas we intended to publish, but who lacked any publishing or distribution expertise or capacity.
- To provide this expertise and capacity by establishing a specialist publishing unit based in Hyderabad.
- At the same time to encourage the development of village libraries and to experiment with ideas for rural book distribution.
- To confine this programme of work within one language (Telugu) and one state (Andhra Pradesh).

We obtained three-year funding from the UK's National Lottery Charities Board for a three-part programme, comprising publishing, distribution and libraries. This has now been extended for a further three years.

There is nothing startling in any of what we are doing; many of the ideas have been tried by others in other contexts. What is unique perhaps is the combination of ideas that we bring together in our programme:

- Working in partnership with publishers, NGOs, literacy and development agencies.
- The linking of development communication with professional publishing expertise.
- Publishing appropriate books, whilst also addressing the issues of distribution and availability.
- Creating a project that is large enough and will continue for long enough to have some real impact.

We are also seeking to bring together the agendas for development and literacy. It is well understood that literacy and education create a platform for development by enabling ideas to spread and allowing people to make informed choices. The development process itself can also be promoted by providing people with relevant information, alongside the sensitisation, training and community mobilisation which is the focus of most development work. And if the books are appropriate and interesting, this in turn will encourage a reading habit and help sustain fragile literacy skills. This creates a virtuous circle of literacy and development, and suggests that there is much more scope for bringing together organisations, resources and efforts in these two distinct sectors.

The Village Publishing Programme

In the two year period 1998 to 2000, we published 84 posters in eight sets on community health and different series of books on forest management (five titles), income generation for rural women (five titles), organic farming techniques (two titles), farmers' rights (one title) and disability (one title). Each series was developed in partnership with one or more development agencies. Our partners included UNDP, Cooperative Development Foundation, Deccan Development Society, PT Reddy Farm Foundation, Centre for Environment Concerns and CARE.

The books were contained between 16 and 48 pages and were well illustrated. Some books were printed in full colour, some in two colours and some in black only. All were printed on good quality paper and published in laminated two or four colour covers. We started with a print run of 2,000 copies for the first titles, but raised this to 3,000 copies in response to demand and with a growing confidence in what we were doing. For distribution, we developed the following outlets:

- We asked each partner to buy back a proportion of the print run for use in their own work. This varied from 250 to 1,000 copies. We believed that we were doing them a service by helping them publish information professionally and cost-effectively, which they could then use in their development and training work and to disseminate their ideas.
- We set up book stalls at conferences and exhibited at book fairs, where there was likely to be an interest in what we were publishing. This often led to bulk sales. In some cases, we joined forces with other specialist publishers (such as Literacy House and Hyderabad Book Trust) to put on a joint display.
- We wholesaled the books through Vishalaandhra, the largest book distributor in Andhra Pradesh and sold copies through our village bookselling schemes (see section on village bookselling programme). We also sold our books to the village libraries we had set up, and to Development of Women and Children in Rural Areas (DWCRA) groups, Mutually Aided Co-operative Societies (MACS) groups and other village level institutions which might have a budget for books.
- We contacted training agencies (such as the National Institute of Agricultural Extension Management), with a request to use the books as part of their training, and development agencies (such as the Integrated Tribal Development Agencies) who might be interested in purchasing bulk copies for their networks.

- We made contact with the National Literacy Mission and the Continuing Education Programme, where there are opportunities for getting books distributed across the network of continuing education centres.

By paying as much attention to the distribution as to the publishing, in the first two years, we were able to recover over Rs 9 lakh out of a total expenditure of Rs 20 lakh from the sales income that we generated (including the bulk purchase of books by our partners). This income plus the value of the stock of books at the end of the period which would continue to be sold (and reprinted when stock ran out) suggests that there is an economic viability for this kind of publishing if the development costs of creating the publication are underwritten, such that at least the printing and distribution costs can be recovered from the sales income.[1]

Deccan Development Society offered us one title to develop with them on 'Vermicomposting'. When we published it, they recognised the impact that this would have both on their work and on the credibility of their organisation, and they immediately set about developing ideas for a series on organic farming techniques that we would publish with them. One of the innovations of our project has been to work with NGOs and development agencies to produce and publish material in a professional and cost-effective way. See Box 9.1 for four examples of how we have done this. Many NGOs and development organisations have important information and ideas created from their experience of working with poor people. With professional support, they can turn this into publications that are interesting and appropriate to their target audience.

Box 9.1: Examples of collaboration with NGOs

1. In Chowdrpally village, a vermicomposting unit has been set up. The project organisers had no information on how to do this. They got hold of our book on vermicomposting which is a simple pictorial step-by-step guide, and used this information to design their unit. They have now purchased 100 more copies of the book, which they will distribute to 100 farmers who set up satellite units in their own fields for composting their own organic waste. This was supported by a local NGO called PEACE.

---

1. A full list of the Books for Change Village Publishing Unit publications is available from Books for Change, 22 Krishnapuri Colony, West Maredpalli, Secunderabad 500 026.

The publication was developed with the Deccan Development Society, who also bought 1,000 copies for their own use.

2. The PT Reddy Farm Foundation had a budget from Oxfam for information dissemination. Instead of producing and circulating their own leaflet, they provided us with the text for a publication called *Buy with Care* aimed at farmers to inform them about dealing with suppliers and how to exercise their consumer rights. Their budget allowed them to purchase 1,000 copies of the publication for their own use, which also helped underwrite the first print run of this useful publication.

3. The UNDP Poverty Alleviation Programme in Kurnool District of Andhra Pradesh had been training local people as community health workers. They wanted to leave behind information with important messages on maternal and child health. We took their training material which we re-wrote into 84 posters published in eight sets, which were distributed within the district, but are now also available for purchase by health centres, hospitals, community centres, etc. The UNDP contributed a grant towards the development costs and paid for 325 poster sets.

4. The Cooperative Development Foundation created a series of five publications to support its training on thrift and credit. A purchaser of one of the titles, *How to Set Up a Thrift Cooperative*, went on to set up a thrift cooperative using information contained in the book.

The Village Libraries Programme

The library movement was an important part of the freedom struggle, and many libraries were set up in towns and villages from the end of the 19th century. But today, where these libraries still exist, they are mostly run down and a shadow of what they were. Libraries were also created as part of the continuing education phase of the literacy programme, where premises were identified and books purchased, but little or nothing was done to make sure that the libraries functioned effectively.

Yet a thriving library movement could be a cornerstone of a reading culture as well as an important outlet for new books being published. This aspiration is contained in 'The Scheme for Continuing Education', the new programme of the National Literacy Mission where the potential is seen of a village library developing into a village information centre.

A Book on Setting Up a Thrift Co-operative Published in Association with the Co-operative Development Foundation

A Book on Vermicomposting Published in Association with the Deccan Development Society

We decided to establish libraries in villages in Nizamabad and Medak Districts and in the Hyderabad slum communities where there were no existing libraries. Working with the Rajiv Gandhi Foundation and local partners, over a period of two years we set up 85 libraries. Each was provided with equipment and around 300 books in the first year with further books in the second year, plus an honorarium and training for the village librarian. In addition, subscriptions to one or two daily news-papers and magazines were taken out. The local community provided the premises.

From carefully monitoring progress of numbers of family members, levels of book borrowing and newspaper readership, and through our interactions with librarians, we were able to identify two barriers to successful libraries.

- Lack of any budget for the continuing purchase of books. Libraries need a continuing supply of new books in order to create interest amongst readers.

- Poor motivation and lack of skills in librarians. The training that is available concentrates on library systems for cataloguing books and lending them out. But the real skills needed in a librarian are to do with creating a sense of excitement about the library so that people want to come and read or borrow books.

To address these, we have undertaken a survey of reading habits, information needs and attitudes to the library with a sample of 1,500 people from 10 villages, and we are now developing a librarian training programme. The overall aim of the training programme is to encourage better librarianship, and to make libraries more user-friendly so that they become a lively community centre for promoting literacy and development.

We have also raised some money to make small grants to libraries for additional book purchase, and we have experimented with the idea of a nodal library circulating books on a rotating basis to a cluster of libraries. Book borrowing figures seem to indicate that these initiatives lead to an increase in both membership and book borrowing.

It now seems to us a priority to make existing libraries thrive. On the basis of 'try, try and try again', we will be trying to develop ways of making libraries work really well, rather than continuing to create new libraries.

The Village Bookselling Programme

If rural publishing is to succeed, then there have to be systems for distributing books to the target readership. This will also help create a reading culture, which cannot exist if books are not available. For this reason, we wanted to include an experimental rural bookselling project alongside our work on village publishing and village libraries.

The idea for our project started with another talk at the Zimbabwe Book Fair, this time in 1996 and given by Arvind Kumar, then Director of the National Book Trust. He described his experiences of taking books to villages and the importance of keeping prices low where they found that people were really interested in books and in buying them. At that time, Rs 3 to Rs 5 seemed to be the barrier, although today it might be around Rs 10 (what people suggest as being a reasonable price might actually not be when it comes to deciding to part with money).

From these observations, we developed the idea of salespeople travelling by bicycle or by bus taking books into villages and selling these in schools, at melas, in markets and to libraries and community centres. We asked two local NGOs, Literacy House (which is part of the state resource centre and the well-known women's college, Andhra Mahila Sabha) and PEACE to develop schemes for us.

Although the results have not been universally good, we found that one bookseller did manage to generate an impressive monthly income

Books Being Sold by Redappa at a Weekly Village Market

from his commission (35 to 40 per cent). He was hard working and committed, and he was extremely thoughtful about how he set about selling books. He was careful to select appropriate books for the people he was expecting to sell to. He also made sure that there was some advance promotion (through posters and a free booklet on the joys of reading that were produced specially for the scheme). He was proud of his success. With the income generated, he was able to purchase a bicycle and a wristwatch for himself, become the first person in his family to open a bank account (in which he deposited Rs 3,000), and buy two calves for his family, all from his first four months of bookselling.

The other booksellers were not nearly so successful. They do not seem to have been sufficiently motivated, and the supervisory structure put in place did not manage to control them. It was also possible that the wrong people were chosen to become booksellers, and that the stock of books was not of wide enough interest. But our one successful bookseller has demonstrated that a demand for books does exist in rural areas and that this might be sufficient to provide a good livelihood for booksellers going from village to village selling books. This is sufficient evidence to indicate that more development work is needed for this idea.[2]

Criteria for Successful Publishing of Information

From our experience in village publishing, we now feel that in order to publish successfully for a rural readership, a publisher needs to think about the following issues:

The Relevance of What is Being Published

- Books should relate to the needs and interests of people. Ideas for books can be generated through discussions with the local community (reader-led), or can stem from the information agendas of those working with them (publisher-led). Books can be for entertainment as well as for information.
- Information books should reflect the lives and situations of the readers and be factually relevant. This requires a process of field-testing. All our books are developed into a draft form and then read to local people for comment and discussion. The ideas generated from this process are used to finalise the text.
- Books should be written in a level of language which is appropriate. This depends on the readership, which should be clearly defined at the outset. For neo-literates, the books need to have a restricted vocabulary, but avoid being childish. Field-testing can identify when the language needs to be simplified. We have commissioned a dictionary of Telugu words for neo-literate publishing from Literacy House, Hyderabad. We also want to look at the idea of publishing the same information in separate publications for different readers, for example, turning our health posters into a range of simple booklets for women with limited reading skills as well as manuals for health workers.
- The text needs to be properly edited. Most people who know about the techniques or the technologies can't write, and when they do

2. A training video of a rural bookseller at work 'Why not be a Village Bookseller' has been produced by Centre for Development Communication, Hyderabad.

write, the manuscripts they produce are over-long, boring and contain too many jargon words. The procedure we have adopted has
been to rewrite manuscripts using a professional editor. Most writers recognise their inadequacies and are happy with this arrange-
ment. Most manuscripts can (and should) be cut by at least 50 per
cent. This is the philosophy of 'less is more'—the fewer the words,
the greater the impact.

- The type size should be reasonably large (we use a very readable 20
  or 22 point typeface), the page layout attractive and there should
  be lots of illustrations. Good design is really important.

Books should inform through giving examples or telling stories, reflecting people's lives back to themselves rather than preaching at them.
Books can also capture local knowledge and ideas. It is here that rural
publishing can be most powerful. A creative publisher can find lots of
ways of doing this, as illustrated in Box 9.2.

Box 9.2: Stories of rural publishing

- ACCORD is a successful development project working with
  adivasis in the Nilgiri Hills of Tamil Nadu. The history of the
  oppression of the adivasis and their fight back is important—
  the 'theft' of their land by tea planters and the forest authorities, their fight back which included a campaign to acquire
  land to live on and now the purchase of a tea plantation by the
  community as a community asset to generate income and create employment. ACCORD plans to document this in a publication for the community.
- Fatima Bi, a sarpanch in Andhra Pradesh, won a United Nations
  award for achievement. The story of her struggle from caste
  and gender oppression to political success could be an inspi-
  ration to others. We would like to publish her biography in a
  series *Heroes of Our Time*.
- A dalit widow in Chowdrpally was given 4 hectares of parched
  land. She planted a variety of drought-resistant crops and used
  organic techniques. During a recent drought, she was one of
  the few farmers in the village to earn a reasonable income. We
  would like to document this as a case study.
- Our very first publication was called *Lakshmi's Teashop*. We
  wanted to show people how to set up a business. We took as
  an example, a fictional couple (Lakshmi and her husband Raja)
  who decided they didn't want to remain poor. Their idea was

---

to start a teashop. The book follows their efforts, showing how they planned their enterprise, calculated the economics of providing a cup of tea and set up a business. Dry information has been turned into a story.

- The Rajiv Gandhi Foundation has run community writing workshops, where local people can document their experiences or ideas for publication. Not everything that emerges from this is publishable, and it will require a good editor to take forward the manuscript.

Affordability of Books

This is a really key issue. If books are to be cheap, then they need to be cheaply produced. But they also need to be nicely produced, so that readers see them as something that is valuable. If they are to be used for reference, they need to be durable. The publisher should ensure the following:

- Production values should be appropriate to the purpose of the book. We have adopted quite high production values for our publications, which are fact books intended to have a long shelf life. We use two or four colour laminated covers, good paper and a 'loose' design with lots of white space and illustrations. But this means higher production costs and, therefore, higher selling price. For our books, we have taken the view that the information we are providing is valuable. Other publishers might wish to drive down the price and the quality.
- Books need to pay for themselves. Subsidy of the production costs is not an answer. If books are sold at below cost, then the more successful the book, the greater the financial cost to the publisher. This is not sustainable. But subsidy is required to keep prices low enough. We believe that there are two areas where subsidy can be effectively applied:
  1. Towards pre-press costs. These are the one-time costs of creating the book. If these are paid for, then this still leaves the production costs to be covered by sales income.
  2. For bulk purchases and other distribution schemes, where the subsidy covers the cost of purchasing a specific number of copies for onward distribution.

- Books should not be handed out free. Much development publishing has been done by a development agency deciding what it wants to publish, paying all the costs of the publication itself, and then distributing copies free to intended readers. This process is producer-led and does not create any feedback link with readers. The books are often irrelevant, badly written and expensively produced. It also provides nothing towards the cost of distribution, as there is no marketing budget and no possibility of offering a discount to a bookseller. What is often found is that bundles of books remain in health centres or panchayat offices unopened and unread.

This question of affordability is for us an unresolved issue. Our books have been priced at between Rs 25 and Rs 12. We would like to reduce this to between Rs 16 and Rs 8, which we feel would be very reasonable for the sorts of books we are publishing. One way of doing this is through a larger initial print run, which would lead to a marked reduction in unit costs. Starting as a new operation, we had to be cautious. But with experience and as our confidence grows, we would like to aim at a minimum first print run of 5,000 for any book we publish.

Availability for Reading and Purchase

To be successful, any book development strategy requires that books be available, either for borrowing or for purchase.

Libraries are extremely important, providing access to books, information and newspapers. We must recognise that the investment in literacy and in continuing education has not yet provided all of the answers. There are libraries now in almost every village in Andhra Pradesh, but most could function a lot better, and we need to invest in this. This means more books and better librarians. It may need different management structures and systems, but it also means more appreciation of the role that librarians can play as centres for development and literacy, and more recognition of their achievements. The libraries that exist are a base for moving forward. We need to build on this to create a 'Second Library Movement'.

But rural bookselling is also important. Our 'bicycle bookselling' is one idea, but a lot more work needs to be done on this. Commercially, Vishalaandhra, the largest book distributor in Andhra Pradesh, has been running three specially converted book buses in rural areas. Non-commercially, the Hyderabad Book Trust and other small publishers are getting together to plan joint marketing in rural areas. Can we turn rural bookselling into a successful income generating activity? With the right books, we just might.

Creating a Reading Culture

The final link in the chain is creating a reading culture, where people value books for entertainment and information, and see books as a catalyst for change in their own lives and communities.

- Low levels of literacy should not be used as an excuse for not publishing and selling books. There is a market there, and even if people can't read, if they know that a book is important, they will find someone to read it to them, for example, children reading to adults. And if people see that books can be useful in their lives, it becomes a great spur to literacy. We have for too long used illiteracy as an excuse for not publishing. Puppet shows, storytelling and songs are not enough. Access to information and the ability to read it is a cornerstone of development. We have spent a generation empowering people; now we should be giving them information to create change for themselves.
- Books must bring hope. This is not a matter of preaching that 'books are good for you'. We should give examples of how books and the written word can and have changed people's lives. We should be collecting together case studies and stories.
- We should give extra emphasis to encouraging reading and book use amongst young people. They are the citizens of the future.

The 'Books for All' Programme in Andhra Pradesh

CIVA is now looking at the next stage in what we do. We have developed the idea of a 'Books for All' programme that will build on our experience of the last three years and foster collaboration amongst publishers, NGOs and others interested in book development to create a major programme in one state.

The components of this programme are:

1. Creating relevant and affordable publications for rural readers. We want to create a consortium of publishers to produce and publish books for a rural audience under the banner 'Books for All'. We have expressions of interest from around 12 so far, including commercial publishers such as Orient Longman, national agencies such as the National Book Trust and the National Centre for Children's Literature, local Telugu language publishers, small independent publishers and specialist agencies promoting books

and reading. We are looking to support a programme of at least 100 books a year on a continuing basis by subsidising the pre-press costs.

2. Stimulating the development of successful libraries as an important community institution. We want to provide training to librarians linked to grants for library improvements and book purchase. This will build on the pilot training programme we are currently developing.

3. Making books available and creating a reading culture amongst rural people. We want to set up a grants fund to support projects which achieve these aims with small grants. We want to build on the ideas and energies of local communities and local projects rather than determine what should be done ourselves. But we will need to bring the message to development organisations that books have a value in community development. The workshops and consultations we have run so far indicate to us that few people in the development world are paying much attention to books and literacy. Yet once we make a case for this, they become enthusiastic.

4. Building collaboration between government, literacy, education and development to support and sustain the effort. We want to work on a reasonably large scale in one state to demonstrate what can be achieved through an interesting partnership between professional publishers and development agencies that provides books but also addresses the issues of availability and use, and that brings the worlds of literacy and development together on a common programme to provide 'books for change'.

We will continue to work in one state, but at the same time we want to encourage others to do similar work in other states and other languages. ActionAid has already set up a Village Publishing Division to produce and publish information in the Hindi belt, which was launched in October 2000. We will have a policy that allows free use of the 'Books for All' material for translation into other languages, but will encourage field-testing of any such material before it is published as changes might need to be made to the text or illustrations if they are to be wholly relevant in another area or language. We will be happy to provide advice and ideas to anyone interested in working alongside us.

We also want to continue to promote the idea of books and reading for development to the development sector and with the government. We will also start to develop our relationships with the National Literacy Mission nationally, and with the relevant ministries in Andhra Pradesh. We wanted positive achievements to show before tackling policy makers. There is a lot we can do to develop a successful partnership with the organs of the government, who have the capacity and the resources to do a great deal more for literacy and book development.

Suggestions for Encouraging Book Reading

These suggestions were developed from consultative meetings with NGOs held in Hyderabad in 1999.

Libraries

Making libraries function more effectively is seen by many people as the most important component of any programme for encouraging book reading. Many libraries just don't function well, and some remain locked. A good library means having interesting and exciting books as well as enhancing the librarian as the key focal point for improving the library. The following are some of the ideas suggested for improving libraries:

More and Better Books

- A book fund so that libraries could obtain a continuing supply of new books.
- A nodal library which could supply books on a rotating basis to a cluster of local/village libraries.
- Publishing a catalogue of available (and suitable books) for librarians, to enable them to see what's available and from where.
- Developing book donation schemes.
- Developing community fundraising to set up a book purchase fund.
- Having a donation slip which can be put into library books so that the donor is recognised.
- Asking readers to contribute towards the book fund, either by sponsoring a book or through a modest cash donation.
- Local book fairs where librarians can see what books are available and make purchases.

More and More Accessible Libraries

- Technical assistance to NGOs and agencies wishing to set up libraries. This could include advice on equipment needed, book selection (and providing a mechanism for ordering books), and induction training for librarians.

- A 'Library in a Box'. A basic library kit comprising books, display material and registers for accession of books, membership and lending, which could be purchased by NGOs or CBOs wishing to set up a community library. This might cost Rs 10,000.
- A mobile library serving a cluster of villages from one central point. Two ideas were proposed. One involved a van with 1,000 books, and the other a pedal rickshaw with perhaps 300 books. The low-tech solution was generally felt to have greater sustainability. The mobile library would be operated by an existing library as an outreach function. Villages would be visited once a week on a regular basis.
- Running libraries on a similar basis to circulating libraries, where a small charge is made per book borrowed. A contribution of Rs 5 per month or Paise 10 or 25 per book was suggested.
- In any community there may be more than one library (in a community centre, a continuing education library, a panchayat library, a school library, etc.). Identify the best library for functioning and accessibility to the community, and strengthen that.
- Form a committee to manage and support the librarian and to take ownership of the village library. The Rajiv Gandhi Foundation has found that it is better to give an existing functioning committee the responsibility for the library than to create a new committee.

Improving Librarianship Skills

- Developing a training course for librarians which concentrates on 'making the library come alive' as a vibrant institution in the community that encourages reading and provides information. This would be accompanied by a certificate.
- Developing activities centred around libraries and continuing education centres, which encourage reading and books.
- Setting up a small grants scheme for library improvement ('Books for All' is proposing to do this).
- An annual 'Librarian of the Year' award at the district level, given at a librarian meeting or workshop.
- Create an enthusiasm in the local community for the library so that the demand is coming up for a well-run library.
- Get the librarian to actively promote the library, and to keep members informed as to what's available, what's new, what's of particular interest or use. This can vary according to the season.

Getting More Resources for Libraries

- Getting the various schemes for supporting libraries to function effectively so that government money achieves some impact. This will involve working closely with collectors, block development officers and local education officials. NGO participants at the meetings felt that there was a great deal of potential here.

- Developing local fundraising for libraries.
- Getting free publications distributed to libraries. There are many of these from government agencies, international agencies, etc.

Schools and Children

Children were seen as the 'future', and an important target for any book development work.

- For developing children's reading habit, the focus of any activity should be the teacher. Training programmes could be organised for teachers on encouraging reading and book usage by children. All teachers should be encouraged to hold reading sessions to encourage reading, literacy and curiosity.
- A book token scheme organised through a school, which provides books for a modest sum, say Rs 2 or Rs 5 per book from a selection provided.
- The 'Library in a Box' idea specifically designed as a children's library that could be run in a school. This could be run by the children themselves, and a simple manual developed for them to operate the library. Every school could be encouraged to have a library. But a budget would be needed for the school to run the library. Consideration might be given to levying a very small charge (for membership or per book borrowed).
- Getting the local/village librarian to run book reading sessions in schools, where various books are displayed and discussed, and the children allowed to borrow the library books. This could be done on a regular (once-a-week) basis.
- Encouraging book reading through children's clubs (and the children's book circles being promoted by the National Centre for Children's Literature).
- Get literate children to read to non-literate children.
- Allow (and encourage) children to take books home.
- A newsletter or magazine was specifically suggested as a good medium for communicating with children.

Community Organisations

The issue was getting people to read, and book development activities should be run through existing community institutions wherever possible, rather than independently. The following were suggested: children's clubs, women's groups, libraries and resource centres, and trainers. It was pointed out that involvement in these institutions may be biased for age, class and gender, and this should be noted in the planning of the programme. Books should not become the sole preserve of adult men.

- Having a poster to accompany each book published by 'Books for All'. This would encourage people to buy or read the book.
- Having a poster displayed at the village-well promoting a book, which would then be read and read out once a week at the women's group. This could become a 'Book of the Week' (or month) scheme, and the reading could be followed by discussion.
- 'Pair Sharing', where two people read the same book and then discuss it together. 'Peer sharing', doing the same in a group. These are many ways in which local community groups can be encouraged to use books positively.
- Readers' clubs and readers' networks to be established at community level.
- 'Barefoot book promoters'. This idea involves selecting volunteers who would be prepared to go round a group of villages with a book to explain it and read from it, for example, educated and unemployed youth travelling by bicycle. There is the possibility of their selling the books as well.

NGO Fieldwork

Creating a book development and literacy component of development programmes. But these should not be created in an ad hoc way, but within the overall development strategy and plans. PLAN would help its project partners develop this aspect of their planning. It was also suggested that some attempt should be made to assess the impact of any book development programme on literacy and social development. The design of any book development programme should also be based on the particular strengths of the NGO, for example, one might be strong on self-help groups whilst others may have lively extension programmes.

- Books can play a role in the development of the capacity and self-confidence of front line workers. A good practice handbook on book development and reading written specially for front-line development workers could accompany a training course for this audience.

- Distribution of books and information via extension workers, trainers and field staff, where the books are linked to the messages being given or the training.
- More collaboration between literacy promotion efforts and development programmes.
- A community media van to provide audiovisual shows, which are then accompanied by written material for reading or sale. Packages of audiovisual material and publications could be produced specially for this purpose.
- Producing books and handout material on such matters as AIDS/HIV and safe drinking water for use in campaigns and distributed through the campaign work. These could be broken down into thematic units of quite small publications (say 16 pages). How and where books fit into the delivery plans would need to be considered.
- Distribution of books via PLAN foster parents to the children they are sponsoring (and other children in the village)—many of the mothers are illiterate, and children could be encouraged to read to them.
- Book reading to become a part of the way group meetings are organised, just as icebreakers, songs and dramas are.
- Needs assessment to find out what information and books people might like to have.
- Create the habit of book reading amongst NGO staff at all levels. This starts with understanding why reading is important, and why we read (and don't read) books. Two proposals were made: to hold an introductory session for NGO staff at HQ who plan and support field programmes so that they come to understand the role of books in development and some of the ways in which programmes can encourage reading; and a practical workshop for field workers so that they understand the importance of books and what sorts of programmes can be run at community level for encouraging reading and book use.
- NGOs can develop an operating strategy which has a books/information/literacy component, and then go on to develop plans and programmes for implementing this. PLAN will be encouraging its NGO partners to 'think books, information and literacy' in developing their strategic plans.

Other Ideas for Encouraging Reading at Community Level

- Encouraging book reading starts with having appropriate and interesting books. This starts with the cover and title (commercial practice might offer a few lessons). It includes having simple user-friendly language. We have asked Literacy House to compile and publish a vocabulary book of 2,000 words suitable for new readers and those who are not fluent at reading. Quality is also important, as books need to be durable if they are not to deteriorate, and this must include both paper and cover.

- For women especially, reading is not of primary importance. We need to create an interest through reading sessions. They must come to know that books have interesting information that is important to them.
- Book encouragement activity should be undertaken at times when women are free, i.e., not in the evenings.
- Creating community information centres. How books could be got together and maintained should be considered.
- Some on-going monitoring of what people are reading and enjoying, so that we could build on this by providing them with material they want to read.
- Books on sanitation and related matters, which could be distributed through the sanitation markets organised by UNICEF.
- Many people (and most women) are illiterate. Book reading is a discipline that has to be developed. Books should contain 90 per cent pictures and only 10 per cent words at the start, in order to get people into the habit of reading.

A Campaign to Encourage Reading

- Campaigns and programmes to create a 'thirst' for reading and a 'hunger' for books.
- An annual campaign as part of National Book Week (14 to 21 November) to get community organisations and groups, schools, community centres, NGOs, and government agencies to do something during that week to encourage reading.
- A journal or newsletter for all those involved in 'Books for All' at all levels to share ideas.
- Propagate books and book reading on local language TV.

Reference

NLM (National Literacy Mission) (1999). 'Scheme for Continuing Education for Neo-literates.' New Delhi: Ministry of Human Resource Development.

PART V

LIBRARIES AND LITERACY

CHAPTER TEN

Creating a Second Village Library Movement

Sarah Kamala

The Important Potential of Village Libraries

It is generally agreed that the development of a community is facilitated by the knowledge and information that is available to it. Knowledge and information can be made available through libraries that are accessible to local people. A library collects, classifies, stores and disseminates information which is relevant to the needs and interests of the people it serves. This includes books, but also other print formats, photographs, video, CD-roms and internet access to the worldwide web.

Around 70 per cent of the population of India still lives in rural areas, and it is also in the rural areas that literacy rates and social development are at their lowest. This supports the idea of locating libraries in rural communities, where rural people can easily access them and the information they contain. A library can be located in a village or be established for a cluster of villages (including hamlets or settlements or thanes).

Village libraries not only need to satisfy the information and recreational needs of the village educated, they should aim to meet the needs of all sections of the community—including women, children, artisans, agriculturists, people of different religions and castes, and especially neo-literates and illiterates.

The village library potentially has a much wider role. It could:

• Become a centre for adult education, by conducting classes.
• Provide facilities for books and newspapers to be read to those who cannot read.
• Deliver books and magazines to the doorsteps of those who are not able to come to the library, either due to distance or due to social restrictions or both.
• Collect and provide information on up-to-date and alternative technologies and techniques of use to farmers, local craftsmen, village artisans and other special interest groups.
• Provide information and advice on matters like public health and hygiene, water and sanitation, contemporary politics, scientific and technological development, etc.

The village library has the potential to become a hub for all progressive activities in the village.

History and Current Status of the Village Library Movement in Andhra Pradesh

The history of the library movement in modern India can be traced back to 1910, when free public libraries were first established in Baroda, Madhya Pradesh state. But, the library movement as a 'public movement' was started in Andhra (which was then a part of Madras Presidency). It was from Andhra that the library movement spread to other parts of the country.

Pre-independence, the library movement was village-oriented. The libraries that were established not only served educational and recreational needs, but also played an important role in adult education as well. This movement was started as a 'people's movement'. Political leaders, social reformers and intellectuals played an important role in establishing, maintaining and developing these village libraries. The cause was taken up with the support of local people as well as philanthropists and library enthusiasts. They all believed that libraries could play a vital role in helping people improve their standard of living, become aware of their rights and responsibilities as citizens of India, and make information accessible to everyone so as to develop a cultured and informed society.

Andhra Desa (which was the earlier name for Andhra Pradesh) took the lead in India in taking the library movement to the villages in far-flung areas. A large number of village libraries were established in Andhra Desa under the dynamic leadership of Andhra Desa Library Association in the 1920s and the 1930s. These village libraries were conceived and shaped to be nerve centres of educational, cultural, social and economic development of the rural community.

Library workers and library enthusiasts all felt that library legislation would act as a driving force for the rapid development of libraries and the literacy movement. With this in mind, various library legislations were enacted in different states in India. The legislation enacted in Andhra Pradesh is the Andhra Pradesh Public Libraries Act, 1960, which replaced The Madras Public Libraries Act, 1948 and Hyderabad Public Libraries Act, 1955.

Box 10.1: Library legislation in India

Library workers and library enthusiasts felt that library legislation would act as a driving force for the rapid development of libraries and the literacy movement. With this in mind, various library legislations were enacted in different states in India.

The main legislation to provide libraries is as follows:

1. Andhra Pradesh (Andhra Pradesh Public Libraries Act, 1960, which replaced The Madras Public Libraries Act, 1948 and Hyderabad Public Libraries Act, 1955)
2. Tamil Nadu (Madras Public Libraries Act, 1948)
3. Karnataka (Karnataka Public Libraries Act, 1965)
4. Maharashtra (Maharashtra Public Libraries Act, 1967)
5. West Bengal (West Bengal Public Libraries Act, 1979)
6. Manipur (Manipur Public Libraries Act, 1988)
7. Haryana (Haryana Public Libraries Act, 1989)
8. Mizoram (Mizoram Public Libraries Act, 1989 and Public Libraries Act, 1994)

The other states and union territories do not have mandatory legislation for the establishment of public libraries.

Even after 50 years of independence, not even half the states have library legislation. Even where there is public library legislation,

---

though this started with great enthusiasm and zeal, the record of organising public library services is very poor.

And where libraries have been established, they are mostly in a run-down condition. The development of libraries has been inadequate in the face of increasing literacy and a growing population. Statistical data relating to the progress of public libraries in these states is barely available.

The Changed Situation After Independence

Enthusiasm for the creation of libraries diminished drastically soon after independence, and these seem to be the main reasons:

1. Politicians who provided leadership for the establishment of libraries for awakening the masses in the pre-independence period lost interest in the library movement after independence was achieved.
2. Public library legislation gave wrong signals to organisations and individuals interested in the library movement. It seemed to signal that the government will do all that was needed for library development, and that the efforts of individuals were no longer needed. The spirit of the library movement dimmed.
3. The State Library System established under the Libraries Acts failed to provide a library service that was accessible to all villages, and the growth in the number of libraries was inadequate for the rapidly growing population.
4. The qualified and salaried librarians started keeping the other library workers and library users at a distance. At its worst, this meant that the books were locked up rather than lent out.
5. Some villages refused to transfer the library cess that was being collected locally to the District Library Authorities (Zilla Granthalaya Samitis) as they had failed to open a library in their villages. Other villages never collected the library cess or never paid the taxes that they had collected to the panchayats or local government, thereby creating a dearth of funds for establishing new libraries in villages.
6. The centralised system for administering public libraries was not appropriate. The local authority and the local librarian are best placed to determine local library and information needs, and their experience and views should have been used to plan the library service.

7. Book acquisition policy was inadequate. The purchase of books was centralised, hence the same sets of books were being supplied to every library when the library was established and there was no choice for selection of books according to local interests and needs or for the rotation of books between libraries.
8. Not enough new books were purchased due to unavailability of funds for this purpose.

The Number of Public Libraries in Andhra Pradesh

According to the State Administration Report (1984–85), Department of Public Libraries, there were in Andhra Pradesh:

- 749 libraries in urban areas.
- Of these 749 libraries, 424 were operating in 30 cities and large towns (with a population of 75,000 or more), which together had a total population of 7,092,928 (including 3,986,638 literates).
- The number of other towns in the state is 222. For these towns, a library service was being provided in 188 towns by 5 district central libraries and 186 branch libraries for a total population of 4,508,535 (including 2,223,729 literates).
- There were no libraries in 34 small towns and 166 urban areas.
- Out of 1,222 villages with a population of 5,000 and above (which must have a library according to the Libraries Act), only 346 villages had a library.
- Out of 12,080 villages with a population between 1,000 and 5,000, only 928 villages had a library. These included 162 branch libraries, 271 village libraries and 495 book deposit centres. In addition, 2,860 villages were provided with mobile libraries and aided libraries.
- All the 16,408 villages with a population of less than 1,000 did not have library service.

There are only 1,540 village panchayats libraries out of 21,943 village panchayats existing in the state as per 1991 census. This amounts to less than 1 in 10 villages having any library facility.

This is the position in Andhra Pradesh, which had a glorious library movement and an early record of library legislation. The coverage of the public library service is very poor especially in the rural areas. The position in most other states could be similar to Andhra Pradesh or even worse.

The Organisational Set-up and Operating Structure

Structure

The Library system in Andhra Pradesh is a centralised system with the Director of Public Libraries at the apex. There are Zilla Granthalaya Samsthas (district libraries, ZGSs) in each of the 23 districts of Andhra Pradesh and in the twin cities of Hyderabad and Secunderabad. The secretary-cum-district central librarian is the head of Zilla Granthalaya Samstha.

The total number of libraries in Andhra Pradesh is 1,274. The various libraries at mandal level, block level, taluk level or middle level are called branch libraries or Telugu Vignana Samachara Kendras. At the village level, there are the village libraries, which are under the administrative control of the respective secretaries of the Zilla Granthalaya Samsthas of the districts.

The libraries presently operational in Andhra Pradesh are categorised as Grade 1, Grade 2 or Grade 3, according to the size of their collection.

Financial Support

The salary cost of the library staff is provided by the Government of Andhra Pradesh. The maintenance cost of the library, including the cost of acquiring books and other relevant reading material and other incidental expenditures, is met by the Zilla Granthalaya Samstha and paid for through the library cess. The libraries receive financial support from Raja Rammohan Roy Library Foundation, Kolkata towards infrastructure and collection development. There is no further assistance either for new books or for maintenance and upkeep.

Book Acquisition

A library will only really succeed if there is a continuing flow of new books, which can attract the reader's interest and gain renewed interest of the readers. The following is the situation regarding the acquisition of new books by libraries in Andhra Pradesh:

- There is a centralised system for the acquisition of books. Zilla Granthalaya Samsthas at district level acquire the books as suggested by the state selection committee. Books are supplied in multiple copies and distributed amongst all the libraries in the district. The books are classified and catalogued centrally, and the catalogue cards are supplied to the library along with the books.

- The books in most village libraries are fiction, short stories, general magazines and other light reading material. Some libraries have a fairly good collection of religious classics, but they do not usually have specific need-based information, which can be used to improve knowledge and enhance livelihoods.

The Librarian

The success of a library will be greatly affected by the quality and competence of the local librarian.

- The librarians at the district and branch level are persons with a degree in library sciences. The librarians at the village level are usually holders of a certificate in library sciences but do not have any formal training in library science.
- The librarians are on a regular pay scale but are not given any further training or guidance and encouragement for running the library. The training that exists tends to focus on library systems and procedures, rather than on developing the capacity of the librarian and promoting good librarianship.

The State of Public Libraries in Andhra Pradesh

The state of public libraries in India, and especially libraries in rural areas, is deplorable. The libraries that do exist tend to have the following features:

1. They cater largely to the recreational and light reading needs of a small strata of the upper and middle classes. They do not reach the illiterate and unmotivated sections of the community.
2. They are a passive institution in the community, rather than an active central point for creating change and development.
3. Their impact on the community and their support base in the community is minimal or marginal.
4. Libraries provide very little relevant information that relates to the issues of social and economic change or to the problems faced by the people in real life. The books have peripheral bearing on

the survival needs of the community. There are few materials relating to vocational knowledge that are relevant to the people. Thus, the impact of these libraries in society is negligible and they are not generally seen as being useful to rural people.

5. The financial support of the government to public libraries is weak.
6. Government and public agencies do not consider libraries as suitable agencies to use for the dissemination of information regarding their own policies and welfare services. They do not deposit their publicity materials with public libraries.
7. The personnel who are in charge of public libraries do not have any autonomy to incur expenditure to pay for bookbinding, repair of furniture or acquiring new books. The impact of this on the working of the library is adverse.
8. With the changing trends in communication and information technologies, libraries could be disseminating audiovisual material, and this would attract more users, especially the illiterates. This is not yet happening on any real scale.

The Role That Libraries Could Play

Today's society is often described as an 'information society'. Information is considered a fundamental resource. The volume and quality of information relating to all domains of human life and activity is unprecedented. Access to this information enables people to solve their problems and advance in society; absence of information sustains poverty and disadvantage. Therefore, providing access to relevant information, and the use of that information to address problems are both critical issues.

A village library is potentially the most effective agency to undertake these functions. People recognise the library as a place where information is available. The library is a community institution and, therefore, can develop an intimate knowledge of the real problems and needs of local people, and also advise on how to apply information to solve problems. It has the potential to reach out to all of the community, which includes non-users, the uneducated and the illiterate. This is not merely a hope for what a village library might be; it is a *sine qua non* for national regeneration and development.

The objective of rural libraries in pre-independence days was to assist in attaining freedom for the country. Today the overall objective of a village or rural library should be to aid rural development and the social advance of rural people and rural communities. This would be at the heart of the second library movement.

Objectives for a Second Library Movement

The library movement today could have the following specific objectives:

- *Education*: To serve as a centre for informal self-education by opening its doors to all sections of the community at all levels—rich and poor, higher castes and lower castes, men and women, older people and children. This would provide the opportunity to develop universal education as a continuing and lifelong process, and to sustain literacy by providing access to books and encouraging reading.
- *Information*: To supply all types of information to the community—including information on culture, health, agriculture, education, both for rural development and for individual benefit—by bringing books to the people, and by serving as a referral point for any specialised information (if this is needed by an individual or by group).
- *Recreation*: To play a vital role in the positive use of people's leisure time, by providing books and other reading materials for relaxation and pleasure.
- *Community development*: To act as focus for community activity and change.
- *Cultural activities*: To act as a centre for cultural activities and to promote active participation and an outlet for the creative talents of rural people. And at the same time, to provide opportunities for leisure and pleasure. In pursuit of this objective, the library could arrange discussions, lectures, musical performances, stage plays, playlets, role-plays, exhibit films, videos, and slide shows, for the children, the youth and the adults of the village.
- *Preserving the cultural heritage*: To preserve the traditional culture and become a centre for folk arts, dance and music. It could become a platform for encouraging traditional artistes provide entertainment, or a medium to impart the latest knowledge and information using these traditional media such as puppetry and street plays, which would help the artistes as well as the community.
- *Information technology*: To link people in the villages to the wider world outside by promoting the library as an information centre and providing it with the latest information and communication technology. With the advance of these technologies, it has become very cheap to reach most remote and inaccessible parts of the world and deliver information effectively. This will aid the process of social and economic change.

Setting Specific Operating Objectives for a Village Library

A village library will only be successful if specific and measurable operational objectives are set for its functioning. Such specific operating objectives might include:

- To increase the *number of people* using the library for reading newspapers and borrowing books.
- To increase the *levels of usage* of each library user (more newspapers read, more books borrowed, more events organised and attended, etc.).
- To ensure that *priority groups become users*, specially encouraging people such as non-literates, neo-literates, women, SCs and STs, and other groups with lower levels of literacy.
- To encourage *book reading and a culture of literacy* among young people and children in school.
- To ensure *continuing interest in the library* by users (so that users don't read all the books and then lose interest). This can be measured by simple attitude surveys as well as by monitoring membership levels.
- To develop a greater sense of *community ownership* of the library and find ways of making it sustainable. This includes creating continuing support for the library, ensuring that there are sufficient funds to run the library and that the quality of service continually improves.
- To develop *links with other village institutions*.

All these factors can be monitored and measured, and this should play a part in developing better management support for libraries. Clear objectives could be set for library improvement with the participation and agreement of the librarian. The changes need not be sudden or spectacular, but there should be a culture of continuing improvement of the library against all these objectives.

Meeting the Information Needs of All Local People

As in the pre-independence era, village libraries should try to reach out to all sections of the community and serve illiterates and neo-literates, as well as literates.

- Every person in every community, urban or rural, and however remote, should have access to books and to the facilities of a library.
- A village library should be kept open for free and equal use of all members of the village, regardless of race, colour, age, sex, religion, language, backwardness, economic or educational attainment. The library should be open at convenient hours for its users.
- The reading matter should be displayed attractively for readers to select what they need. The library should lend books (and other reading material) for home reading. Ideally, the library should also contain a reading room where people can sit and read the books.
- The village library could create or raise awareness of people on a variety of issues—social and economic development, local history and culture, history of the state and the nation, the contemporary political scene at all levels, health and hygiene, environment and ecology, agriculture, livelihoods and traditional crafts, local resources and their effective utilisation, the caste system and religion, peace and communal harmony, government policies and programmes and how to access these, poverty and its eradication, and aspects of personal development and the role that people can play in creating a better future for themselves and their communities.
- The library could develop special collections for women, children and other priority groups addressing their particular interests and information needs. This could include 'do-it-yourself' books, providing information on all sorts of subjects: engineering, tools, local artisan workmanship for improving their skills, tips for construction of various types of houses (including estimation for house construction, information regarding construction tools and methods, architectural design, exterior and interior decoration, vaastu), gardening, kitchen gardening, agricultural implements, low-cost farm technologies, watershed and rainwater harvesting methods, information regarding latest farm technologies, improved seed varieties, plant pest and disease identification, plant protection, marketing, food processing and storage, health and hygiene, sanitation, first aid and nutritional requirements, home management, people's rights and using the law, and other legal information for the benefit of the rural masses (to enable them to deal with exploitation).
- The library could address the needs of neo-literates by providing them with suitable literature and prevent them from falling back into illiteracy. This is a key function for a village library to sustain literacy and build on the work of the Total Literacy Campaigns.
- The village library could link its activities with the work of educational, cultural and social agencies such as schools, universities, museums, labour unions, study clubs, adult and continuing education

organisations and non-governmental organisations. Creative links could include keeping books in the library that are relevant to the needs of these institutions, sharing information budgets for the purchase of such materials, organising joint events, etc.

• The village library could act as a focal point for capturing local knowledge and ideas. It could facilitate community documentation, capturing and passing on traditional knowledge and wisdom, and assisting with the publishing of books written by local people with their ideas and their stories.

At the same time, it should be seen as important to increase public participation in the running of the library. This could be done by establishing local library committees to oversee the running of the library and by involving local people in library extension work as volunteers, using those who have time on their hands such as the retired.

Becoming an Information Centre for the Community

What is needed is a vision that the village library becomes a centre for fostering social change and economic development. Ultimately, this should prove to be a cheap and effective method for disseminating information, for providing training and adult education in the widest sense, and for contributing to the eradication of poverty. The revised library manifesto of UNESCO in 1994 highlighted this role for village libraries.

• Appropriate literature should be available including books, newspapers and periodicals, according to the needs of the locality, the interests of the readers, the age range of the readers and the levels of literacy of the readers. Some good material is already published, but much more attention needs to be paid by publishers and development agencies to creating appropriate information to meet the needs of poor people.

• Every library should have an annual books acquisition budget so that it can add new books. Without this, the library will fail. The library can also display or circulate information published by other organisations.

• The resources of the library should be used to provide other rural organisations with literature that is helpful for their work (this includes youth clubs, mahila mandals, co-operative societies, thrift

Information is Power. Give us Empowerment

and self-help groups, water users associations, vana samrakshana samithis, joint forest management communities, panchayati raj institutions, janmabhoomi committees, etc.).

- A village library should play a part in promoting literacy and numeracy. It might run evening classes, with books available in the library to support this. The village library should function as a Jana Sikshana Nilayam or Community Education Centre.
- The village library should function as a '*Charcha mandal*' (a common platform for group discussion) for discussing common problems and issues of interest to local people. Books can be used to support this.
- The village library should function as a training centre for simple and short-duration courses relating to health, public health, family welfare, vocational training, new developments in agriculture, animal husbandry, conservation of energy and improved crops.
- Other functions could include putting on recreational and cultural activities, arranging exhibitions and book displays, showing instructional and other videos and providing access to community radio and the worldwide web.

Information technology is sweeping across the world, and this has the potential to revolutionise social change. Recent advances in communication technology have heralded the age of digitally encoded information, an increasing number of networks of television channels (terrestrial, cable and satellite), fibre optic and wireless communication and much more user-friendly computers. Prices are falling all the time, which has made it reasonably cheap to enter this world; and it is reaching even the most remote and inaccessible parts of the globe to deliver information effectively.

Libraries need to take account of these changes when planning their future. Each library simply needs electrical power, a television set, a reasonably new and versatile PC, a telephone line and access to the Internet.

Increasing the Resource Base of the Library

Lack of resources is one reason why libraries are not thriving. The village library needs a proper resource base for its proper functioning and for new book purchase. This can be provided through library membership subscriptions supplemented by local fundraising. But underpinning this should be a proper allocation of resources by the government as recognition of the important role that the library can play in sustaining literacy, supporting education and promoting development. Where there are provisions to collect a cess tax, this should be collected and applied to the running of the library.

There are many imaginative ways of raising library finances:

- Charging a small monthly membership fee to readers for borrowing books. The Rajiv Gandhi Foundation libraries charge each family Rs 2 per month for membership of the library.
- Charging a small monthly fee for reading newspapers. A fee of, say, Rs 2 to Rs 3 per person per month could be collected from the readers of newspapers. If there were 35 to 50 people visiting the library to read the newspapers daily, this would provide an income of Rs 70 to Rs 100 per month, with which the librarian could then pay for the newspaper and for a local magazine (like the agricultural Telugu magazine *Annadata*), which in turn will attract more number of readers and visitors to the library.
- Getting the purchase of publications sponsored. The cost of a subscription of a magazine or a newspaper can be underwritten by

naming an individual landlord or rich eminent person in the village or a local leader as its sponsor, who could easily afford to pay the subscription price of a single magazine (which might cost about Rs 6 to Rs 10). Using this technique, you might get between two and four people to pay the subscriptions, and their names can be exhibited on the noticeboard of the library and also on the publication so as to provide recognition for their generosity. This will enhance the prestige and esteem of these donors, and it might also encourage others to follow their example.

- Charging a fee for certain services such as photocopying (if this is provided), inter-library book loans, etc.
- Approaching philanthropists, local banks and companies for donations. Local villagers who have migrated or working in the cities or urban areas, or who are now resident in other countries, might also be approached to provide funding for the library. They might be designated 'Honorary Members of the Library' and the librarian can be encouraged to maintain good contact with them.
- Getting grants from foundations and charitable endowments, and from other funding sources.
- Community fundraising: local panchayat members and presidents can be approached to subscribe to a fund for new books. Local self-help groups, DWCRA members and co-operative society members, youth clubs and other associations in the village can be approached for funding, and with their support, books or magazines that relate to their particular interests can be purchased. An agreement can be drawn to sponsor a subscription for six months or one year, and the donor's name can be displayed and acknowledged in the meetings and at gram sabhas.
- A donation box can be placed in the library to collect donations from willing donors, visitors and dignitaries. This fund can be utilised for repairing furniture, binding books, and fumigation and treatment of the books.
- Gifts in kind: old books, and magazines can be collected from villages that can donate them to the library and the names of the villages can be labelled to the book. Donations of furniture or pictures for the library could be encouraged from local industrialists, banks and philanthropists.
- Other activities could also be organised. Cultural programmes, melas, traditional dances, folklore, dramas, painting competition, *rangolis*, elocution, one-act plays, and rallies can be arranged and a small fee can be collected from the audience.

> ### Box 10.2: How a library can generate funds: A case study
>
> A private library in an urban area collects a monthly subscription amounting to Rs 60 per month charged at a daily rate of Rs 2 per Telugu magazine, and Rs 75 per month charged at a daily rate of Rs 2.50 per English magazine.
>
> Every day a person will deliver a book or magazine to the home of a subscriber. While delivering the new book, he will collect the book he delivered the previous day. If the reader does not return the book on that day, it will remain with that person for another day. On average, 75 to 100 books are supplied each day to the readers, producing a daily income for the library of Rs 150 to Rs 250. In this way, the library collects between Rs 4,500 to Rs 7,500 each month. This provides a surplus of Rs 1,000 to Rs 2,500 after allowing for the cost of the magazines and newspapers and paying the librarian's salary.
>
> If similar techniques were used to generate resources, a village library could become much better resourced, and this would enable it to play a much more significant role in its local community.

The Importance of Having a Good Librarian

The key component of a successful library is an active, enthusiastic and competent librarian. This requires two things: raising the status of the job, and providing appropriate training. In addition, the management structures for operating the library need to give the librarian the authority to run the library effectively. Dealing with these issues is urgent if the village library is to be transformed from a dull institution that carefully guards its books to an active, lively and successful contributor to community life and local development. The librarian needs to start by redefining his or her role in the community and should also be skilled at all systems required for operating the library. These are some key aspects of the librarian's role:

- An effective communicator and disseminator of information.
- An information manager supplying information relevant to the needs of the community.
- An advice provider to the community.
- A leader in the community, which includes being a co-ordinator and rapport builder, maintaining contact and good relations with user groups, officials, village elders and other village institutions.

- A catalyst for documenting information about the community.
- A planner and a resource mobiliser.
- A media extension worker.

The librarian will need to be trained to undertake the following functions with a degree of competence:

- Outreach and community development activity.
- Identifying and linking up with useful sources of information.
- Literacy promotion and support.
- Developing and maintaining links with schools and the education system.
- Undertaking skills training.
- Undertaking community publishing to capture local knowledge, ideas and stories.
- Using media resources.
- Developing community ownership and support.
- Creating sustainability for the library, including resource mobilisation in the local community.

Village Librarians are the Tools for Information Decimation. Strengthen Them

- Developing and maintaining links with government, local departments and non-governmental organisations.
- Dealing with influential local people and officials to win their support, and strengthening people's involvement in local self government.

All this will require a new approach to the training of librarians, who up to now have concentrated on the skills of cataloguing and lending out books. But this extended role of librarians is feasible. Such training is now being developed in Andhra Pradesh as part of the 'Books for All' programme, in partnership with the Rajiv Gandhi Foundation.

CHAPTER ELEVEN

Door Step School: If People Can't Go to Books, Let Books Go to People

Rajani Paranjpe

Door Step School started its work in 1988–1989 in Dalit Ambedkar Nagar, a slum in Cuffe Parade, Mumbai. Today it is working in 10 different slums in the same area and has a branch in Pune. Since its inception, the organisation has been working single mindedly for the spread and retention of literacy skills among poor urban children. Our focus is on the 3–18 year age group. Our objective is to offer them the following services:

- Pre-primary education for the 3–6 age group;
- Study classes for 1st and 2nd standard children;
- Literacy classes for out-of-school children with the aim of imparting skills up to a functional level that enables children to read a newspaper and express themselves in writing;
- Mobile libraries, primarily for children but even adults interested in taking books on loan;
- Mobile school called 'School on Wheels' to cover out-of-school children who do not have any fixed place of residence, not even a slum or pavement dwelling;
- Bus service for children in the 1st and 2nd standards.

We named our organisation Door Step School (DSS) because of our goal to take all these services to the doorsteps of children, wherever they may be. Hence, we run our *balwadis* (pre-primary education centres), study classes, Non Formal Education (NFE) centres, literacy classes and library centres in slum dwellings, work sites, and even on pavements. Our *balwadis*, study classes, NFE centres and the mobile libraries have been running from the very beginning. The last two services, namely, the School on Wheels and the school bus service were added in 1998.

We started our first mobile library centre in Mumbai in 1991 and in Pune in 1993. We have continued with the activity since then and have tried a variety of methods to reach out to children, sometimes as an alternative to the previous method and sometimes as an addition to the existing mode of dissemination. Our mobile library programme was planned mainly to provide reading material to children who have recently acquired reading skills either by joining a regular school or through our NFE classes. Our experience has been that even those children who attend regular schools hardly get any opportunity for additional reading. They simply do not have access to books other than textbooks. Since reading is basically a skill, it requires practice to retain. Therefore, it is important to run libraries as a supportive activity to any literacy programme.

Presently, I discuss our experience of running the abovementioned services and a few related activities that were added with a view to strengthen the literacy skills acquired by our children. The first part deals with the different strategies by which we try to reach out to readers and disseminate books. The second part discusses the learnings from our experience.

Library Incarnations and Activities

Breadman on a Bicycle or Hand Delivery?

We began with the idea of running a library in the slums in which we were actively running literacy centres. The idea of mobile libraries emerged because of an obvious problem—the unavailability of a fixed place to store books and run a library from within the slums. Therefore, the next best option was to take books right to the doorsteps of our target readers. The idea of a mobile library was appealing. Inspired by images of a breadman carrying a box of bakery products attached behind his bicycle, our plan was to similarly carry books on a bicycle. This idea was rejected outright by our literacy workers who were mostly teenagers from the same community. They simply refused to carry books in this manner due to the risk of becoming objects of ridicule for their friends and neighbours. Instead, they preferred to carry books in their hands and go from door to door and change books on fixed days and at fixed times. Thus, it was agreed that each worker, whom we called a library volunteer, would cover about 100 houses in his/her neighbourhood and issue books twice a week. The library volunteer was to conduct an initial survey of these 100 families, make a list of potential readers and fix their timings. This method of issuing books also did not last long because it is not easy to carry books in hands. They are heavy and also get damaged while being carried in a bag.

Adults or Children?

Our readership in those days included both adults and children due to our interest in catering to all readers. This posed a problem of book selection. Adult readers wanted us to buy books suitable to their tastes, such as, novels, murder mysteries, film magazines, and so on. In our enthusiasm we did whatever possible without compromising on the quality of books selected for the library. However, we could not continue with this approach, first, because the books for adults cost much more than the books for children, and second, we could not cope with their growing demand. Even though the number of adult patrons was not very high, our ability to supply a sufficient number of books was rather limited. Therefore, we stopped catering to the reading interests of adults and decided to concentrate only on children. This does not mean that we stopped giving books to adults. We still do, but the selection of books is done keeping a child reader in mind.

Public Garden as Library

Given our failed experience of carrying books from door to door, the book circulation method changed to the idea of operating the library from a nearby public garden. We announced the days and timings that the library would run from the garden. This failed miserably. The workers soon got tired of waiting for the readers to come as only a dedicated few showed up. Seeing the sense of helplessness among library workers, this method of distribution was also stopped soon after its launch.

Home as Library

After the public garden debacle, volunteers started operating the library from their homes itself. Readers were expected to go to these Home Library Centres (HLCs) and get their books exchanged on fixed days and timings. HLCs were open twice a week for two hours a day. Every HLC was to cover 100 houses as before. Thus, there were several small library centres scattered all over the place. While this method worked to some extent, and continues to this day, it is not free from problems. The number of readers we used to cover by going door to door dwindled when library centres became stationary. There is also a problem of getting library volunteers. Running a library requires storage space for books, and within the areas of our work, there is, as it is, a paucity of space in people's houses. Library books lead to further cramping. Besides, parents often refuse to take responsibility for keeping books at home. The readers too tend to visit the HLC at any time causing great discomfort to the household, and the two hours allotted by the household to this activity is generally exceeded. Moreover, a library volunteer is obliged to stay at home on the days and timings fixed, regardless of whether readers turn up or not. The turnover of books is also not very smooth as many readers keep the books for a long time, affecting the supply and availability of books at the HLC. Our policy is to keep 50 books at a time at every centre and rotate them periodically between centres. Returning books late not only creates a supply problem in one HLC, it also affects other centres. The number of books lost or damaged has also gone up. In addition to these problems, parents often find that the HLC activity hinders their children's studies, consuming a lot of time with very little remuneration. Therefore, there is a large turnover of library volunteers and due to this, a problem of fluctuation in readership.

Attracting Readers

The number of library patrons has grown steadily over the years (Table 11.1). The available data from the four communities in Pune shows that the number of patrons has increased from 294 in 1994 to 642 in 1999. Readers as a percentage of the 6–14 age group population that is literate, has also grown substantially. Although no exact data is available for 1998–1999, the estimated figures show a sharp increase.

The data clearly shows that readership fluctuates considerably. This is mainly due to the fluctuation in the number of library volunteers in the concerned area. During 1994–1997, at best we could cover only about one-third of the potential readers from a given area, however, the

**Table 11.1: Number and percentage of readers, aged
6–14 in Pune centres**

Year	Number of readers	Readers as % of literate people in 6–14 age group
1994	294	30
1995	239	28
1996	371	39
1997	249	32
1998	418	42*
1999	642	64*

Note: * Estimated figures based on the 6–14 year literate
population in previous years.
Source: DSS records.

estimated figures in 1998 and 1999 indicate greater coverage. A concern
with our coverage is that the majority of our readers are boys. Household responsibilities, unfortunately, leave girls with very little free time
for reading at home. Children who have dropped out from school are less
likely to become members of our libraries than those presently in school.
Ironically, it is the former group that is in danger of losing their literacy
skills. We have yet to find an effective strategy to attract school drop-
outs to our libraries.

Readers' Weeks During Vacations

In order to cater to the needs of girl readers, we started organising 'Readers' Weeks' during Diwali and the summer vacations. During this period
our library centres are open every day for four hours, two hours each in
the morning and evening. Prizes are given to children who read a certain
minimum number of books during that period. The number of books is
fixed depending on the number of library days available in that vacation.
For example, if our library is to run for 10 days, we announce a prize for
all those readers who read a minimum of five books. Prizes are not given
only by looking at the number of books issued to a given child. We make
a list of those eligible candidates and take a small test of each child to
ascertain that he/she has not only read the books but has also retained
at least a part of what was read and is able to recount it. Children appreciate the Readers' Weeks and enjoy receiving prizes. Other activities are
also organised, such as, quiz contests and essay competitions. A small
collection of essays written by children was published in booklet form,
and priced at Rs 5. Other children buy this book with interest, saying that
it will be useful for them in their studies. The Readers' Weeks have helped

in encouraging community participation and in publicising our activity. The local *mandals* (groups) get involved by sponsoring Readers' Weeks and prizes.

Perhaps the most important point of success of Readers' Weeks is that they are successful in attracting girls. During vacations, girls have relatively more free time than when school is in session. However, the total number of days covered under this activity remains small, hence, the need emerged for our school library programme.

School Library

Approaching Municipal Corporation Schools

In every municipal school, every class has two periods per week allocated for supplementary reading. However, in most schools these periods are hardly ever used for the purpose of reading. The teachers do not distribute the library books they have in their cupboards for fear of losing them. According to the rules, teachers have to pay for the loss of books or if they are damaged beyond repair. This acts as a deterrent to giving books to children. Therefore, we requested permission to use the library time and the school premises, for which we were granted permission, to experiment in 10 schools in the Karve Road area of Pune and 2 schools in Mumbai. Our library volunteer, whom we recently started referring to as '*pustakpari*' (book fairy), goes to the classes during the scheduled library time and distributes books to children, mostly for in-class reading. The teacher is supposed to be present in the class along with the *pustakpari*. However, very few teachers do so. Permission to use the school library books has also been sought, including a willingness to pay for any loss or damages at the end of the year. Permission is awaited. Selected children get to take books home on the basis of their capacity to read independently and, of course, their own desire to read at home. Under the school library programme, we are able to reach out to over 4,000 children on a regular basis. Of these, only 169 children take books home on a regular basis. This experience has given us ample opportunity to observe children's reading preferences, become aware of the availability of books in the market and contemplate ways to improve the situation. These are discussed later in the chapter.

Book Fairies Helping Academically Weak Children to Read and Write

Reference Library

As a recent addition to the library programme, a reference library was opened in a slum community on an experimental basis. The idea of starting a reference library originates in children's expressed need for textbooks. Hence, textbooks, workbooks, guides, dictionaries and other useful reference material is kept in this library. Students of Standard V onwards are the primary users of this facility. The reference library is open for two hours each in the morning and evening. Children come, sit, and study. They even pay a nominal entrance fee of Rs 0.25 per entry. During the last six months the membership of children who use the facility regularly has increased from 2 to 45.

Libraries in Study Classes and NFE Centres

In addition to the library centres described earlier, books are issued regularly by the teacher or instructor to children who attend our study and NFE classes. After the School on Wheels was initiated, we started keeping books and daily newspapers on the bus. Surprisingly, the response to newspapers has been rather lukewarm.

Readers' Clubs

Readers' clubs were created for children who have been our students in the past. These clubs meet regularly to discuss current issues. For example, during the elections, the topics of discussion are democracy, the voting system and so on. Other issues taken up include water problems, problems of sanitation, and other such issues that touch upon their lives. Our workers attend these meetings to facilitate the discussion. However, it has been our observation that it is difficult to hold the interest of the group for long. Generally the attendance starts to fizzle out after the first few meetings.

Other Activities

Hamara Akhbar (our newspaper) is published bi-monthly. In it, children write in their own handwriting and words. This provides them with an enjoyable opportunity to express themselves and participate in the entire creation process. Children are encouraged to compile important news items from the newspapers and put them up in their classroom like a college wallpaper. This encourages newspaper reading while offering points for classroom discussion.

Learnings from Experience

Background of Readers

From the above account it should be clear that it has not been easy to run library centres in slums under tremendous resource constraints. The challenge of inculcating reading habits among children who have never seen a book in their parents' hands is daunting. In addition, the onslaught of TV and video parlours in slum localities adversely affects the desire to read books. The surroundings in which a slum child grows up is hardly congenial to reading. There is little space, erratic and infrequent power supply, and in all probability, not much leisure time or quiet at home. In this situation it is difficult to nurture good reading habits and expect a sustained response from readers.

Paucity of Suitable Reading Material

Compounding the challenges in the spread of the library movement is the paucity of suitable reading material for neo-literate children. Neo-literate children need books in simple language and large type. By simple language one means two things. The language should avoid the use of *jodaksharas* (compound syllables). In our school libraries we have over 4,000 books for an equal number of readers. Out of the readers who had completed II, III and IV standards in April 2000, only 50 per cent could read books with *jodaksharas*, nearly 35 per cent could read only the books without *jodaksharas* and the remaining 15 per cent struggled even with the basic syllabary. If this is the level of reading in an average public school, it is clear that books without *jodaksharas* are badly needed in large numbers. Unfortunately, such books are seldom available. For example, we could literally unearth only about 150 such books after an extensive search in both the Mumbai and Pune markets and after visiting a few book exhibitions.

There is another aspect of simple language relating to the selection of words. Most books use words which are not in common usage. The neo-literate person, in particular, finds it difficult to understand these words. For example, words like '*nitya*' meaning every day, '*snan*' meaning bath, need not be used at all when simpler words used in everyday life exist. Possibly, the storywriters think that they must use complicated words if the stories are to be published, and to some extent this may be true. If writers simply use everyday language in their books, the problem of *jodaksharas* will automatically get reduced.

The third problem is that of good dictionaries for school children. There are many words which we understand but whose meaning is difficult to explain in simple language to children. This difficulty was experienced while preparing a glossary of words not easily read or understood by our children. During 1999, the library volunteers were asked to keep track of such words. The idea was to bring out a dictionary for use by our children. While working on the prepared and manageable list of words, we sometimes came across words like *adwait, samudra-manathan*, *pratidnya*, and so on—clearly words that are beyond the understanding of our target group. Therefore, it was decided to make a list of difficult words used in a given book and attach a page at the back with their meanings expressed in simple language. This makes the child's task easier and is also helpful to a person like a library volunteer or school teacher, who may also find the words difficult.

Apart from the language difficulty, another problem is with regard to the types and fonts used for printing. They should be chosen so as to facilitate reading by a neo-literate. Somehow, this simple consideration has escaped us. Even the comic strips available in the market use a small type, whereas the picture occupies a bigger share of the page. This may be justified for children already proficient in reading but is inappropriate for our children. We do need many more books in the style of comic strips but with carefully chosen font types. Such books would go a long way to promote interest in reading. In many developed countries, such as Japan or America, comic and cartoon strips are very popular even among the adults. Writers use this method to make difficult subjects interesting to readers. For example, there are books written on subjects like statistics using cartoons to simplify difficult concepts.

Why Not More Libraries?

Some issues make it difficult for people to take up a library project. The initial investment in purchasing books is considerable. Book-buying is also a recurring cost. The books need to be stored well, numbered carefully and closely followed up to minimise loss and damage.

Book loss and damage is a major concern. In many public schools, children are deprived of the opportunity to read simply because the teacher fears loss or damage to books. Our experience shows that while the number of books lost is negligible, the number of books damaged beyond repair is substantial. During 1999, nearly 20 per cent of the total books had to be replaced because of wear and tear. There is no doubt that children handle books roughly, but one cannot also forget the quality of our books and their loose binding. This probably is necessary to keep production costs low. Nevertheless, this is a major factor contributing to the high maintenance cost of books. Together with the high initial investment to start a library, book maintenance further conspires as a stumbling block for the spread of library initiatives.

Readers' Responses

Children enjoy reading and handling books, if there is an opportunity. Teachers find that children's grasp of the written word improves even if they are allowed to handle books frequently by themselves. There are a large number of adults in poor localities who would like to read. Even our own library volunteers as well as the municipal corporation teachers are interested in taking books home to read. Special efforts are required to collect material suitable for them. Our experience has taught us that there are a large number of potential readers but there are not enough opportunities to get books easily. However, not many people are willing to pay for reading. We have seen the number of readers go down every time we try to introduce a small fee, say, of Rs 2 per month per reader. We have also seen that children do pay for the use of our reference library. Parents look upon reading as a leisure time activity. They are even known to object to additional reading, particularly during the exam months, since many see it as a distraction from studies and a wastage of their child's time.

Donor Response

The library activity is not as popular among donors as the literacy class or a *balwadi* centre. Obtaining funds for running a library is difficult. It is also difficult to show concrete gains in statistical terms resulting directly from making books available. That reading ability improves with practice seems self-evident and without continuous practice, a neo-literate person is bound to relapse into illiteracy. The donors, in the absence of clear statistical data, do not appreciate this fact and are reluctant to sanction money for library activities.

Concluding Remarks

A large number of Municipal and Zilla Parishad school libraries hardly ever issue books to children. This needs to be looked into and ensured that children are able to make optimum use of existing facilities. There is a paucity of reading material for neo-literate and semi-literate children. It is, therefore, necessary to produce reading material suitable to their needs taking into consideration their social backgrounds and levels of reading competence. Writers and publishers need to be provided regular feedback regarding the needs of this newly emerging group of readers and potential customers. Finally, we need to sensitise the public as well as donor organisations regarding the importance of the library movement in the literacy movement.

CHAPTER TWELVE

Joy for Reading in the City of Joy: Libraries in Kolkata Slums

Saswati Roy

'Books are my companion.'

—Binita Sadhana Devi, 69 years, widow, slum library member.

Any lover of reading will attest that books make for intimate companionship. Unfortunately, a large section of India's population is deprived of this intimacy because they cannot read. People may never have gone to school. Those fortunate enough to begin schooling may have had to leave at an early stage. Later, due to sheer lack of practice many find themselves gradually reverting back to illiteracy. What learners in school or elsewhere do immediately and simultaneously with their newly acquired skills of reading, writing and numeracy is critical for sustained literacy. Innovative measures are needed so that children and others can practice their developing skills in a multiplicity of contexts while learning to read and write in a formal or non-formal setting. Driven by this concern, the idea of creating libraries specifically for neo-literate dwellers of Kolkata slums emerged.

Before initiating this project, our experience in Swadhina[1] had taught us that creating libraries is not merely the act of opening a facility, stocking books and hoping that it will run. A library, especially in disadvantaged contexts, also involves the development of appropriate learning materials, promotion of a congenial atmosphere and the facilitation of learning and people's cultural participation that is fun.

The Beginning

Beginning in July 1998, 15 libraries were opened in the slum areas in and around Kolkata with the idea that this would be a two-year effort, following which all the libraries would become self-reliant. The space for the library was selected and provided by the community. With external support, minimal furniture was bought.[2] Every library received two cupboards, two chairs, a wall clock and a table. Library stationary was provided in Bengali. The community was encouraged to regularly supply the library with at least two newspapers. When approached for newspapers, some community members agreed to offer their own daily newspaper to the library after reading it in the morning. In the initial stages, the librarians went door to door to encourage people to become members. Later, the library committee of each library was entrusted with this responsibility.

Librarian as Social Animator

The librarians were carefully selected. Educational qualification was not an important criterion; an ability to maintain registers and accounts was. The most important basis for selection, however, was a person's capacity to act as a skillful social animator. Thus, among those selected in the area, there were three homemakers, three college students, six unemployed youths with some education, and three non-formal education facilitators.

1. Swadhina is working in 150 villages and 15 slum areas spread across four states—West Bengal, Bihar, Orissa and Tamil Nadu. Since its inception in 1986, Swadhina has been involved in non-formal education activities among women and children.
2. Funding for all the libraries in this case came from the Rajiv Gandhi Foundation (RGF), New Delhi.

Prior to the opening of a library, training was imparted on the techniques of book management and maintenance of a library. However, a thorough orientation emphasised the librarian's role and responsibility as 'social animator', over and above that of a 'librarian' in a strict sense. The librarian's training attempted to inculcate in them:

1. an ability to identify and analyse problems in the slum areas;
2. an appreciation for the need for such a library in the community;
3. an understanding of the difference between a library for neo-literates and a regular library, especially, vis-à-vis the need to motivate membership; and
4. skills to encourage a culture of learning from books among all members.

Every month, a one day interaction is held among the librarians, called 'sharing meet'. At the sharing meet, librarians report on the previous month's activities, share the failures and successes and brainstorm about concerns and possible solutions. These monthly meets also serve the purpose of constant reorientation related to standard book-keeping duties, the special needs of neo-literates and the librarian's function as a social animator. The sharing meets, thus, play a pivotal role in enthusing community participation while preventing indifference and apathy by instilling a sense of healthy competition.

Library Committees: A Key to Success

In the formative stages of a library, the most important task is to motivate people from the community to form a library committee—the stronger and committed the committee, the greater the possibility of achieving sustainability. Ensuring gender balance in the committee was an important factor considered. A library committee of five to nine members was constituted for each of the 15 libraries. Of the total 102 committee members, 57 members are women. Like the librarians' sharing meets, the library committees meet every month to discuss, among other issues, ways to increase membership, and collection of fees and books (from local donors). Policy decisions on library timings and membership fees are also made at these regular meetings.

Books

Books were supplied to the libraries in phases. Utmost effort was made to select books that are appropriate for neo-literates. Books were selected keeping in mind the objective of engendering and sustaining the reading habit and to ultimately empower members through the widening of their knowledge base. The librarians were consulted periodically for the selection of books, based on their experience of what the members desired. What members seemed to like most were simple and short stories, ghost stories, humour and books on vocational guidance. Children's books were also very popular. Initially, school textbooks were not included since the libraries were not specifically intended for students. However, in due course, as the members increased, the demand for textbooks also arose. Presently, some librarians have, of their own initiative, started collecting textbooks locally. Thus far, 757 textbooks have been collected in 13 libraries, entirely through the efforts of the respective librarians. Textbooks are maintained in a separate section in the libraries.

Present Status

Libraries are open every day for two hours. Timings are decided according to local convenience. Each library now has an account in the local bank or post office where the monthly membership fee is deposited. The relationship between the librarian and library members tends to be very cordial. Some librarians are even known to take books to people's houses when they cannot themselves come to the library, such as homemakers with small children. Such gestures are vital in strengthening the bond between the librarian and community members, thereby drawing more people to the libraries.

There are several indicators that the libraries are turning into sustainable institutions. Library membership has increased from 607 members in July 1998 to 975 in June 2001 (Box 12.1). This has contributed to a general growth in the reading population and book borrowing. Book donations, collection of membership fee and a steadily growing bank balance are testimony to the health of the libraries.

Box 12.1: Kolkata slum libraries at a glance (June 2001)	
Library members (15 libraries) July 1998: 607 June 2001: 975 (417 female, 558 male)	Increase in membership 368 in 3 years
Total number of newspaper readers: 176	Child newspaper readers: 36
Female adult newspaper readers: 45	Male adult newspaper readers: 95
Total books collected as donation: 1392 (Other than textbooks)	Total membership fee collected: Rs 37,964
Total expenses so far: Rs 4376 Cash in hand: Rs 4026	Total bank balance: Rs 29562
Total number of library committees: 15	Total number of library committee members: 102 (57 female and 45 male)

Strategies

Since the libraries target school drop-outs and neo-literates, several activities are undertaken to sustain their involvement in reading and writing.

Special Reading Awards

In the first year, a special prize was given to the members who read the highest number of book. This assessment was based on the number of books loaned by a member within four months of the establishment of the libraries. Although this is not a strict measure of the number of books read, the fact that these members had come to the libraries on several occasions to check books out exhibited their interest in the library and book reading. Altogether, 12 members received this prize, of whom nine were women.

Quiz Contest for Library Members

On 15 August 2000, on India's 53rd Independence Day, a quiz contest for library members was organised at four of the libraries. In all, 97 members participated. There were separate categories for children, women and men. Different questions were asked based on the books available in the library. Simple prizes were given to those answering the highest number of questions. Donations were collected locally for the prizes. The event further enhanced the interest of the existing members and encouraged many more to become members. For instance, at Nayapatti Library, the total number of members increased from 84 before the event to 102 as a result of it.

Sarodotsav Essay Contest

Since the beginning, an essay contest is organised during Durga Puja, called Sarodotsav Essay Contest, open to library members only. The participants have typically included students, homemakers and school drop-outs. The contest is helping several members to revive their writing skills. The choice of topic in the first year was 'A Great Soul' or 'An Indian Festival', while in the second year participants were asked to write on 'Our Library'. The latter was an invitation to members to write on what they liked most about the library, their dreams and wishes with respect to the library and how it had influenced their lives. In the first year, 101 essays were received from 12 libraries, whereas the next year, only 71 essays came from 9 libraries. Bibhas Mohanta, a Class VII student living in the Nayapatti slum area wrote in his essay, 'After becoming a member in this library we have met so many authors through their books.... Without the library, life would not have been so much fun. There should be a library in every lane in India.' At specially organised functions, all the participants received some prize or the other in appreciation of their contribution.

Promotion of Wall Magazines

Some library committees have plans to bring out their own wall magazine, for which, contributions will be invited from library members. The magazine will then be put up on the library wall or in a prominent place in front of the library. The library fund is to cover the expense for paper and pens. This activity is intended to give regular writing practice.

Cultural Programme at Nayapatti Library

Motivating Librarians

The success of a library depends very much on the librarians. Therefore, it is very important to motivate them well. Swadhina awards prizes to the librarians to augment their enthusiasm. At the refresher training organised in the second year, an assessment exercise was held to judge their performance and give away prizes (Box 12.2).

Box 12.2: Prizes given to librarians

Highest membership
Ms Itu Dey (123 members), Ms Sarmistha Basu (100 members), Ms Soma Poddar (83 members)

Highest bank savings
Mrs Sumati Mondal (Rs 1400), Mr Ataul Haque (Rs 810), Mrs Shyamali Chandra (Rs 700), Ms Sarmistha Basu (Rs 700)

Least expenses
Mr Arman Hossain (Rs 10), Mrs Sibani Das (Rs 26), Mrs Sumati Mondal (Rs 30)

Highest collection of donated books
Mr Ataul Haque (119 books), Ms Itu Dey (104 books), Mr Prabir
Banerjee (91 books)
Overall best performance
1st Prize: Mr Prabir Banerjee (Jana Sevak Library); 2nd Prize: Mr
Ataul Haque (Dent Mission Library)

For the essay contest, a special prize was declared for the libraries
contributing the highest number of essays. Punctuality is an important
quality of a librarian, hence, during the initial sharing meets, an award
for punctuality was also given away.

Libraries as Social and Cultural Centres

One of the goals of the libraries is to become centres for social and
cultural interaction. Different types of activities were organised toward
this end, some by Swadhina and some others through local initiative.

Children's Cultural Programmes

Several cultural programmes for children were organised since the
project began, promoting an atmosphere conducive to the healthy growth
of children in the slums. Sound mental, psychological and social growth
is a need for children, especially in the slum areas.

Children's Drawing Contest

Children from the slum libraries participated in a drawing contest
organised by Swadhina in August 1998 in Kolkata. Each child drew a
picture of his or her choice. At the end, all the participating children
received a prize.

Children's Day

On 14 November 1998, on Children's Day, a children's gathering was
organised at the Bangla Academy. This was a rare occasion for children
from slum areas to perform in such a large hall. They sang songs, shared
jokes, danced together and staged a drama.

Shishu Utsav

On 30 January 1999, a children's festival was organised in Kolkata where children from the libraries presented various cultural items.

Rabindra Jayanti

On the occasion of Rabindranath Tagore's birthday, cultural programmes were organised on local initiative at three of the libraries, in 1999. Children presented songs, dance and drama for the entertainment of the community.

Empowering Women

Development initiatives often fail without the active participation of women. It is also a fact that a disproportionately high number of non-literates and neo-literates are women. Therefore, we have actively endeavoured to attract and involve women library members. This is reflected in the proportion of librarians and library members who are women. We also believe that women's education is extremely important for any kind of social development. Some of the activities with women are described below.

Women's Handicraft Exhibition

A women's handicraft exhibition was organised at three libraries in May 1999. Women exhibited their handicrafts, some of which were made by them before their marriage but preserved carefully for many years. Many people from the community came to see the exhibition. Women of varied age who participated felt proud and happy to see their work appreciated and recognised by all. Prizes were given to women whose work was selected. The different types of items exhibited revealed the tremendous potential and creativity latent in these women, creativity which unfortunately goes unrecognised very often.

Members of Bagpara Library at Their Craft Exhibition

Celebration of International Women's Day

For two successive years, International Women's Day was celebrated on 8th March with the women from the slum areas where the libraries are located. A spacious hall was booked for the occasion. Instead of inviting special performers, women from each library were asked to perform at the programme. Some sang songs, some spoke about their lives —shattered dreams and unfulfilled desires and expressed their thoughts about the day. Most of the women performers were shaking visibly but ultimately gathered enough courage to face the audience. A few even seemed to have shed all their shyness and inhibition. Women went back home feeling confident and empowered through their active participation in the programmes.

Sustainability of the Libraries

If people are convinced about the importance of libraries, they will come forward to support the cause. Over the last two years we have seen that the libraries have been able to secure much support from the community in terms of getting space, newspapers and books as donation. A high community involvement is an important factor in sustaining the libraries. Apart from the formation of library committees, local interest towards the affairs of the library was also slowly generated through the participation of community members in the various activities organised periodically. Regular election of the committee members is also necessary to ensure a dynamic and democratic process while also contributing to rolling duties.

Creation of the Library Fund

The library fund was created with membership fee which continues to be deposited in the bank or post office. The membership fee, decided by the library committee, varies from library to library. Generally it is Rs 2 to Rs 3 per month. The librarians are encouraged to keep expenditure from the library fund to a minimum keeping in mind the issue of financial sustainability. The interest accrued from the account, even though it is a small amount at present, is re-deposited. A creative effort is necessary to generate extra income for the library so that the fund is sufficient for the librarians' honorarium and other expenses.

On a recent visit to the libraries, the librarians were asked about their plans for future sustenance of the libraries. They seemed confident of running the libraries creatively and efficiently even if the external financial support stops. Discussions have been initiated on ensuring a continuous supply of new books to the libraries. Some measures identified are raising donations to buy books, increasing book donations, especially from schools and big libraries, and exploring places where second-hand books are sold at nominal rates.

Concerns

During the initial months, considerable effort was required to attract people to the library and encourage them to read. Moreover, the librarians too needed time to clearly understand their special role within the community. With the initial effort behind us, the project is at the stage of grappling with some concerns.

Increasing Female Members

In at least four localities, it has been the experience that women do not become members because the librarian is a man. At the same time, it has been difficult to find a female librarian. Hence, the number of female members in some libraries is very low. Men, having greater mobility, can come to the library more regularly than women to read newspapers. As a result, against an average of 95 men who are regular newspaper readers, there are only 45 women.

Getting the Right Books for the Community

There is a shortage of books appropriate for neo-literates. Therefore, the development of reading material ideally suited for them is a prime need. There is a continuous demand for simple books befitting the reading skill levels of a neo-literate. In the absence of such books, readers are discouraged. Books appropriate for neo-literates are pictorially rich, printed in large fonts and written in very simple language.

Regular Supply of New Books

The members' interest wanes if they do not get new books regularly. There should be a continuous supply of new books at the library. This is a significant issue from a sustainability point of view, especially when there is no external financial support.

Conclusion

Running the slum libraries has been a very unique and rich learning experience. Time and experience have deeply influenced the adoption of new ideas and strategies. The libraries have created a culture of reading and writing among a large population for whom practising literacy skills was otherwise infrequent. What is more important, however, is that the libraries have introduced a sense of self-dignity in the members' lives. They feel empowered in their newly acquired knowledge from books and this is changing their attitude towards life. As Mrs Binita Sadhana Devi said on International Women's Day, after receiving a prize for her essay, 'We always think that we do not know anything. I am happy that I have written something for which I have now won a prize.'

Swadhina has also opened 50 libraries in remote areas of rural Orissa and Tamil Nadu states. Running them is proving to be a far greater challenge. The experience gathered from the libraries in Kolkata slums, however, are enabling Swadhina to meet the challenge.

Appendix

Popular Books

Title of Book	Author
Children/Adolescents	
1. Boromamar Kirti	Sanjiv Chatterjee
2. Majar Majar Magic	P.C. Sorcar
3. Chuttir Ghanta	Sunil Ganguli
4. Rahasya Romancha	Syed Mustafa Shiraj
5. Shera Hasir Galpa	Arun Kumar Das and Sanjib Chatterjee
Adults	
1. Aalor Pathe	Gurudas Patnaik
2. Loukik Aloukik	Bibhuti Bhusan Banerjee
3. Saat Taka Baro Ana	Sanjiv Chatterjee
4. Nijhum Rater Atanka	Syed Mustafa Shiraj
5. Sarkari Daptare Hasya	Tushar Kanti Basu

PART VI

MEDIA AND LITERACY

CHAPTER THIRTEEN

Same Language Subtitling: A Butterfly for Literacy?[1]

Brij Kothari, Joe Takeda, Ashok Joshi and Avinash Pandey

Introduction

The 'Butterfly Effect' is a term coined in 1961 by meteorologist, Edward Lorenz. His contention was that a butterfly flapping its wings in one part of the world could alter the weather somewhere else. Is there such a butterfly for literacy? A butterfly that could flutter ever so gently to transform the literacy forecast of a nation that is one billion strong and home to one-third the world's illiterates? Possibly, even if it sounds somewhat overstated! And that simplest of creatures is Same Language Subtitling (SLS). As the term implies, SLS refers to the idea of subtitling

---

1. This chapter has been reprinted from the *International Journal of Lifelong Education* (2002), 21(1): 55–66. It is reprinted here with permission from Taylor & Francis Ltd. (www.tandf.co.uk).

motion media programming in the same language as the audio. No translation, just verbatim matching of audio and text in the same language—Hindi programmes subtitled in Hindi, Tamil programmes in Tamil and so on in all the 24 official languages and numerous other dialects. Unbelievable as it first sounds, what the multihued butterfly can do for the weather, potentially, SLS in its linguistic diversity can do for literacy in India.

Relapse and Low Levels

At the turn of the millennium, India's literacy rate, for a population of over one billion, is estimated to be 65 per cent. That makes India a country of roughly 560 million literate and 300 million non-literate people in the 7+ age group. There are, however, no statistics available on the skill levels of the 560 million whom we call 'literate'. What percentage is literate at competencies above Grade V or even Grade III levels? How many of the so-called literates can read a newspaper? Write a letter? Fill out applications? These are important questions in a country where an ability to merely sign one's name often gets equated with literacy.

A conservative guesstimate of the semi or neo-literate[2] population is 325 million. This is roughly 60 per cent of those we consider to be literate. Thus, a challenge of gargantuan proportions facing India is not only to make one-third of its population partially literate but also to create opportunities for another one-third to move from partial to functional and irreversible literacy.[3] This move is necessary in a lifelong sense since literacy skills beyond a minimally functional level have the potential to expand the scope of informed choice, decision making, and opportunities for the family, in unpredictable ways. The National Literacy Mission (NLM), created in 1988, has enjoyed considerable success in creating large numbers of early literates through its Total Literacy Campaigns (TLCs). However, the post-literacy (PL) (read post-neo-literacy) agenda has lacked imagination. In fact, according to the NLM's own Report of the Expert Group (1994), neo-literates' relapse into illiteracy could be as high as 40 per cent.

2. A semi or neo-literate person is defined here as someone who is at risk of literacy skill erosion and/or possible relapse into illiteracy.

3. Functional literacy is used simply to mean the ability to independently draw information from the most common sources (e.g., newspapers, bus destination signs), articulate thoughts in writing (e.g., letters), and do basic arithmetic on paper to the extent necessary in everyday life.

Everyday Literacy

Literacy skills, like any other skill, need constant practice for maintenance or improvement. Unfortunately, literacy transactions are often absent in the lives of many neo-literates because they have not yet attained the minimally functional level. The PL agenda of the NLM has relied heavily on neo-literates' enrolment in PL centres. Generally the classes are held in the evening or night. Nationally, actual participation was found to be as low as 31.51 per cent of the 'proposed' 13.4 million neo-literates (NLM, 1994). As it is, the proposed number of neo-literates targeted by the NLM is a small fraction of the national pool of people with some but lower than functional literacy skills. And here too, participation in PL centres is less than a third of the target. Furthermore, participation in PL and/or Continuing Education (CE) centres is programmatic and therefore limited in duration. How does a partially literate person, then, continually improve one's skills throughout life? This is where the concepts of everyday and lifelong literacy transactions assume critical importance.

In the everyday context, the national strategy has depended on the creation of libraries and making available wallpapers, magazines and other reading material designed for neo-literates. Both the PL/CE centre approach and the creation of learning spaces and material for literacy, as pursued by the NLM, are necessary but grossly insufficient in terms of sustained and broad-based reach. Generally, in these situations, the contact with participants tends to be short-term and costly, serving only a small percentage of the partially literate population. Most seriously, these strategies require the learner to be highly self-motivated for post and lifelong literacy.

Lifelong literacy cannot be achieved through fixed duration projects but requires the integration of skill-practice into everyday life. For 325 million neo-literates, this is impossible to achieve without a creative use of the mass media. National policy on literacy has been lacking vis-à-vis mass media. According to the NLM's website, 'All India Radio (AIR) and television (Doordarshan) are playing a positive role in: disseminating the message of literacy, broadcasting radio plays and telecasting short films on adult education, organizing interviews, quizzes and 'quickies' to sensitise the viewers about the objectives of the NLM.'[4] The role of the media is primarily seen to be motivational—to disseminate the message and sensitise viewers, but not create an environment in which direct literacy interactions can be unleashed between the people and media.

---

4. http://www.infoindia.net/nlm/lit.htm. Checked on 27 January 2000.

SLS is one approach that can spawn through television an endless volley of effortless reading transactions. In the long run, it can not only promote a culture of literacy but, almost surreptitiously, raise the skill levels of a nation.

According to the annual report compiled by the Audience Research Unit of Doordarshan (national television), 479.1 million, a little less than half of India has access to television (Table 13.1). On the whole, there are nearly 27 million more rural viewers than urban viewers.

Table 13.1: TV homes and viewers (million)

	Urban	Rural	Total
Home viewers	191.4	170.7	362.1
Other viewers	35.0	82.4	117.4
Total viewers	**226.4**	**253.1**	**479.5**
TV homes	36.9	32.2	69.1

Source: Doordarshan (1999), p. 29.

From 27.8 million TV homes in 1990, TV had arrived in 69.1 million homes by 1999. In the 1990s, increase in the number of TV homes was 10–14 per cent annually. Recently this figure has stabilised to an annual increase of 10 per cent.

Television clearly commands an overwhelming share of media presence in an average Indian household. The dominance of television is matched in programming only by the insatiable appetite for film-based entertainment. SLS capitalises on this powerful union of television and film to infuse everyday entertainment with reading practice. This simplest of additions in popularly watched song programmes can contribute to literacy, not by compromising entertainment but by enhancing it. The potential of SLS in India and its popularity with viewers has been discussed elsewhere (see Kothari, 1998, 1999, 2000; Kothari et al., forthcoming). d'Ydewalle et al. (1991) have tracked eyeball movement to prove that reading of television subtitles is automatic and unavoidable. Parks (1994) cites a number of research studies that have found that captioned TV enhances language and literacy, including reading skills, comprehension and vocabulary, among students of English as a Second Language (ESL). Presently we describe a controlled experiment conducted in a primary school, to explore the effects of SLSed songs on the reading skills of neo-literates.

Same Language Subtitling of Hindi Film Songs in Hindi

School Experiment[5]

Methods

A two phase study design with a pre- and post-test was followed. The experiment was conducted over a three-month period at the Memnagar Primary School, located in the heart of Ahmedabad city. The school is representative of most government primary schools. The medium of instruction at the school is Gujarati, and Hindi is taught from Grade V. Enrolment at the school is entirely from low-income families—primarily children of migrants from the states of Madhya Pradesh, Rajasthan and rural Gujarat. They now live in nearby slums and generally work as labourers, hawkers and small traders. The total number of students enrolled in Grades I to VII (the maximum attainable at the school) was

5. Funding for this experiment was provided by the Research and Publications Unit of the Indian Institute of Management, Ahmedabad.

458 at the time of the experiment. No fee is charged. Children automatically progress from Grade I to V regardless of internal exams. Teachers are instructed from the school administration not to fail anyone because that could lead to child drop-out. In Grade V, children take the state board exam which is the only filtering point up until then. As a consequence, it is not uncommon to find children in Grades IV and V who can barely read from their own textbook. Since many children are first generation learners, parents' role in their education at home is minimal. The school has no electricity despite being in the heart of the city. For the experiment, electricity had to be 'bought' from an adjoining residential flat.

Three mixed groups were created from all students of Grade IV and V. Each group had 46 children. The groups had an equal number of children from both grade levels and had the same male-female ratio (58 per cent male and 42 per cent female). Hindi film songs recorded from *Chitrahaar*[6] were subtitled earlier. Groups received one of the following treatments:

- *Subtitle*: five subtitled Hindi film songs were shown in each session, three sessions per week, generally;[7]
- *W/O Subtitle*: the same film songs, but without subtitles, were shown in each session (three sessions per week); and
- *Control*: Control group, which saw no songs.

---

6. *Chitrahaar* is the first film-song based television programme of its kind initiated by Doordarshan. Still very popular, it is a half hour programme that is currently broadcast two times a week.

7. This experiment explores the acquisition of Hindi skills through Hindi film songs/subtitles, in Gujarati children studying in Gujarati medium schools. Hindi songs were chosen, and not Gujarati, due to practical considerations justifiable within the experimental context. Hindi songs with subtitles were readily available due to earlier efforts with subtitling directed at nationally telecast Hindi film-song programmes. Hindi and Gujarati scripts (and languages) are quite similar yet different enough to assure a sizeable sample of neo-literates in Hindi among those studying in Gujarati medium schools. This in turn facilitated the 'measurement' of improvement in reading skill. The choice of language also enabled an understanding of the impact of subtitled Hindi film songs in non-Hindi speaking states, at least those with not too dissimilar languages. Hindi is not only the language of the largest and most popular film song industry, the Hindi belt is home to nearly half the country's non- and neo-literate population. This is not to say, however, that a more intuitive first experiment would not have been to show Gujarati songs/subtitles to Gujarati speakers. In fact, such an experiment is now underway. Both approaches can offer different but equally relevant insights for the Indian context.

Watching Subtitled Songs in Memnagar School, Ahmedabad

A session comprised of five songs to mimic the 30-minute duration of the *Chitrahaar* programme. A test was designed, not to measure functional literacy and its various dimensions, nor reading and its facets of comprehension, fluency, etc., but very narrowly, recognition/reading of syllables and words. Within the short time frame of the experiment and the basic levels of literacy we were working with, at best one could expect improvement in syllable and word reading ability. If improvement even in this narrow sense could be proven to result from subtitling, then it is confirmed that viewers don't just ignore the subtitles but read them and one can expect higher order improvement with more frequent and longer term exposure to subtitling.

The test contained four blocks of unconnected words. In the first block there were 38 mono-syllable words and in each of the second, third and fourth blocks, there were 20 words of two, three and four syllables respectively. The mono-syllable words were created to cover all the sounds and *matras* (roughly translated as vowels) existing in Hindi. The two to four syllable words were taken randomly from the songs shown. Children's reading of the words was recorded and simultaneously marked for mistakes—syllablewise—on a separate sheet. Syllablewise marking means that in each word, only the syllables read wrongly were marked. This ensured an accurate measure of changes in reading ability at the syllable level. Since all the words were unconnected, it is unlikely that merely practice in the pre-test could have led to any significant improvement in the post-test conducted after a gap of over three months. The exact same pre- and post-test instrument was used to measure reading ability. The post-test was conducted after a total of 35 viewing sessions spanning a period of three months.

Scoring of the tests looked at the number of syllables read correctly in the mono-syllable block and the number of syllables and words read correctly in each of the two to four syllable blocks.

Test scores are reported as follows:

T-1: Number of syllables read correctly in the mono-syllable block.
T-2: S = Number of syllables read correctly in the two-syllable block.
     W = Number of words read correctly in the two-syllable block.
T-3: S = Number of syllables read correctly in the three-syllable block.
     W = Number of words read correctly in the three-syllable block.
T-4: S = Number of syllables read correctly in the four-syllable block.
     W = Number of words read correctly in the four-syllable block.

For two group comparisons, t-tests were used. For three group comparisons, an analysis of variance was done.

Pre-test

The pre-test results confirm that no two groups were significantly different from each other at the $p \leq 0.05$ level. Group means for the above test
scores were very similar. The slightly higher scores tended to be in the
Control group. There was no such pattern of difference between the
Subtitle and W/O Subtitle groups (Table 13.2).

Table 13.2: Pre-test means

Group	T-1	T-2		T-3		T-4	
		S	W	S	W	S	W
Subtitle	19.91	23.71	8.34	36.56	7.10	54.20	7.98
W/O subtitle	20.93	23.86	8.47	34.33	6.44	53.07	7.67
Control	21.80	23.40	8.98	35.24	7.76	56.73	9.46

For all the three groups, the results of the reading exercises were
independent of sex. As expected, the pre-test means of certain scores
were significantly higher for Grade V as compared to Grade IV students.

Post- and Pre-test Comparisons

Table 13.3 shows the mean improvements in reading skills for each
group.

Table 13.3: Comparison of treatment groups: Post-test minus pre-test result (means)

Group	T-1	T-2		T-3		T-4	
		S	W	S	W	S	W
Subtitle	**1.57**	**2.93**	**1.51**	4.15	1.29	**5.27**	1.39
W/O subtitle	0.62	1.33	0.44	2.49	0.86	3.72	0.95
Control	**−0.56**	**0.84**	**0.35**	1.95	0.55	**1.49**	0.39

On average, a child in the Subtitle group read 1.57 syllables more in
the post-test score for the mono-syllable block. He/she read 2.93 syllables more and 1.51 words more in the scores for the two-syllable block
and so on. On every score the mean improvement of the Subtitle group
is the highest, followed by the W/O Subtitle group and lastly the Control
group. Group comparisons of means that were found to be significantly

different (p ≤ 0.05) are shaded. For instance, improvement in the Subtitle group was more than in the Control group on several scores (T-1, T-2-S, T-2-W, T-4-S) at p ≤ 0.05. There were no statistically significant differences found between the Subtitle and W/O Subtitle group and between the W/O Subtitle and Control group, on any score.

These findings can be interpreted as follows but would need to be borne out by a much longer study: Gujarati children's Hindi reading skills can improve, at least initially, simply from exposure to the language, even through unsubtitled songs. However, this is not likely to result in rapid or sustained improvement for most people. A surer approach to reading improvement is to show subtitled songs (since improvement was also statistically significant).

Comparison of the performance of boys and girls (Table 13.4) reveals that girls in the Subtitle group improved more than boys in the same group while reading the two-syllable block (p ≤ 0.05). Girls also tended to have higher means than boys in the Subtitle group, but not all of the scores were statistically significant. Although it is premature to explain this finding, it is possible that girls tend to know the lyrics of popular songs better to begin with (since they are more home-bound and thus listen to the radio and watch TV more). However, we do not know this for sure. A longer-term experiment comparing girls and boys is required.

Table 13.4: Gender comparison: Post-test minus pre-test result (means)

Group	T-1	T-2		T-3		T-4	
			Male				
		S	W	S	W	S	W
Subtitle	1.52	**2.24**	**0.88**	3.60	1.36	5.76	1.68
W/O subtitle	0.59	1.08	0.12	3.15	1.19	3.35	0.96
Control	−1.08	0.67	−0.08	1.96	0.38	**0.21**	**−0.21**

Group	T-1	T-2		T-3		T-4	
			Female				
		S	W	S	W	S	W
Subtitle	1.65	**4.00**	**2.50**	5.00	1.19	4.50	0.94
W/O subtitle	0.67	1.71	0.94	1.47	0.35	4.29	0.94
Control	0.05	1.05	0.89	1.94	0.78	**3.29**	**1.24**

For every block, the score at the syllable level was combined with the score at the word level to arrive at a consolidated score (C), reported in Table 13.5. Half credit was given for correctly read syllables in otherwise incorrectly read words. For example, the consolidated score for the block of three-syllable words was calculated by assuming that six syllables read correctly, in otherwise incorrectly read words, is equivalent to correctly reading one three-syllable word. This further analysis confirmed, more firmly, a similar pattern of statistically significant improvement in the Subtitle group over, both, the Without Subtitle and Control groups (Table 13.5).

Table 13.5: Group comparison of consolidated score: Post-test minus pre-test result (means)

Group	T-1 or C-1	C-2	C-3	C-4
Subtitle	**1.57**	**1.49** [*#]	1.34	1.35
W/O subtitle	0.62	**0.55** [#]	0.84	0.94
Control	**−0.56**	**0.38** [*]	0.60	0.38

Statistically significant differences ($p \leq 0.05$) were found on C-2 score between the Subtitle and Control groups (marked '*'), and between the Subtitle and W/O Subtitle group (marked '#'). Reading improvement seems to have occurred most in the Subtitle group and this improvement is most observable in the mono- and two-syllable word blocks. This is not surprising. In 35 viewing sessions this is the extent of improvement one can expect from a neo-literate sample that could, to begin with, read only about 20 mono-syllables out of the 38 presented. For improvement to be measurable in three- and four-syllable words, more sustained exposure to SLS may be required.

This three-month experiment has shown that subtitling does indeed lead to syllable and word reading improvement, most apparent with mono-syllables. A safe corollary is that greater exposure to subtitling will also lead to reading improvement in general. If this is possible in a short span of less than 18 hours of exposure to subtitled songs, one can speculate what it can do over a lifetime of subtitled viewing. To hazard a guess, with the plethora of film-song programmes shown on TV, the average person probably watches at least two hours of song-programming a week. Improvement comparable to that found in the experiment can be expected in nine weeks if all the songs that are telecast are also SLSed. Imagine the lifelong impact that SLSed songs could have on the millions of people in India. What would have already happened to reading skills by now if policy makers could have taken a decision to subtitle all songs since the 1970s, when TV expanded rapidly, or in the late 1980s, when NLM began generating millions of neo-literates through the campaign mode?

Same Language Subtitling: A Beginning in Gujarat

Same Language Subtitling is no more an idea with potential for 'experimental study' only. Gujarat is the first and only state where it recently became a reality. This has been possible due to the institutional collaboration of: (*i*) Indian Institute of Management, Ahmedabad (Ravi J. Matthai Centre for Educational Innovation, RJMCEI), (*ii*) Doordarshan Kendra (DDK), Ahmedabad,[8] and (*iii*) Development and Educational Communication Unit, DECU, of the Indian Space Research Organisation (ISRO).[9] Since May 1999, the weekly telecasts of *Chitrageet*—a programme of Gujarati film songs—are being subtitled in Gujarati. The subtitled words change colour to exactly match the audio, making it easy for neo-literates to follow along with the song. To measure the impact this would have on the reading skills of adults, 516 neo-literates are being monitored closely in Surendranagar and Ahmedabad districts of Gujarat. Data from the post-test are still being collected. A cursory comparison of pre- and post-test scores suggests that adults who watched the subtitled *Chitrageet* more frequently improved their syllable and word recognition skills 'measurably' more than others who did not watch the programme at all or watched it rarely.[10]

Hundreds of postcards received from literate and neo-literate viewers alike have almost unanimously been in favour of subtitling. From the responses, it is clear that adults too read the subtitles, feel that subtitling enhances the entertainment value, and make conscious links with learning. For example, improvement in language, reading, spelling and vocabulary are ascribed to SLS, not only for themselves, but also for their children. Generally, people enjoy SLS because it helps them sing along, know the song lyrics, even write down parts of the song. Due to the complementary effect of sound and subtitles, many claim to 'hear' the songs better. For instance, Rameshbhai Naik, a painter from Kadi village in Mehsana district, wrote, 'A partially deaf member in my family started dancing while watching this programme.'

---

8. State television for Gujarat.

9. At these institutions, several people have shown tremendous initiative and encouragement. At DDK, one acknowledges Mr Satish Saxena, Director, and Nirali Joshi, Isu Desai and Urvish Dave. At DECU, Mr B.S. Bhatia, Director, and S.R. Joshi have contributed greatly.

10. Results from this experiment with adults are still to be analysed and will be reported in a separate publication. Hence, it cannot be argued convincingly at this stage that SLS will also contribute to the skill-enhancement of adults.

Ridiculously Economical

Same Language Subtitling weaves lifelong literacy transactions in a home environment at a ridiculously low per-person-cost as compared to what the NLM and states are spending for post-literacy today. Let us take the example of Gujarat. According to the 1993–1994 figures of the NLM (1994), a total of US$ 616,000 were sanctioned for a proposed 0.815 million neo-literates in the state. Thus, the combined centre and state allocation for PL in the state is around US$ 0.73 per person per year. Based on the 1991 census, the population estimate of Gujarat in 1993 was 43.2 million. This makes the 7+ population estimate in the same year around 37.2 million. The estimated literacy rate at the end of 1993 was 64.7 per cent. That means that Gujarat then had around 24 million people considered to be literate. Here's where the first assumption is made. Neo-literacy will be higher in states with lower literacy rates. To suggest a rough scale for neo-literacy, in a state with 100 per cent literacy, 30 per cent of the 'literate' population is assumed to be neo-literate. In a state with 50 per cent literacy, 70 per cent of the 'literate' population is assumed to be neo-literate. Thus, at the end of 1993, 58 per cent of the 'literate' or 14 million can be thought to have been neo-literate. Of the 0.815 million neo-literates enrolled in PL programmes in Gujarat, only 0.331 million participated. Hence, the state PL initiatives covered only 2.4 per cent of the state's neo-literate population at a US$ 0.73 per person per year cost (Table 13.6). [11]

As mentioned earlier (Table 13.1), almost 50 per cent Indians have access to TV. Since neo-literates would tend to be in the lower income groups, it is a fair assumption that at least 35 per cent of them have access to TV. In 1993, TV in Gujarat would have given at least 3.5 million neo-literates reading practice through SLS. The cost of subtitling one 30-minute programme of songs per week is approximately US$ 23,000. With these figures, the cost of giving 35 per cent of the neo-literates in Gujarat, half an hour of weekly reading practice, comes to US$ 0.0065 per person per year with SLS on TV (Table 13.6). This compares rather favourably with US$ 0.73 per person per year for covering a mere 2.4 per cent of the neo-literate population through PL centres. Besides, access to TV is rapidly increasing, it is a medium that has lifelong presence and one can easily increase the frequency of SLSed song or even other programmes. Following a similar approach, cost comparisons of PL and SLS are given for selected states in Table 13.6.

---

11. Figures based on a conversion rate of 1 US$ = Indian Rs 48.

Table 13.6: Comparison of expenditure (US$) and coverage (million)

State	Post literacy projects			Subtitling on TV		
	Government expenditure (pp/annum)	Neo-literate coverage (million)	%	Expenditure (pp/annum)	Neo-literate coverage (million)	%
AP	1.47	1.158	5.6	0.0042	7.266	35
Gujarat	0.73	0.331	2.4	0.0065	4.903	35
Karnataka	1.52	0.678	4.5	0.0060	5.272	35
MP	2.69	0.002	0.0	0.0042	7.335	35
Maharashtra	0.98	0.417	1.4	0.0029	10.500	35
Orissa	0.24	0.185	1.8	0.0089	3.517	35
Rajasthan	3.53	0.035	0.3	0.0067	4.743	35
Tamil Nadu	1.58	0.868	4.7	0.0049	6.489	35
West Bengal	1.24	0.522	2.2	0.0038	8.267	35
Hindi belt	—	—	—	0.0007	42.689	35

The economics of SLS becomes more attractive in states with larger populations. In the Hindi belt (Bihar, MP, Rajasthan, UP and HP), which accounts for almost half the country's illiterates and neo-literates, SLS of one weekly episode of *Chitrahaar* would give weekly reading practice to over 42 million neo-literates (35 per cent), at a lowly US$ 0.0007 per person per annum (3 paise!). In reality, many more people all over India (outside the Hindi belt) would also benefit. The maximum coverage of PL programmes in any given state is less than 5 per cent of the estimated neo-literate population.

This is not to imply that the PL or CE programmes should stop. Nonformal classes, support for libraries, wallpapers, magazines and other reading material designed for neo-literates must not only continue, but they also need to be strengthened. However, relegating the mass media to a motivational role only is not recognising the power of learning through subliminal processes. The same process on television that makes one buy a bar of soap can also be tapped to unleash household reading. Thus, organisations like the NLM could, for instance, launch a plethora of their own subtitled song programmes, nationally and in every state/language. There is no reason why these programmes could also not be commercially profitable. Every channel already shows tens of song-programme-clones (without subtitles) at a substantial profit. The NLM could also tie up with newspapers to bring out editions specially designed for neo-literates, and sold at an affordable cost. Clearly, the NLM needs to create an environment in which literacy transactions can occur habitually and automatically. For this, the mass media are not good, they are inevitable.

Conclusion

The power of SLS lies in the fact that it is covertly educational and 'adds' to the entertainment value. While enhancing the entertainment value of popular song programmes, SLS simultaneously makes reading practice an incidental, automatic and subconscious process. The popularity of SLS has been established through the overwhelmingly positive viewer feedback from viewers in Gujarat. Now the important question is whether the weekly subtitled telecasts of *Chitrageet* also lead to mass-scale improvement in reading skills. Further, what secondary and indirect effects are there in terms of generating an interest and environment for reading? Patelbhai Jeetendra's comments (from Nanikadhi village in Mehsana district) provide a window on what may be happening:

> The subtitles that you have added to *Chitrageet* will help the cause of literacy. I say so after noticing the behavioural change in my child. My son Parth is studying in Grade I. Whenever *Chitrageet* is on, he tries to read the writing at the bottom. Because of this his interest in reading has also increased. It is my belief that many underprivileged children will also benefit. Now TV is in almost every household. In low-income neighbourhoods, even if there are a few TVs, people go there and watch this programme. They will learn a lot because they already like to sing Gujarati songs. They just don't know how the words are written.

The most effective context for the implementation of SLS, especially for neo-literates, is songs—film and folk songs, bhajans, ghazals, and various other forms. This is not to suggest that it is not also effective in dialogue. However, songs provide some advantages that ordinary dialogue does not. There is widespread interest in knowing song lyrics. In songs one can anticipate the lyrics. Repetition is inherent. Both these factors make it easier for the neo-literate viewer to follow along with the subtitles. Songs also come in a variety of speeds, presenting reading challenges for the whole range of literacy levels.

The target viewership of SLS on television is broad. It includes school going children who can get out-of-school reinforcement, school dropouts who can relearn eroded skills and the millions of adults who enthusiastically picked up basic skills under the literacy campaigns but had few opportunities or perhaps lacked personal motivation to engage in regular practice. A major advantage of SLS is that it invites reading without dependence on personal motivation for 'literacy' practice. If SLS is dependent on anything, it is an interest in film songs and here the passion of one billion Indians is unquestionable. SLS can infuse the idiot box and the lives of millions of neo-literates with automatic reading practice. Now it is up to media and education policy makers in different states and at the centre to release this simple and low-cost butterfly. The transformational butterfly-effect for literacy is not a writing on the wall, it is a subtitle on television.

References

Doordarshan (1999). *Annual Report: Doordarshan '99.* New Delhi.

d'Ydewalle, Gery, Caroline Praet, Karl Verfaillie and **John Van Rensbergen** (1991). 'Watching Subtitled Television', *Communication Research*, 18(5): 650–66.

Kothari, Brij (1998). 'Film Songs as Continuing Education: Same Language Subtitling for Literacy', *Economic and Political Weekly*, 33(39): 2507–10.

———— (1999). 'Same Language Subtitling: Integrating Post Literacy Development and Popular Culture on Television', *Media and Technology for Human Resource Development*, 11(3): 111–19.

———— (2000). 'Same Language Subtitling on Indian Television: Harnessing the Power of Popular Culture for Literacy.' In Karin Wilkins (ed.), *Redeveloping Communication for Social Change: Theory, Practice and Power*, pp. 135–46. New York: Rowman & Littlefield.

———— (2000). 'Same Language Subtitling for Literacy: Small Change for Colossal Gains.' In Subhash C. Bhatnagar and Robert Schware (eds), *Information and Communication Technology in Development*, pp. 176–86. New Delhi: Sage Publications.

NLM (National Literacy Mission) (1994). *Annual Report 1993–94: Literacy and Post-Literacy Campaigns in India.* New Delhi: Directorate of Adult Education.

Parks, Carolyn (1994). http://www.cal.org/ncle/Digests/PARKS.HTM checked on 27 January 2000. Also in Eric Digest, National Clearinghouse for ESL Literacy Education, July 1994, EDO-LE-94-02.

Report of Expert Group (1994). *Evaluation of Literacy Campaign in India.* New Delhi: National Literacy Mission.

CHAPTER FOURTEEN

Velugubata, the Chittoor Post-literacy Newspaper: An Evaluation

D. Janardhana Reddy

This chapter is based on an evaluation of a weekly post-literacy newspaper developed in Chittoor district of Andhra Pradesh. The sample of respondents comprised 216 neo-literate people selected at random from 18 PL centres in three revenue divisions of the district. The evaluation attempted to understand how the newspaper was being used and what neo-literate people thought about its relevance and usefulness. The newspaper had been in existence for about six years at the time of the study.

Introduction

The Total Literacy Campaign (TLC) was formally launched in Chittoor on 2 October 1990, but the actual teaching learning process was undertaken in 1991. As many as 61,000 volunteers came forward to impart literacy to 6.06 lakh (0.606 million) learners; finally, 5.56 lakh (0.556

million) learners participated in the programme. The National Institute of Rural Development, Hyderabad, and the Central University, Hyderabad, evaluated the TLC. The achievement rates reported by the two agencies were 82 per cent and 86 per cent, respectively. The post-literacy campaign was then launched. About 10,000 Jana Chaitanya Kendras (post-literacy centres) were established, and 20,000 volunteer monitors appointed. Thus, each centre was managed by two monitors, who provided post-literacy services to about 50 neo-literate people.

The *Zilla Saksharta Samiti* then designed a weekly newspaper, *Velugubata* (a road of light), specifically for neo-literate people, in 1992. Chittoor thus became the first district in Andhra Pradesh to start a weekly newspaper. The newspaper has two pages. It is printed at one of the *mandal* (block) headquarters, which is about 50 km from the district headquarters. It is a single colour (black on white) paper with 18-point letter size. Five copies are supplied to each centre by post. The paper is registered with the Registrar of Newspapers.

Objectives

The National Literacy Mission has provided guidelines for the preparation, production and distribution of books for neo-literate people. These guidelines provided the backdrop for the evaluation that was undertaken. Reading material should be educationally sound, attractively produced and interesting. The content may be related to the following: (*a*) recreational topics/fiction, (*b*) social and developmental issues, (*c*) civics and values, and (*d*) knowledge related to work and development of skills. The material should contain elements of entertainment. It should also promote a scientific temper. The language used should be simple. The content should be relevant to the needs of the target group. The letter size may vary from 16-point light to 24-point light.

The specific objectives of the study were the following:

1. To assess the extent to which the newspaper was used by neo-literate people.
2. To analyse the content of the newspaper, and the relevance of this content to the needs of neo-literate people.
3. To examine the distribution mechanism evolved by the Zilla Saksharta Samiti.
4. To ascertain the opinions of neo-literate people on the get-up: size, colour, letter type, number of pages and pricing.

Related Studies

A few studies of the Chittoor newspaper had already been done by the time this evaluation was undertaken. Alan Rogers (1994) making some observations on the Chittoor attempt, remarked that each issue contained some political news, an article on social development, a short story, a cartoon, a song and a few poems. Agriculture, however, was the main focus. Questions and answers, competitions, and quizzes were regular features. The material was not pre-tested. He also pointed out that the paper was largely the work of one man, and that very few people would be willing to pay one rupee for the paper. Venkatappaiah developed a case study of the newspaper in 1993. He observed that neo-literate people found the paper useful for sustaining their reading skills. He remarked that there was no material for women readers in issues 6, 7 and 8. In 1997, the State Resource Centre for Adult Education, Hyderabad analysed the weekly newspapers of various districts for their content, presentation styles and language load. In Chittoor, it found that in a sample of 10 issues, most of the features fell under the broad category of civic education (social, political, legal and environmental issues). Information related to health and hygiene constituted a second important cluster. Features on agriculture had become fewer. More importance was attached to information than to light reading material. The narrative form was predominant, and the percentage of conjunct words in the 10 issues ranged from 31 to 49 per cent.

Methodology of the Evaluation

An interview schedule was prepared and field-tested on a sample of 20 respondents belonging to four villages. Then, 216 neo-literate people were selected through a three-stage random sampling technique. Chittoor district has 65 *mandals* spread over three revenue divisions. At the first stage, six *mandals*, two from each division, were selected. In the second stage, 18 villages (three from each *mandal*) were chosen. Finally, 12 neo-literate people were selected from each village, at random.

Profile of the Sample

About 48 per cent of the sampled neo-literate people were in the age group of 26–35 years. About 88 per cent were engaged in agriculture, either as farmers or as labourers. Close to 62 per cent were married. About 72 per cent belonged to the Backward Classes and Scheduled Castes; 3 per cent belonged to the Scheduled Tribes (this reflects the low proportion of Scheduled Tribes in the district), and the rest belonged to the general category. In general, this sample was reported to be fairly representative of the district's population profile.

Discussion of the Findings

Extent of Use

Knowledge of Newspaper Name

A simple but not very accurate way of assessing the awareness about a newspaper is to ask the respondents the name of the newspaper—in this case, *Velugubata*. About 73 per cent of the sampled neo-literate people named the paper correctly. This indicates that a large number of the sampled learners are aware of the post-literacy newspaper being circulated in their villages.

Reading Habit

Each centre was supplied with five copies of the newspaper in the hope that these copies would be read regularly. About 47 per cent of the respondents read the paper very regularly, and about 25 per cent read it only occasionally.

Reasons for Not Reading

The reasons for not reading the newspaper were identified by 57 learners, who were not at all reading the paper or who read the paper only rarely (Table 14.1).

Table 14.1: Reasons for not reading the newspaper

Reason	Frequency of responses	%
Lack of leisure time	31	30.3
Inability to read	23	22.5
Irregular supply of paper	21	20.6
Lack of interest	15	14.7
Absence of co-operation from monitors (instructors)	12	11.8
	102	

Note: Multiple responses from 57 learners.

Of the five main reasons cited by the learners, three reasons—lack of leisure time, inability to read and lack of interest—are personal in nature, whereas the other reasons—irregular supply of paper and absence of co-operation from monitors—are organisational reasons over which learners have no control.

Time Taken for Reading

How much time a learner spends on reading the newspaper is determined by the speed with which he or she reads, or the amount of leisure time that is available (Table 14.2).

Table 14.2: Time taken to read the paper

Days	Frequency	%
2 to 3 days	132	61.11
1 day	84	38.89
	216	

Given that many readers take two to three days to read the paper, the present periodicity, one week, may be considered appropriate.

Relevance of Content

One of the main objectives of the post-literacy campaign is to improve the social, economic and health status of learners. Therefore, the content of post-literacy material should have relevance to the daily life of the learners. Nearly half the respondents (47 per cent) felt that the content was useful to a large extent; 30 per cent felt that the content was useful only to some extent. However, about 15 per cent of the sample could not make any comment on the usefulness of the content, and another 7.8 per cent remarked that the content was not useful. The diversity of the material may need to be increased since needs and interests vary from individual to individual.

If one looks at the specific instances of usefulness of the newspaper, nearly two-thirds of the respondents cited one or more situations where the knowledge acquired from the newspaper helped them in their day-to-day life. A few specific situations cited were:

- Knowledge about procedures for bank loans for buying cows.
- Information about the incentive scheme for inter-caste marriages.
- Information about photo identity cards and the availability of photographers.

- Need for administering polio drops to children under the pulse polio programme.
- Knowledge about first aid for burns, cuts, snake bite, dog bite, etc.
- Use of oral re-hydration solution for diarrhoea in children.
- Information about demands by women learners for equal wages for equal work.
- Information about reservations for women in employment and admissions into educational institutions.
- Information about sources of seeds of high yielding varieties of sunflower.
- Knowledge about appropriate doses of pesticides and fertilisers for crops.

Distribution of the Newspaper

The newspaper was being printed at a place about 50 km from the district headquarters. The Zilla Saksharta Samiti had one co-ordinator exclusively for handling the printing and dispatching. Copies are sent directly from this place to all the centres by post. About 39 per cent of the learners were receiving the copies only once in 10 to 15 days. Close to 17.5 per cent of the learners had not received copies during the three months preceding the evaluation. The reasons attributed by the monitors for delays in supply or for non-receipt of papers were:

- interior location of centres and inaccessibility of centres,
- postal delays,
- delay in posting the papers at the place of printing,
- resignation of monitors, and
- monitors' negligence.

At the village level, it is the responsibility of the monitors to see that all the learners read the newspaper regularly. The monitors are expected to circulate the copies to different learners. The monitors were asked to state where the learners read the paper (Table 14.3) and how the paper was circulated to the learners.

Table 14.3: Places where the paper is read

Place of reading	Frequency	%
Reading at home leisurely	90	41.6
Reading at the centre	82	37.9
Reading at public places (panchayat office, temple etc.)	44	20.3
	216	

Most of the 41.6 per cent of the learners who read at home get the paper through the co-learners or the monitors. The 20.3 per cent who read at public places return the paper to the monitors or pass it on to their co-learners.

Improvement of Reading and Writing Skills

One of the basic objectives of the PL programme is the retention, consolidation and improvement of literacy skills. The views of the neoliterate people on the role of the PL newspaper in improving their reading and writing skills are reported in Table 14.4.

Table 14.4: Role of the paper in improving reading and writing skills

Extent of improvement of reading/writing skills	Frequency	%
Reading/writing skills improved to a large extent	103	47.7
Reading/writing skills improved to some extent	62	28.7
No improvement	21	9.7
No response	30	13.9
	216	

Slightly less than 10 per cent felt that the paper had not helped in improving their literacy skills, and about 14 per cent did not offer any comments. These two groups account for slightly less than a quarter of the sample, and may not have benefited much from the paper. However, it appears that quite a number of learners—about three-fourths of the sample—perceive that they have benefited through an enhancement of their literacy skills.

Language: Level of Difficulty

One of the essential characteristics of reading materials is that they should be easy to read and understand. The learners were asked to state whether the language used in the newspaper was easy to read and understand. The majority of readers did not experience difficulties in reading the paper. However, a few learners (14 per cent) felt that the language was difficult to read, and a substantial number could not comment on the difficulty levels (Table 14.5).

Table 14.5: Levels of difficulty

Level of difficulty	Frequency	%
Very easy to read	88	40.9
Moderately easy	51	23.7
Difficult to read	30	14.0
Don't know	46	21.4
	215	

Appearance

The get-up of the newspaper is also equally important in attracting the attention of adult learners.

Paper Size

As far as the size of the newspaper is concerned, two types are in vogue in Andhra Pradesh. One is the standard size (56×40 cm) and the other is the tabloid size (40×28 cm). The former is a two-page paper and the latter is a four-page paper. However, the printing space in both is more or less the same. In Chittoor district, the standard newspaper size (56×40 cm) of two pages is used. In this study, the two models were shown to the sample learners and their preferences found out. Opinion was divided, with slightly more than half of the sample (52 per cent) preferring the tabloid size.

Size of Letters

The speed and ease of reading is influenced by the size of the letters. Selection of letter size depends on various factors like age and ability of the readers. At present, the publishers of PL newspapers in the various districts are using a variety of letter types and sizes. In order to ascertain the preferences in Chittoor, two types of newspapers, one with 16-point size and the other with 18-point size, were shown to the respondents. More than three-fourths of learners preferred the 18-point size letters. This finding meshes with the recommendation of the National Literacy Mission.

Colour

At present, in Andhra Pradesh, some PL newspapers are printed in black and white and some in colour. Two types of PL newspapers—one with partial colour print and the other with black and white print—were shown to the learners to assess their preferences. The results indicated that the overwhelming majority of neo-literate people (79.1 per cent) preferred the colour paper.

Summary and Conclusions

This study in Chittoor district of Andhra Pradesh examined some of the factors associated with the use of a post-literacy newspaper. A sample of 216 neo-literate people was selected randomly from 18 post-literacy centres spread over three revenue divisions. Over 72 per cent of the sample were aware of the circulation of the newspaper in their villages. About 47 per cent were found to be reading the paper either very regularly or fairly regularly. However, over one-fourth (26.2 per cent) did not read the paper. The reasons for this were shortage of free time, inability to read, irregular supply, lack of interest, and absence of co-operation from the organisers. Fast learners read the paper in one sitting, whereas slow learners (61 per cent of the readers) took two or three days to complete the reading of the newspaper. About 47 per cent remarked that the PL newspaper was very useful to them in their daily life, since it helped them gain knowledge in the areas of health, agriculture and development. However, about 8 per cent were not happy with the content, and another 15 per cent did not express an opinion. The newspaper was reported to have improved reading and writing skills of learners.

Regarding the distribution mechanism evolved by the Zilla Saksharta Samiti, about 43 per cent of the respondents were happy with the prompt supply of the newspaper, but about 39 per cent reported some delay. A number of learners (17.5 per cent) had not received any copies during the three months preceding the study. The reasons attributed for this were the following: villages not being easily accessible, postal delays, change of monitors and monitors' negligence, and delay in filling up vacant posts.

Reading patterns varied from individual to individual. While 38 per cent of the respondents were found to be reading at the centres, about 42 per cent were reading at their homes and another 20 per cent at public places (temples, public buildings). Most of the respondents preferred double colour printing and 18-point letter size; more than half of the learners (52 per cent) preferred a tabloid size of 40×28 cm—the standard newspaper size is 56×40 cm. The language used in the paper was felt to be appropriate and easy to follow. However, about 14 per cent found the paper difficult to read and understand, and about a fifth of the sampled readers could not comment.

Overall, one can conclude that the newspaper has had a positive impact. However, there are areas for improvement. Evaluations such as the present study are of use to district-level literacy authorities since they not only point out areas for improvement, but also indicate what other PL newspapers can learn from the learners' perceptions about the format of a PL newspaper.

References

Rogers, Alan (1994). *Using Literacy: A New Approach to Post-literacy Materials.* Education Research Report No. 10, Overseas Development Administration. London.

Venkatappaiah, V. (1993). 'Broadsheet in Telugu: A Case Study'. *Indian Journal of Adult Education*. 54(3).

PART VII

BRIDGING PEOPLE'S MATH AND FORMAL NUMERACY

CHAPTER FIFTEEN

The Meaning of Numbers: Understanding Street and Folk Mathematics

Anita Rampal

Introduction

A young man Chandru, who happens to be a school drop-out, is asked to solve the substraction '200–45'. When he does it in writing he writes the numbers one below the other, then starts from the units going on to the tens and then the hundreds. Intuitively, he says aloud 'five out of zero, nothing; four out of zero, nothing; two left; leaves two hundred.' But when he does it orally he proceeds confidently with, 'If it were 50 I'd get back 150, but now I'll get 155'.

It is generally seen that while doing mental arithmetic people usually begin by estimating the larger quantities and then fine tune their answers by taking into account the smaller ones. In the above example the boy begins by subtracting 50 from 200, and later makes the correction by considering the additional five. However, in written procedures we always start from the smaller ones, that is, from the units to the tens, then the hundreds, and so on. Thus, if there are any mistakes in the initial steps these amplify as we go on (Reed and Lave, 1981).

Indeed, in different studies of street mathematics it has been observed that people who depend on oral arithmetic make very few errors and have efficient ways to prevent straying from the correct results. Such oral strategies help preserve the meaning of the numbers and the operations they perform on them. Detailed studies comparing the strategies used by the same children while selling their wares in street markets and later using written mathematics were conducted for almost a decade in Brazil under a research programme of the Universidade Federal de Pernambuco, Recife (Nunes et al., 1993). Some of our own investigations were also influenced by the approach of the Brazilian studies (Rampal et al., 1998, 2000)

An Unschooled Mother, A Schooled Daughter

We first got some insights into people's mental strategies when we interacted with Draupadi, who was trying to help her school-going daughter in mathematics. We look at a brief sketch of Draupadi's background so that we may understand her cognitive history as reflected in her life trajectory. Draupadi, a middle-aged woman, had struggled for many years to survive in a city through rag-picking and, later, as a labourer at construction sites. Only for the last 15 years has she managed to feel somewhat more 'settled', working as a domestic-help in several middle class urban homes. She had missed out on school education due to her turbulent childhood spent in a small village. At a very young age she had had to take full charge of her younger brother and sisters after the death of her father and her mother's mental breakdown. After being married off at the age of 13, she had moved to the city with her husband and her siblings in search of work. She learnt to read a little in her 30s from one of her sympathetic domestic employers. The driving force in her life was a need to protect her children from the deprivations of her own childhood. Thus, she strove to send them to school as a way to release them from the vicious cycle of disadvantage. Much to her disappointment, she later realised that schooling by itself did not really fulfil her aspirations. Instead, schooling had managed to instil in all her children a debilitating sense of failure. Her eldest daughter barely managed to stay in school for six years. Her middle son, who initially took interest in his studies and attended classes regularly, finally gave up disillusioned after failing twice in the Class X examination. Sunita, her youngest daughter, was studying in Class V when we first interacted with Draupadi who still hoped that her starry-eyed child would manage to complete school and perhaps even study further.

Ten-year-old Sunita had been very upset at not being able to cope with math at school. She told us that her teacher was constantly reprimanding her for it. When we probed to understand the nature of her problem with numbers, we realised that Sunita was totally confused by the algorithms and methods taught at school. She was unable to use her own life experience to operate upon numbers the way her non-literate mother rather effortlessly could. Sunita's difficulties were not just with more involved operations like 'division' but also with simple sums. 'But you know how to do division, isn't it? See, if your mother wants to divide Rs 180 equally between her three children, how much would she give you?' we asked her reassuringly, expecting her to give a pat reply. Sunita seemed confounded and stared blankly. But, her unschooled and barely literate mother laughingly provided the right answer instantly.

On probing further it became clear that Sunita does not make sense of the problems she attempts at school and manipulates numbers almost mindlessly, often randomly guessing what she thinks the teacher wants to hear. For instance, when the problem is stated in words, Sunita first desperately tries to translate it into some mathematical operation between the numbers 180 and 3, and often cannot decide which operation to use, the '×' or the '÷', or some other. Even when she is told she has to divide 180 by 3, she can only visualise the school method of writing numbers in what is a meaningless and strange pattern to her (e.g., a 'long division'). She says the method involves bringing one down, writing something on the right side, some number above, and so on, but is unable to make much meaning of the sequence of operations. Not surprisingly, she soon gives up. Her mother, on the other hand, relates to the word problems most easily as an actual transaction and applies her own methods to get correct answers almost instantaneously.

This is not an isolated case of a 'slow learner' and her 'amazing mother'. This is the general situation faced by the majority of children enrolled in school but who are soon compelled to drop-out because of their inability to cope with the demands of school. Indeed, most surveys and interviews of out-of-school children have shown that they find studies in school to be 'uninteresting' and 'difficult'. Indeed, mathematics epitomises all such troubles. Appropriately, it is called the 'killer' subject. On the contrary, Draupadi, like the majority of adults engaged in everyday mathematics as part of their life activities, did not suffer from school-induced 'math phobia'. She was extremely confident of applying a variety of mental algorithms when faced with mathematical challenges.

Street Mathematics and Oral Strategies

While performing mental operations people stay close to the meaning of numbers and also work through visual images of the whole number, not just each digit, as we might do in writing. Thus, when Draupadi is asked how much money she needs if she were to give Rs 180 to each of her children, without batting an eyelid she responds to our amazement, 'Rs 180 for three, Rs 540, that's it'. Without knowing any tables and without writing any figures how does she manage to calculate it? How does she do it so fast and, more importantly, so correctly? She says that she *visually* pictures three 180s, and mentally gives 20 from the last to the first two, to complete 200 in each. Then she adds 200+200+140 to get 540! In addition to such quick algorithms she also has sound mechanisms to crosscheck her answer, if ever in doubt, and thus hardly ever goes wrong. In fact, she laughingly but proudly confesses that she has often challenged her husband, a skilled and literate mason, that she can perform more complicated computations faster than he can by his schooled written methods.

Draupadi is not exceptional in this respect. Most adults who have learnt to deal with numbers themselves through everyday mathematics are capable of sophisticated mental computations. We found that oral numeracy is more natural among unschooled adults than literacy, which means that they are more familiar with numbers, operations, measurements, and so on than with alphabets. Yet, in adult education classes they are taught written numeracy without any understanding of their prior knowledge, especially of the effective oral strategies they used in everyday mathematics. Moreover, those who design primers for adult learners insist on imposing upon them written routines that make little sense to them. Expectedly, they end up in boredom, frustration and failure, similar to the 'school math syndrome' suffered by millions of school children.

There are undeniable advantages of written algorithms for doing mathematics. For instance, in written arithmetic there is the advantage that we do not need to think about the relative value of the numbers involved, since we look at only the relative positions, such as units, tens, hundreds, etc. For the number 444 we would symbolically write it as 4 4 4, where only the placement of each of the 4s matters. However, when working with the number orally we always look at each of the 4s as different, depending on its relative value of 'four hundred', 'forty' or 'four'. This added feature only ensures that we stay close to the magnitude of the numbers and the meaning of the operations. Thus, to perform orally we necessarily need to preserve the *relative value* of each number and manage to keep track of it throughout our calculations. This is why we do not face the baffling situation as that done by Chandru above who wondered what to do with 'five out of zero'. This is also why the rule of 'carry over' does not come naturally in mental arithmetic, and becomes a major problem if it is not introduced thoughtfully.

Written arithmetic thus gives us the advantage of being able to follow the general rules and forget about the magnitudes or relationships of the quantities we are dealing with. Using the decimal point, a person need not know what changes of units actually take place after the decimal. However, as we have seen above, oral practices help us preserve *meaning* since, at each step, we need to keep track of the quantities and conversions involved, and cannot just follow mechanical algorithms. For instance, in writing we can mechanically add 1.5 m to 3.75 m and straight away get 5.25 m, without actually bothering about the relationship between m and cm. In oral arithmetic we would have to note that the '1½ m' was really 1 m 50 cm, and when added to the '3 m, 75 cm' give us '5 m and 25 cm'. Thus, at each step we are conscious of the relationship between the units used and cannot proceed without knowledge of the meaning of each transaction.

Ironically, the generalisations offered by written algorithms have not been used effectively by the teaching methods in our formal education system. Such algorithms have only aggravated the alienating 'distance from meaning' created by written procedures, and even led to the point where students may carry out computations properly but fail to interpret their results correctly. A typical example is taken from the National Assessment of Educational Progress carried out on 45,000 students in the US. Students were asked to compute the number of buses required to transport 1,128 soldiers, when one bus can take 36 soldiers. Over 13,000 students divided the numbers correctly but gave '31 and "remainder 12" buses' as the answer, while another 8,000 students wrote '31 buses' (Carpenter et al., 1983)! Such examples abound in every school and country causing much concern among educationists the world over. In the haste to promote writing in schools we seem to have failed to reckon with the writing on the wall!

Indeed, it has been seen that the algorithm for long division requires a sequence of steps devoid of associated meaning and is not a natural method of calculation used in everyday transactions. As argued, it tends to create problems of interpretation for children as well as adults. Oral arithmetic uses repeated grouping for both multiplication and division, where the person consciously keeps track of subsequent groups, at times, by using stones or sticks. If oral practices are suitably encouraged, written procedures can serve as appropriate supportive tools, especially in the case of large numbers and long chains of successive steps. Moreover, repeated grouping, especially repeated division by 2, has been the basis of most traditional number systems. This is the reason why most ancient oral civilisations used number systems with the base of 12, 16 or even 20—numbers that allow repeated division by 2. This way people could easily halve or quarter and sometimes even work with one-eighth units orally. In contrast, the modern decimal system with base 10 only allows one division by 2, and this had caused problems for people accustomed to oral mathematics. In fact, the metric system faced tremendous public resistance in France where it was first introduced, as well as in many other countries subsequently.

'Deficit' Learning or Problematic Teaching?

Just as we do not start by teaching adults how to speak before teaching them to read and write, we do not have to teach them to count simple numbers or to add before teaching them written numeracy. Moreover, adults are aware of the limitations of using only their memory for keeping numbers in their mind, especially when they tend to lose track of subtotals during complex calculations. They would find it a great help to be able to write numbers, but they do not want to be taught only how to write 1 or 8 or 22. They *quickly* want to learn to write larger numbers, and our numeracy programme must reach this level of teaching 'useful' skills at an early stage. We must also reinforce their mental arithmetic skills instead of replacing or ignoring them. They may need assistance with different types of record-keeping of practical use in their daily lives. Unfortunately, our adult literacy primers did not seem to respect this fact.

The literacy primers used as part of the Mass Literacy Campaigns laboured through numbers in a boring and often absurdly linear fashion, with numbers 1–10 in Chapter 1, numbers 11–20 in Chapter 2, etc. Normally, the first literacy primer contained numbers 1–50 and simple addition and subtraction. The second primer dealt with numbers 1–100, some idea of place value, further exercises in addition and subtraction and an introduction to reading clock time. The third primer included operations of multiplication and division, measurement and basic concepts in decimals, fractions, money transactions, etc.

We had found that adults were treated as children and were taught slowly and in a painfully linear manner. Pictorial illustrations too were taken from children's books, where they were asked to count eight ducks or five apples. The curriculum committee at the national level tended to patronisingly 'dilute' the expected competencies each time it was forced to deliberate on such issues. When the poor mathematical performance of adult learners was brought to its notice, the knee-jerk reaction was to remove the more challenging concepts, such as decimals or fractions, in a misguided attempt at further 'simplifying' the curriculum.

On the contrary, we found that the process of learning in an adult is far from linear. It is contextually related to the mathematical knowledge acquired through everyday life experience. Moreover, adults do want to move on fast to more sophisticated and challenging tasks in mathematics to help them in dealing with market transactions more confidently. A number such as 97 may seem large to a child but not to an adult. Therefore, it does not justify postponement to the second primer. Further, operations like addition, multiplication, etc., make sense to adults as contextual problems if stated in words. Just as Draupadi could solve the problems of division and multiplication of 180 by 3 effortlessly through her own strategies, adults are capable of doing 'word problems' much before they learn to read and write. In fact, stating arithmetic problems in words helps keep the meaning and context alive, maintaining a real world link for adults. However, curriculum planners are influenced by the school mathematics myth of 'word problems being too difficult'. They, therefore, diligently avoid using these, even with adults. In addition, various calculations involving money, in particular those related to profit and loss, simple interest on loans, or even probability of winning or losing a lottery, are considered to be important by learners themselves, but do not find a place in the curriculum.

We had seen that adults who came to literacy classes were using not only their own oral arithmetical strategies, but were engaged in a host of other mathematical transactions, such as sorting, measurement, estimation, etc., as part of their activities related to life and labour. In this respect too the teaching practice was completely divorced from their knowledge and skills, and often even dismissive of the 'non-standard' methods they used. For instance, metric units of measurement were cursorily defined as constituting the standard and 'canonical' system without any attempt to link those to the systems they normally used. It is well known that adults do not acquire and internalise new skills, ideas or knowledge in a vacuum, but need to mediate them through the praxis of reflection and action. New ideas or skills have to be reinterpreted through their own mechanisms of assigning meaning to them, and codifying them according to the categories they have evolved. More importantly, all new learning must be given a chance to be tested out in real-life settings. However, teaching practices used in adult literacy classes rarely attempted to encourage such mediation and failed to engage learners in reflection of any kind.

There was thus a mismatch between the learning strategies of adults and the methods for teaching math adopted in the campaign. Thus, those who were mobilised to come to literacy classes, through tremendous efforts in the campaign, soon became disheartened and dropped out, often dampening the spirit of the campaign leaders. Indeed, this fact had been witnessed not just in our country but also in the literacy campaigns and adult education programmes across the world (Dalbera, 1990).

A Mason Uses His Plumb-line to Check the Alignment of a Wall at a Construction Site

The last decade has witnessed much soul searching in both the UK and the USA about large numbers of educated 'innumerate' citizens who suffer from deep 'math anxiety' and are incapable of solving simple arithmetical problems. Despite having achieved universal schooling, these industrialised countries are expressing concern about their adults' level of mathematical performance. At the same time, they are also questioning the efficacy of teaching mathematics in schools. The 'Mathematics Report Card' caused a furore in America. Samples of 80 per cent of 17-year-olds at school were taken. The study showed that only 40 per cent of the nation's students could solve moderately sophisticated problems such as finding '87 per cent of 10', while only 6 per cent could locate the square-root of 17 between two consecutive integers that were given. In his critique of the educational system, Paulos (1990) has shown that widespread innumeracy exists in even professionally educated adults who misinterpret statistics or take incorrect decisions. For instance, quoting a study done by two doctors at the Washington University, Paulos showed that most doctors' assessments of risks involved in various operations, procedures and medications were often way off the mark by orders of magnitude.

Taking Account of our Inherent Sense of Numbers

Several interesting developments in recent research have revealed new facets about how the brain deals with numbers. Some of these studies directly relate to how adult learners mentally deal with numbers. It has been known for some time that humans (and even some animals) have an innate 'number sense' and that we can compare numerosities related to small numbers, typically, less than three, without actually having to count. Psychologists have also known for almost 20 years that each of us attaches meaning to every counting number we encounter. Response time tests have shown that we take much longer to answer questions such as 'which is the larger number' when the numbers are themselves larger, even if the difference between the pairs is constant. Thus, choosing the greater of 1 and 2 is quicker, than choosing between 2 and 3, and is much longer for 52 and 53. Moreover, if the difference between the pairs is greater we find it easier. More interestingly, if the symbols are in different sized fonts, we seem to flounder more. For instance, it takes longer to decide that the symbol 3 is larger than the symbol 8, than to decide that the symbol 8 is larger than 3. Subjects are unable to forget that the number 8 is larger than the number 3. This shows that 'digits are not just symbols to which meaning *can* be attached; they are indeed symbols to which meaning *is* attached, and closely' (Devlin, 2000).

Several tests that have been conducted suggest that the symbols we use for numbers seem to become 'hard-wired' into our intuitive number module in the left parietal lobe of our brain, and this is distinct from the way we use ordinary number words. There are brain-damaged people who are unable to read words but can read aloud single or multi-digit numbers presented through numerals. Conversely, there are persons who can read words, including number words and word expressions for multi-digit words, but are unable to read aloud a number presented to them in numerals (Butterworth, 1999). Other studies too have pointed to the fact that even though a number system, such as the Arabic one, may serve as a language, yet symbols are handled in a special way and in a different region of the brain from normal language.

Interesting observations of 'mathematical wizards', or 'human calculators', such as India's Shakuntala Devi, have also led researchers to look at how the brain uses linguistic and auditory patterns for fast computations. A mathematician Arthur Benjamin was once giving a demonstration of his mental feats. He insisted that the air conditioning must be turned off, since its hum interfered with his calculations. He said he had to 'hear the numbers' otherwise he forgets them, and certain noises tended to blur the sounds of his numbers. People known for such wizardry with numbers have a strong sense of associated meanings, such as Wim Klein who said that as soon as he looked at 3,844, he thought of it as a familiar friend and said 'Hi, square of 62!' Ramanujam was also known to have had strong associations with the meaning of numbers and their properties. In fact, educationists now stress that most people who feel they are 'no good at maths' lack a sense of meaning with the symbols they encounter.

The significance of the linguistic 'sounds' of numbers has also been noted in our ability to use multiplication tables. We recall the sound of the number words we had first spoken in our efforts to memorise these tables, rather than the numbers themselves. While computing multiplications we invariably revert to the language in which we first memorised the tables. This affects the computation time of bilingual persons whose first language (or the language they learnt tables in) happens to be different from that in which they now operate. These experiments have again made a connection between the computational ability of the brain and its language faculties. Researchers have also seen how Chinese and Japanese children have an advantage in memorising multiplication tables and performing other calculations because the number words in their languages are short and simple. One significant fact regarding the almost universal difficulty with multiplication tables, especially with number facts such as 8×7 or 9×6, has led to the conjecture that the human brain has evolved for pattern recognition and not for storage or computation of exact computations. Why is it that the above multiplication facts give us problems, and how is it that most of us come up with specific wrong answers, such as 64 or 48, not *any* arbitrary number like 53 or 57 and so on? It has been found that the numbers we come up with as incorrect answers are normally from among the multiplication facts we have learned as part of our tables. Our brain only gets confused because it tends to retrieve similar 'associated' numbers stored in our memory. Thus the brain is only doing its job of 'looking for similar patterns' it has stored in the memory.

The number sense of the human brain has thus evolved for pattern recognition and associative memory, different from a computer's ability to retrieve exact data. This was in response to the survival need for quick decisions with often relatively little information, such as in the case of 'fuzzy logic'. Thus, the part of the brain that deals with estimation does not effectively perform accurate computations. For exact computation, the brain tends to use other areas, normally devoted to speech and language. These ideas help us focus more on the verbal strategies that non-literate adults use in their mental calculations, differentiating them from the written algorithms devised for computations.

A brilliant example helps elaborate this point about how the associative memory of similar patterns creates problems for our brain while dealing with multiplication tables (Dehaene, 1997). Suppose we had to remember the following three names and addresses:

- Charlie David lives on Albert Bruno Avenue
- Charlie George lives on Bruno Albert Avenue
- George Ernie lives on Charlie Ernie Avenue

These facts seem to present a challenging task for memory recall. The similarities between them seem to cause each fact to interfere with the others. However, these are simply entries from our multiplication tables, where the names Albert, Bruno, Charlie, David, Ernie, Fred and George stand for the numerals 1, 2, 3, 4, 5, 6, and 7. Thus, substituting these in the first three sentences give the multiplication facts:

- $3 \times 4 = 12$
- $3 \times 7 = 21$
- $7 \times 5 = 35$

Pattern interference in the brain causes our problems in recalling such multiplication tables. That is also the reason why we take longer to realise that $2 \times 3 = 5$ is false than to realise that $2 \times 3 = 7$ is wrong. We are so conditioned by the fact that $2 + 3 = 5$ and our brain is so familiar with that pattern that it takes longer to recognise the difference. This phenomenon of pattern interference also affects the learning process of children and non-literate adults when they first begin to write similar equations.

There is a need, therefore, to devise appropriate teaching methodologies that take such pattern recognition and interference into account, and build on the oral strategies that adults efficiently use as an integral part of their daily lives. This is what we attempted to do through a process of action research in close collaboration with adult learners. We began by trying to understand the role of folk mathematics in their numeracy practices. We documented in detail their different methods of sorting and counting, of estimation and measurement of weights, lengths, time, and so on. Based on all these inputs, we worked out teaching practices that would meaningfully address the lives of our learners and enable them to deal with real world mathematical challenges.

Tapping the Treasure of Folk Mathematics for Teaching Adults

> *It is impossible to count father's money*
> *And impossible to fold mother's sari*
> *What are these?*
>
> (Answer: stars in the sky)

Oral societies have invested tremendous effort and ingenuity in devising mnemonic techniques to memorise, preserve and transmit their rich bodies of knowledge to future generations. *Shlokas, mantras and sutras* rendered through elaborate rhythmic patterns were all means to ensure that the rich knowledge available to societies was made memorable for posterity. Moreover, verse and rhyme, which help in memorising long pieces of complicated information, have been woven creatively with the empirical observations and philosophical moorings of oral civilisations. Voluminous bodies of early scientific texts existed for centuries in purely oral form, composed and recited through the use of complex techniques (Rampal, 1992). Such techniques for oral transmission also make use of elaborate hand and facial gestures with bodily movements that virtually inscribe the words into the 'motor memory' of the body (Daniels-Ramanujan and Harrison, 2001). Moreover, numerous such poems, narratives, riddles, games and songs exist not only in the repertoire of classical oral literature meant for the limited consumption of the 'learned' elite, but more so in the folklore of ordinary people. Even today the older generations living in villages savour and enjoy this rich repertoire of folklore received through their ancient traditions of orality.

Innumerable poetic puzzles and stories about numbers exist in the folklore of different regions of the country. These are often non-trivial to solve, even with written algorithms. However, people enjoy enumerating these and try to give answers more through their familiarity using intuitive and empirical strategies. The number riddle given below is simple, and yet, is more than a mere enumeration of the fingers of one's hand. It reflects an important characteristic of *homo sapiens.* The ability that allows us to touch each finger separately with the 'opposable' thumb is known to be responsible for humanity's most cherished creations, through the use and manufacture of tools. Thus, the riddle is meant not just to help us think of numbers but also to instill an appreciation for the special construction of the human hand.

> *Brothers there are five*
> *Without the help of the eldest*
> *The younger ones can barely survive.*
> *What are these?*

Through our involvement in the literacy campaigns we had learnt that learners use various oral strategies in their daily transactions. We attempted to document the rich folk knowledge of our adult learners as part of our study on their numeracy practices. Subsequently, many of the numeracy practices were incorporated as examples in our books, titled, *Numeracy Counts!* in English (Rampal et al., 1998) and *Zindagi Ka Hisaab* (Life's Accounts), an enlarged version in Hindi (Rampal et al., 2000). These books were not to be seen merely as a collection of esoteric examples. They were meant to serve as handbooks for all those actively engaged in the literacy campaign, to help them redesign their teaching practices. Indeed, the initial findings and ideas were disseminated at a national workshop among representatives of various institutions who regularly design teaching learning materials for adults. In addition, a pilot 'math *mela*' was organised, along the lines of a traditional village fair, to give a first hand account of how creative activities could be conducted by neo-literate women themselves, making math learning more exciting and challenging. During the workshop, worksheets on various mathematical themes were designed for use in adult primers, based on people's folk and street mathematics, and were included in the Hindi book.

In the concluding section, we give some examples from our work on the teaching methods we devised to deal with the 'meaning' of numbers. Beginning with the initial introduction to numbers, encouraging learners to consciously think of numbers in their lives, we go on to more sophisticated ideas related to large numbers. We also briefly describe the potential of transforming such learning exercises into group activities, which address crucial issues of community resources through methods of participatory resource management.

The Meanings of Numbers: Changing Our Teaching Strategies

In teaching reading and writing skills, we usually try to follow the methodology of introducing letters through meaningful words, instead of directly beginning with alphabets. Paulo Freire's work in literacy has had a significant influence and practitioners and academics by now acknowledge that the alphabet approach lacks meaning, while words loaded with life help adults decode letter and life better. For some reason, this point is forsaken in the context of numeracy. A similar approach

Members of the 'Didi Bank' (the Women's Thrift and Credit Group) Initiated by the Literacy Campaign in Dumka, Jharkhand, Discussing Their Accounts and Loans

is worthwhile in the context of numbers as well. One may begin by asking what numbers mean to learners and what numerical operations actually signify. But what *can* numbers mean to learners? Once a group of learners were asked to think of what each number, said aloud, actually meant to them, that is, what is it that they thought of when they heard the number. In response to 'hundred', many thought of flowers which they bought or sold in units of hundreds, some thought of mangoes, some of the number of paise in a rupee, and so on. We continued with different numbers, small and large, to get a feel of people's experiences and the meanings attributed to numbers. However, when it came to 'one hundred forty four', there was a stunned silence. One woman, after some thought, excitedly said it made her think of the '144 benches in the local cinema hall'. We learnt that numbers evoke vivid mental pictures and associations in most adults and they thoroughly enjoy such exercises.

Based on our experiences with adults, we suggested to the volunteer teachers to maintain a number diary for their literacy centre. It was basically to be a compilation of numbers and their meanings, arising out of such discussions in class. Non-literate adults initially claimed that they had very little to do with numbers and somehow never connected their rich living experiences with what they thought was the core of the numeracy curriculum. Therefore, to begin with, the teacher would ask the learners to make a simple number statement about themselves. For instance: 'I weigh 53 kilogram', 'My uncle has 11 toes', 'There are 7 people in my family' The group would then be encouraged to continue the process, and each person was expected to state as many number facts about herself as possible. The teacher would next initiate the discussion with a series of questions:

- How many persons are there in this room?
- How many toes do you have?
- How many members does your family have?
- How old are you?
- How many films do you remember having seen in the last five years?
- How many mangoes can you expect to buy for ten rupees?
- What is the number of the bus you take to go to .... from .... ?
- What is the cost of one kilo of wheat?
- How many stars do you have on your *lehenga* (skirt)?
- How many buckets of water do you use everyday?
- How many trees are there in your village?

The teacher was asked to make it as interesting as possible and to record these numbers as well as their significance in the number diary. She was further instructed to give only exercises based on the numbers that had arisen out of these discussions in the class. The idea was that when an addition or multiplication problem was given later on, if the learners seem baffled, a real life interpretation could be quickly provided in terms of the meanings recorded earlier. Moreover, this exercise helped remind learners about the regularity with which they encountered numbers in life.

Another way of continuing this exercise was for the teacher to say a number aloud and for the learners to respond with some objects of the appropriate quantity. For instance, the teacher would say '100' and a learner may respond with '100 jasmine flowers'; then the teacher could say '50' to which another learner would respond, and so on. In addition, learners would also be encouraged to ask questions (of the type listed above) to each other, to look consciously for numbers and report in the next class, and thus contribute to the growing collective database of familiar numbers.

How Numbers Grow

Expecting that learners would typically tend to think of only small numbers as meaningful in everyday life, it was felt that they must be encouraged to also think of large numbers. This was necessary to motivate the study of arithmetic and to give them a feel for numbers they may later encounter. Thus, questions were deliberately posed as follows:

- How many mangoes does a tree yield in a year?
- How many days are there in a year?
- How many leaves does a typical mango tree have?
- How many *chapatis* do you make in a year? How many do you eat yourself?
- How many stars are there in the sky?
- How many people live in our village?

It was important for learners to give estimated answers to these questions. Teachers were asked not to accept any response of the 'I do not know' or 'No idea' variety. The main idea was not to arrive at exact numbers, which in any case is a tall task if not impossible. The purpose was to use the process of estimation to decide whether the answer was in hundreds, thousands, or tens of thousands, etc. Besides increasing familiarity with large numbers through a practical feel, a discussion on whether the number of leaves on a *neem* tree is in hundreds or thousands, makes for a very lively discussion.

Experience with such discussions showed that learners did understand that there is no limit to the growth of numbers. A good game to challenge learners took the form of bidding, 'whatever number you tell me, I will tell you a greater number'. One can begin with small increments. Gradually, when numbers get into the thousands, the teacher can go for much larger ones. For instance, when learners came up with '5,000' the teacher would respond with '10,000' (and not '6,000'). This game becomes challenging if at least half the class knows words such as thousand, lakh, etc. (they need not know that hundred thousands make a lakh, but should only know that a lakh is 'much bigger' than a thousand).

While the basic numeracy curriculum worked with small numbers, typically less than hundred, we saw that learners needed to have an understanding of large numbers as well. This did not mean asking them to add 5-digit numbers such as 67,432 and 43,728, as is done in somewhat irrelevant exercises in primary schools. It meant giving them a feel for orders of numbers and honing their skills in estimation and manipulation of large numbers, which they regularly encountered in real life situations. For instance, where leasing of fruit trees is done, it is common for contractors to estimate the likely yield of a tamarind or mango tree using similar techniques.

Exercises chosen for large estimates were based on a series of Fermi-type questions, named after the famous physicist Enrico Fermi who not only loved to pose such questions but whose estimates showed uncanny accuracy. We began with posers such as, 'What is the number of leaves on this tree?' or 'What is the number of cups of tea drunk this morning by the entire village?' We combined such exercises with interesting group activities of planning, say, a menu for a village feast. This exercise involved detailed estimates and quantities, as well as elaborate descriptions of the recipes for each of the items on the feast. Such group activities were extremely popular among adult learners and were conducted in a highly participatory manner. Needless to say, volunteer teachers were required to be trained to handle such sessions effectively.

More advanced exercises also involved the study of the village resources, where the literacy volunteers helped learners to conduct participatory resource mapping. They could begin by trying to estimate the number of children below the age of 10 years, the number of cows and buffaloes, and so on, and later graduate to more systematic enquiries, which also generated valuable databases. In several places, detailed maps were drawn by the neo-literates themselves and were used as part of watershed management programmes. This group activity not only gave them a chance to enjoy mathematics but also helped the group develop a better understanding of their world, with more control over their lives. Indeed, a neo-literate woman who had calculated the number of *rotis* she had cooked in her life claimed that the exercise had changed her perspective about her own life and suggested a new course for the future!

References

Butterworth, B. (1999). *The Mathematical Brain.* London: Papermac Publishers.

Carpenter, T.P., M.M. Lindquist, W. Mathews and **E.A. Silver** (1983). 'Results of the Third NAEP Mathematics Assessment: Secondary School', *Mathematics Teacher,* 76: 652–59.

Dalbera, C. (1990). *Arithmetic in Daily Life and Literacy.* Paris: International Bureau of Education, UNESCO.

Daniels-Ramanujan, M. and **K. Harrison** (eds) (2001). *A.K. Ramanujan: Uncollected Poems and Prose.* Delhi: Oxford University Press.

Dehaene, S. (1997). *The Number Sense.* London: Penguin Books.

Devlin, K. (2000). *The Maths Gene.* London: Weidenfeld and Nicholson.

Nunes, T., A.D. Schliemann and **D.W. Carraher** (1993). *Street Mathematics and School Mathematics.* London: Cambridge University Press.

Paulos, J.A. (1990). *Innumeracy: Mathematical Illiteracy and its Consequences.* New York: Vintage Books.

Rampal, A. (1992). 'A Possible "Orality" for Science?' *Interchange,* 23(3): 227–44.

Rampal, A., R. Ramanujam and **L.S. Saraswati** (1998). *Numeracy Counts!* Mussoorie (India): National Literacy Resource Centre, LBSNAA.

——— (2000). *Zindagi Ka Hisaab.* Mussoorie (India): National Literacy Resource Centre, LBSNAA.

Reed, H.J. and **J. Lave** (1981). 'Arithmetic as a Tool for Investigating Relations between Culture and Cognition.' In R.W. Casson (ed.), *Language Culture and Cognition.* London: Macmillan.

PART VIII

CONCLUSION

CHAPTER SIXTEEN

'To Keep Them Literate'

P.G. Vijaya Sherry Chand

The foregoing chapters have drawn attention to the role that initiatives and innovations in 'lifelong literacy' education can play in contributing to the larger debate on literacy and literacy policy. These innovations which have been evolved in a variety of specific socio-cultural contexts focus on social development that needs the 3 Rs while furthering the retention and development of these basic literacy skills. Thus, they offer lessons in an area in which policy discussion has been relatively weak—sustaining literacy and locating the learning of the 3Rs in the context of a 'literate society'. This concluding chapter is a 'reading' of some of the general themes that these lessons illustrate—a reading that people concerned about literacy and educational policy making and analysis may find useful. These themes include the role of semiotics in shaping literacy policy and influencing thinking about lifelong literacy, the role of 'political will' in focusing attention on helping people become sustainably literate, the links between good quality formal basic schooling and literacy, the issue of language as a medium of instruction, the need for well-planned research to underpin strategies for the development and evaluation of lifelong literacy, and the issue of lifelong sustainability of literacy skills.

Semiotics and Literacy Policy

One theme that many of the cases presented in this collection highlight is the influence that the language of policy can have on the programmes that are actually implemented. The significance of terms like 'post' and 'phase' in hindering the conceptualisation of a model for effective retention of neo-literacy skills has been pointed out (see Introduction). In effect, 'making' people literate has influenced action in the field of literacy education, whereas as this volume points out, it is neither desirable nor easy to separate making people literate and 'keeping' people literate.[1] While it is beyond the scope of this chapter to trace the history of literacy policy since its first formulations in the 1920s, it needs to be pointed out that concepts like campaign, post-literacy, eradicating or liquidating illiteracy, are not of recent origin. Rather, their endurance since pre-independence times indicates the ease with which these seemingly simple terms lend themselves to melding with political rhetoric.[2] At the same time, they have perhaps hindered the development of alternative conceptions of dealing with the-development of literacy.

Adult education, as it is understood at present, has a long history, going back to the adult education schools set up in 1920–1921 in the Punjab and Bengal. The role of literacy in agricultural development and rural development and the role of female literacy in the literacy of future generations were also recognised as early as 1928, by the Report of the Royal Commission on Agriculture (quoted in Shah, 1989: 164–66). By the 1930s, the experience of the then Soviet Union (which in 1919 became the first country to adopt a 'campaign', as we understand it today, to 'liquidate' illiteracy) was becoming known in the rest of the world. The Report of the Adult Education Committee of the Central Advisory Board of Education, brought out in 1940, and various policy documents which have followed it into the 1990s, have pointed out the need to undertake 'campaigns'. However, international experience with campaigns (even the ones conducted before the Soviet Union adopted the modern form

---

1. It is not that literacy policy has been unaware of this distinction. The Report of the Adult Education Committee of the Central Advisory Board of Education (1939–1940) quoted in Shah (1989: 13) stressed that the 'primary aim of the campaign must be not merely to make adults literate but to keep them literate.' The phased-action approach in later years, however, led to a predominant focus on the 'making people literate' stage.

2. Shah (1989) contains excerpts from various official policy documents that have dealt with adult education and literacy, either directly or indirectly. These documents date back to 1928.

of the campaign) indicates that literacy provision has been merged with the socialisation of the young through a system of schools for basic education. A good example is the Reformation in 16th century Germany. We will return to this linkage later. Suffice to say that in the absence of this linkage, 'making' people literate remains a necessary and powerful but insufficient goal of literacy campaigns.

The chapters in this book also focus attention on the irreducibility of the retention of literacy skills to a 'post-literacy' phase. 'Post-literacy' also has a long linguistic history in our policy making. If the logic of making people literate first is accepted as a prime goal, then it is one easy step to applying the stage-wise instruction logic of formal education to adult literacy education. In other words, 'learning to read' precedes 'reading to learn'. This dichotomy, even in the field of early childhood education, has come to be questioned (Guillaume, 2000: 247). Initially, phrases like follow-up education and public library education were used in Indian policy discourse. Later, the Adult Education Programme adopted the phrase post-literacy, and a 1979 Committee under the leadership of J.P. Naik specifically dealt with the arrangements that were needed for post-literacy programmes (Government of India, 1979).

Illiterate or non-literate? The authors of the case studies in this volume have grappled with this question in their own ways. A few deliberately choose the term non-literate. For such authors, the question is not just one of semantics. The term illiterate, for many people, has come to signify a person who is deficient in some respect, and the 'meanings' that are then constructed tend to devalue the personal knowledge and systems of knowledge of such 'illiterates'. This syndrome is powerfully evident when one uses the vernacular. And so, for instance, 'abhan' in Gujarati, is no longer a neutral term to describe a non-literate person, but is a label which is used as a weapon to deride individuals, or even social groups.

The point about groups is important, since the interaction of literacy achievement with group status (like caste) needs to be better understood. Educational performance of girls in relation to that of boys, and educational performance of the Scheduled Castes and Tribes, have become important issues in recent times. For instance, under the District Primary Education Programme, reducing the gender gap and social gap in enrolment, retention in the schooling system and learning achievement, has been an area for targeted attention. But in most parts of India, it is the relatively smaller caste groups, usually in the middle of the caste hierarchy, which exhibit very low group-levels of literacy. In a survey of 424 villages in a district of Gujarat, it was found that two such communities, which constituted about 37 per cent of the population, accounted for about 56 per cent of the out-of-school children (Vijaya Sherry Chand,

1998). A similar pattern of disadvantage is likely in the case of literacy rates—though information on community literacy was not collected, female literacy rates in these two communities (as conventionally reported), varied from 3 to 7 per cent in the various blocks of the district. Such performance on the literacy front is possibly responsible for the categorisation of these (and similar) communities as '*abhan qom*' (illiterate communities), leading to the construction of derogatory characterisations of the communities. Though specific innovations dealing with retention of literacy among such groups are not reported in this volume, more attention on the methods of reaching such communities is needed. Perhaps, just as we need to focus more on isolate non-literate households (see Introduction), we need to focus on isolate predominantly non-literate communities.

We need not labour the point about 'eradicating' or 'liquidating' illiteracy here. Such terms still find a place in policy as well as popular discourse. Some may argue that not much need be made of the use of such language. Others (including this book) may point out that such terms are better confined to the medical and public health arenas, and that they fit in well with the once and for all 'making'-people-literate approach.[3] Lifelong literacy, which calls for a continuous developmental approach, would aim at building on neo-literacy skills and keeping people literate. In sum, it is instructive to reflect on the role that the language of official thought on literacy education has played in influencing action and the signals that the various actors involved in this action receive. This is especially important in our context, where the state more than any other social agent directs literacy policy.

'Political Will'

The importance of the state in evolving and implementing educational policy leads us to the much-discussed concept of political will. Many of the foregoing chapters touch upon this aspect indirectly—through a discussion of the will that is needed to support innovations in lifelong

---

3. In this context, Foucault's exploration of the institutionalisation of disciplinary and surveillance practices is interesting. He traces some of the origins of these in the attempts of the civic authorities to control and eradicate plague epidemics in early modern Europe. And among the institutions in which these practices have been replicated over the centuries have been prisons, hospitals factories, military establishments and even *schools* (Foucault [1975] 1985: 138–229).

literacy or to ensure adequate funding, or to ensure that interpretation of policy by the 'street-level bureaucrats' aids the cause of literacy. For instance, Sasidharan and Madasamy in their chapter have noted the help given by the district's top-level bureaucrats in supplying adequate printed material. At the same time, one can go back to an incident from the early days of the TLCs, to illustrate what can happen when political will is used to subvert the development of literacy. Pondicherry was the second area, after Ernakulam, to be declared 'totally literate' in November 1991. The literacy primer in Pondicherry had a lesson that discussed poverty and unemployment. The 'crime' it committed was that it asserted that resources were unequally distributed and called for a struggle for a just society. In a locally well-publicised incident, the then Speaker of the legislative assembly used this lesson as evidence to malign the campaign, and called the campaign 'anti-national'. As a result of this stand, the post-literacy budget was not sanctioned and reading material for the 530 post-literacy centres could not be produced (Rao, 1993: 915).

However amorphous 'political will' may be, it is important since it highlights the fundamentally political nature of literacy. As far back as 1929, the Auxiliary Committee of the Simon Commission commented that a literate electorate 'will be potentially more capable of understanding issues submitted to its judgement and hence *prima facie* better equipped to exercise political power' (quoted in Shah, 1989: 169). However, even today, the reliance on symbols in the Election Commission's repertoire—axe, banana, car, dam, elephant, frock, glass tumbler, hand, jeep, kite, and so on—continues. These symbols are necessary so that people who *cannot read the names of parties or their candidates can exercise their franchise* in what is arguably one of the largest events in the practice of democracy. The last general election involved hundreds of millions of voters, nearly 200 political parties and more than 4,000 candidates, and 1 million voting centres. By all accounts—even taking into account a few endemic blemishes like booth capturing and electoral violence—the event is well managed. But removing the plethora of symbols from the ballot paper has proved, up to now, a very difficult task. Ensuring the right to exercise a political choice through the ballot has been easier than ensuring the development of reading ability in most, if not all, people. No doubt the freedom that I enjoy when I am able to cast a vote by recognising my preferred animal or fruit is important. But there are other personal and social freedoms which open up to me when I do not have to rely on reading only through pictures. The will which ensures that 300-odd million are not excluded from a political process also needs to ensure that this population continues to remain included in the political process even in the absence of symbolic representation of parties or candidates.

This is not to say that expression of political will to tackle illiteracy has been lacking. The Total Literacy Campaigns themselves constitute a concrete example of such concern. No doubt, the context of the 1990s as a decade of internationally co-ordinated strategies to 'eradicate illiteracy' and ensure universal primary education has helped in focusing attention on the campaign mode to tackle the problem of illiteracy. Examples of political will contributing significantly to making entire populations literate in other countries are also available. China is an example of the intensive application of political will to the process of overcoming illiteracy in an underdeveloped economic context (Bhola, 1982). Arnove and Graff (1987), an edited volume containing accounts of campaigns beginning from 16th century Reformation Germany, reiterates this point. It also points out that, usually, literacy campaigns have been part of larger transformations in particular societies, which have aimed at integrating individuals into 'more moral' social orders or more stable political orders. And, these transformations have provided the impetus for sustaining the initial push for literacy. Perhaps, in the absence of a larger agenda, the phases of a campaign are seen as ends in themselves, and the political will that makes large scale mobilisation possible in the first phase is not necessarily sustained in subsequent 'phases'. Reinventing and reformulating the 'will' that will ensure acceptable levels of permanent literacy skills, is an urgent task. One is not talking of the kind of political will which decreed in the Soviet Union in 1919 that the People's Commissariats of Enlightenment could draft citizens to teach, and that a refusal to learn or to teach would be treated as a criminal offence. A will that facilitates local initiatives and the expansion of successful innovations, and supports the longstanding demands for more financial support for basic education (see Introduction) would be more appropriate. Our inability to allocate 6 per cent of the GDP to education, a figure initially recommended by the Education Commission (1964–1966) on the basis of its calculations regarding projected enrolment and national income, has already been noted. Another crucial area which political will and policy need to refocus on is the linkage between formal basic education and literacy.

Schooling and Literacy

The importance of the school as an institution that is designed to merge the functions of socialisation of the young, and provision of basic education is well recognised. Historically, initiators of literacy campaigns who saw literacy as a means towards a more moral/religious or stable society have tried to achieve the same final purpose through socialisation of the young by 'teachers' who themselves were agents in the transformation towards the desired social order. This association between mass literacy and basic education through the institution of schooling has been an important feature in the creation of literate societies. Wherever this association has been weak, primarily on account of an inefficient basic schooling system, societies have been stumbling and floundering towards an ever-receding goal of education for all—a sort of Derridean 'deferral' of an important indicator of human development.

In the move towards education for all, ensuring access to schooling and keeping children in school, are both necessary if irreversible literacy is to be attained. As far back as 1929, the Auxiliary Committee of the Simon Commission (chaired by Sir Philip Hartog) noted that primary education 'is ineffective, unless it at least produces literacy. On the average, no child who has not completed a primary course of at least four years will become permanently literate' (quoted in Ghosh, 2000: 154). The Committee was also concerned that out of every 100 boys (*sic*) admitted to Grade I in 1922–1923, only 19 were in Grade IV in 1925–1926. Similar concern had also been expressed at various points of time during the 19th century. While one may, in the 21st century, legitimately feel relieved that the picture of 'appalling waste' and 'ineffectiveness' noted by Hartog no longer exists, the 'waste' and 'ineffectiveness' that is still evident erase that relief. 'About 35 per cent of those who enroll drop out before completing the primary school cycle.... About 15–20 per cent of the children enrolled do not attend school regularly' (World Bank, 1997: 4). In 1991–1992, 'One-third of all children aged 6–14 years (about 23 million boys and 36 million girls) were out of school' (Probe Team, 1999: 9). The latter situation leads to the claim that 'India's primary education glass is two-thirds full, one-third empty' (World Bank, 1997: 1). Perhaps, it needs to be added that the glass is more like a strainer that does not pick up everyone and does not manage to retain all those it picks up.

Efforts to keep children in school for a certain number of years (especially given that an Indian adult, on the average, has put in only two years of schooling), and to ensure that a certain level of skills is attained, are no doubt being made. The full impact of the District Primary Education Programme, and the implementation of the Sarva Shiksha Abhiyan, are yet to be assessed. However, it is likely that the need for lifelong literacy among young adults who have not spent sufficient time in school and among those who have not been able to gain access to school, will continue to exist in the foreseeable future. Perhaps, some of the recommendations of the Education Commission (1964–1966) need to be revisited, for instance, part-time courses of about one year for 'drop outs' in the age group 11–14. Recommendations regarding making the system more flexible, including multiple levels of entry (lateral entry), flexibility in the structuring of schooling (part-time instruction) had also been made prior to the Commission's work. Pulling these together into a coherent strategy for lifelong literacy of this section of adults will be a necessary constituent of any plan for lifelong literacy education.

Some of the cases in this volume describe initiatives that have targeted the young adult population. Saswati Roy describes an initiative in the slums of Kolkata that provided libraries to young adults (school drop-outs and neo-literates). The innovation described by Kothari et al. has the potential to reach such a population directly through television; perhaps, programmes specific to different literacy levels should be possible in the future.

Language of Literacy

The issue of language of instruction in education is a vexed question. India has, in addition to Hindi, 14 scheduled languages. Another 41 languages are used for educational purposes and there are nearly 200 recognised language varieties. Besides these, we claim about 1,600 mother tongues. This diversity is not just a matter of multilingual complexity, but is also a problem of contestation of power and assertion of cultural identity. Modern debate on the language of instruction goes back to the late 18th and early 19th centuries, with the Anglicist-Orientalist debates giving way to a discussion on the roles of English and the vernaculars in the mid-19th century. Later, Mahatma Gandhi would argue for the instruction of children in their mother tongues. His philosophy of *nai talim* (more popularly called basic education) relied heavily on the principle that all curricular transactions had to be in the mother tongue. He justified this principle on pedagogical and ethical grounds (Gandhi, 1951). It is possible that Gandhi had in mind what are today called the scheduled or regional languages when he spoke of the mother tongue.

During the independence struggle, three value orientations underpinned the contestations over education: justice, progress and identity (Kumar, 1991). The quest for identity took the form of a confrontation with the colonial model and system through an emphasis on 'Indian classical' culture and a religio-cultural revival, through a shedding of foreign associations. This cultural revivalism, unfortunately, only achieved the entrenchment of a sanskritised Hindi in large parts of northern India as a symbol of a liberated identity.

This, according to Kumar (1991), had the effect of slowing down the spread of mass literacy. Perhaps, this process is at least in part responsible for the poor performance on the literacy and primary education fronts—and there is a positive correlation between the two (Sinha, 1998: 22)—of states like Uttar Pradesh and Bihar. The post-independence linguistic reorganisation of Indian states, and the numerous committees which have gone into the question of the medium of instruction starting with the University Education Commission (1948–1949), indicate the highly contested nature of the medium of instruction.

The scheduled languages usually dominate a particular state or region, but even within this geographical space, there are likely to be many large linguistic groups which may respond to the dominant language in a variety of ways—ranging from active resistance to acceptance. Preeti Soni's case in this volume highlights the tension that exists between Kachchhi (the language widely spoken and understood in the region of Kachchh in western Gujarat) and Gujarati, the scheduled language used in the state of Gujarat. The large number of languages claimed as home languages or mother tongues adds another dimension to the responses that smaller groups may make to the use of the dominant language in the region.

Such responses are, however, tempered by the recognition that the choice of language for education reflects official language policy and the opportunity for social advancement that the dominant language offers. Thus, very often, literacy means learning the dominant language in the region, irrespective of whether the learner speaks a non-standard form of that language or a totally different language at home. For instance, sizeable sections of the Bhils in Gujarat speak a variant of Gujarati that has incorporated features of other languages like Marathi. This group's language of education is, however, Gujarati. Children of the large number of immigrant labourers from other states become literate in Gujarati. Similar patterns elsewhere result in the development of bilingual or multilingual capabilities among a large number of Indians, but generally at the cost of a certain loss of esteem for and alienation from one's own mother tongue and its culture (Kumar, 1996); see Faust and Nagar (2001: 2879–82) for a description of similar effects of education in the English medium. At the same time, it has to be acknowledged, practical considerations dictate that literacy instruction follows the formal education language policy of the state. Within the schooling system, the three-language formula, in whatever manner it is applied, does provide an opportunity to become literate in multiple languages. An issue that deserves serious consideration is how lifelong literacy can offer this choice—a menu of languages—so that non-literates who have grown up in a language, and whose identity is tied up with that language and its attendant culture, can benefit from literacy in their own tongue and perhaps regional/national 'lingua francas'.

Research and Lifelong Literacy

Kemmis and Wilkinson (1998: 26–31) offer a useful typology to distinguish the various aspects of practice that are researched. A combination of focus (individual or social) and perspective (objective or subjective) leads to four types of practice: practice as individual behaviour, seen in terms of performance, events or effects (objective-individual, behaviourist and most cognitive approaches), practice as social interaction (objective-social, social systems and structural-functionalist approaches), practice as intentional action, shaped by meaning and values (subjective-individual, most constructivist approaches) and practice as socially structured (subjective-social, for instance, interpretive and post-structuralist approaches). When both perspectives are combined with both foci (a reflexive-dialectical view of subjective-objective relations and a similar view of individual-social relations), we obtain an understanding of practice as socially and historically constituted, but reconstituted by human agency and social action. Critical social science and action research would best fit into this fifth cell (Figure 16.1).

Figure 16.1: Traditions in the study of practice

Focus Perspective	Individual	Social	Reflexive-dialectical view of individual-social relations
Objective	Practice as individual behaviour	Practice as social interaction	
Subjective	Practice as intentional action, shaped by meaning and values	Practice as socially structured	
Reflexive-dialectical view of subjective-objective relations			Practice as socially- and historically-constituted, and as reconstituted by human agency and social action

Source: Adapted from Kemmis and Wilkinson (1998: 29, Figure 2.3).

The current state of research in lifelong literacy in the Indian context indicates that a variety of research perspectives (possibly all the five cells indicated above) need to be promoted, especially since a substantial body of literature is still to be built up.

The cases in this volume reiterate this need for incorporating as many research perspectives as possible. Janardhana Reddy evaluates the responses of individual readers of a post-literacy newspaper, an example of an objective-individual research. Shrivastava touches upon the limitations of the primer *Khilti Kaliyan*, and describes the evolution of a more 'open' syllabus which also incorporates a feminist perspective. Sasidharan and Madasamy describe a variety of trials in reading—reading aloud as a social experience, joint reading, use of riddles and puzzles, and so on. Obviously, a literacy practitioner has to undertake such 'local' research if the best use of resources provided is to be ensured. These two approaches adopt a subjective perspective and a social focus. At another level, Kothari et al. describe an experiment that explores Same Language Subtitling (SLS) of songs as an effective way of integrating reading practice with entertainment on television. This approach is more strategic in nature since it tackles the issue of keeping neo-literates literate through a medium that has wide reach and is cost-effective because of that reach. Lifelong literacy needs to incorporate all these varieties of research, if a sound body of knowledge is to be built up as fast as possible.

One cannot expect practitioners alone to undertake this task. Literacy practitioners will continue to modify and adapt their innovations and interventions on the basis of their experience. But a more systematic effort through networks of academic institutions/individuals and organisations/individuals involved in literacy practice needs to be mounted. As pointed out in the Introduction, recent research in the area of early childhood education has a lot to offer literacy education among older people.

One area which has been touched upon in the Introduction is phonemic awareness. This area of research has come to be recognised, at least in the English speaking world, as an important contributor to improving the practice of reading. However, more applied research in the context of lifelong literacy, and more importantly, within the framework of Indian languages, is needed. The various phonemic awareness tasks (Lewkowicz, 1980) offer themselves not just to developing methodologies for post-neo-literacy education, but also to evaluation of the current status of reading abilities: sound-word matching (recognising within a word a previously identified phoneme), word-word matching (recognising that two words have a common phoneme in a specified position), recognition of rhyme, isolating a sound, phonemic segmentation, counting phonemes in a word, blending phonemes, deleting a phoneme and specifying the deleted phoneme, and phoneme substitution. Tests to determine phonemic awareness have also been developed in the western, and early childhood, contexts. Exploring this area of research in our contexts, for lifelong literacy purposes, is bound to be fruitful. It should also be noted that the purpose of such exploration in adult contexts is different from using phonemic awareness to improve future reading abilities among children. The magnitude of the task indicates that a network of departments of education and researchers needs to be developed in order that such research may contribute to improved practice.

This research may be usefully tied to a study of the concept of 'prior knowledge' which is now considered, at least in early childhood education, as being a crucial factor in ensuring success in reading. That is, an immersion in literate environments, being in a context where others use print for various purposes, helps pre-school children understand the semiotic and functional nature of language (Raban, 2000). Adults bring their 'incidental exposure' to print (see Introduction) to the task of further development of their literacy skills. This does indicate that closing the Vygotskyan gap between actual knowledge and potential knowledge is a task that deserves more attention.

Another area that the case studies point out as deserving of serious attention is the provision of relevant and effective material for lifelong literacy. The uses to which literacy is put include personal enrichment and entertainment. Research in the field of content literacy development among young children highlights the importance of four types of textual material (Guillaume, 2000: 248): textbooks, trade books, fiction with content information, and other kinds of print like newspapers and magazines written specifically for young children. Similar material would be applicable to lifelong literacy also. The Introduction has referred to the somewhat unanticipated use of neo-literacy skills to read fashion magazines in Brazil in a literacy development programme; it also points out the existence of the fund of stories available in almost any subculture of India as a source for entertaining and educating texts. Sushama Merh-Ashraf (this volume) provides an interesting example of the adaptation of a Gujarati play, *Lala Patel-Ni-Laibary*, first published in 1938, into material in Hindi for neo-literates. Sarma et al., in their case study, describe an innovative use of participatory land-use mapping exercises for post-literacy education. This exercise, though limited in its scope, 'aimed at improving the skills of observation, visualisation and quantification. It was also expected to result in better decision-making processes and to provide a platform for collective activity.'

Some of the cases have directly addressed this important issue of producing relevant and appropriate material for post-neo-literacy education. Preeti Soni's and Shalini Joshi's cases on a newsletter and a magazine are good examples where the relevance has to be seen in the context of more mundane considerations like get-up, distribution and pricing. Michael Norton's case highlights the need for relevance to be tied to the imperative of affordability and distribution networks. Sarah Kamala and Saswati Roy discuss the role of libraries, though they do not emphasise the need for a deliberate selection of relevant content that is in the most appropriate format. All these cases, however, highlight the weaknesses that exist as far as delivering books or magazines to readers (distribution channels) is concerned. This is where the potential of the mass media is most relevant. Television, for instance, need not be just limited to exhorting people to become literate or asking people to join in the 'crusade to eradicate illiteracy'. Its use as a directly educational medium, as Kothari et al. point out, is possible through an integration with popular culture and entertainment.

Developing Numeracy

K.S. Ram, in his case study, touches upon the development of accounting and calculating skills as part of a post-literacy intervention. Some of the other cases also hint at the development of number skills. These examples, however, do not directly address the issue of developing numeracy among adult learners. This task is undertaken by Anita Rampal in her chapter, 'The Meaning of Numbers: Understanding Street and Folk Mathematics'. She highlights the need to realise that developing numeracy skills among adult learners requires an approach that is different from the conventional approaches used to teach children 'number skills'. Neo-literate adults bring with them certain already developed numeracy strategies, heuristics and indigenous algorithms. These comprise what may be termed oral numeracy strategies, or 'street and folk mathematics'. Written numeracy, as it is taught at present, does not build on this foundation. Thus, Rampal makes the point that, pedagogically speaking, written procedures need to complement an encouragement of oral practices. This would challenge many of the faulty assumptions teachers of adult learners make—for instance, large numbers are indeed too 'large' for adult learners, or that adults do not bring with them a 'sense' of numbers to the learning situation. This leads to another important point that Rampal makes: the processes of curriculum development and preparation of primers or texts need to be reformed. For instance, the nature of examples may have to be more daily life oriented, or riddles and mnemonic devices may also have a place (see also Rampal et al., 2000). In sum, during the process of developing numeracy skills among neo-literate adults, it is important to recognise that people bring with them a learning platform which may be in a different idiom, but which needs to be recognised and built upon.

Sustainability of Literacy Skill Learning

In an assessment of the sustainability of literacy skills, one needs to consider the extent to which literacy skills have been scaffolded on to other skills in the learner. One way of looking at the issue is by adopting a psychological conception of learning, under which the establishment of a cognitive skill is expected to transform related behaviours. Therefore, if new cognitive behaviours related to literacy practice can be identified, one can say the first step has been taken. But the linkage of the literacy practice with the context—in other words, the embedding of the literacy practice in activities (community or individual) that learners consider important, is equally important.

To understand this point better, we need to review how the impact of literacy on thinking processes has been understood—only a brief summary of the discussion can be provided here. What are called the direct benefits of literacy (not just an ability to read the printed word, but a transformation in the generalised ability to think) have occupied one strand of research (for instance, in the work of J.S. Bruner). In this way of looking at literacy, the printed word becomes a cognitive amplifier— a tool for using resources available in a particular culture. Literacy, therefore, would amplify the ability to think differently (for example, to go back to the use of symbols in elections, 'reading' not just the name of the candidate and party, but being able to think differently about the process of voting itself). This 'reading the world', in a narrow sense, would be a direct effect of literacy. In addition, the possibility of overcoming context-dependent oracy with the relatively context-free written word, and the possibility of reading and reflecting on frozen speech, would lead to higher levels of abstract thinking skills.

A second school of research has explored the effects with a view to isolating the effects of schooling, since many studies compared non-literates with *schooled* literates. This line of thinking (beginning with an interesting study of Liberia's Vai community by Scribner and Cole [1978] which had unschooled literates) has focused on the indirect effects of literacy on cognitive processing, and the functionally specific effects of literacy. These effects result from the learners' involvement in the activities of a literate society. The higher the integration of literacy practices with community practice, the greater the benefits to the learners, in terms of sustaining literacy skills. If literacy is practice, becoming literate has a specific effect on the cognitive processes related to that literacy practice. Also, the indirect effects are mediated effects; that is, the nature of activities changes once literacy is incorporated into them, thereby requiring modified cognitive skills from individuals engaging in such activities.

Some of the cases in this volume bring out the importance of nurturing the indirect effects of literacy in sustaining lifelong literacy. For instance, K.S. Ram's case describes the incorporation of reading and writing skills into literacy practices; examples include preparing applications, the *Zara Sochiye* experiment, group discussion followed by writing (writing being seen as more important than reading in this context), and so on. These in turn lead to community practices like the *purchi* (procurement slip) system, the *Naya Bastar* newsletter, the Imli Andolan as an organisation that has woven the literacy practices into its developmental work, and the systematic calculation of interest. (It should be mentioned here that this case is perhaps the only one in this volume which deliberately incorporates numeracy into the literacy practice of preparing accounts and interest statements.) Jaya Shrivastava provides examples of linking recognition of letters to discussions on words and webbing off into other meanings of the words—a specific example being *chadar* (a sheet of cloth), the *dakhila abhiyan* and exposure to courts. It should be possible to extend this literacy practice into a community practice; one example given is the linking of names of garments and figures of measurement with the activity of stitching. Paranjpe's example of Readers' Week (held during the vacations) to determine learning from reading, and Saswati Roy's special reading awards, library committees, essay contest and handicraft exhibitions, are other examples of integration of literacy practice with community development work. Sasidharan and Madasamy discuss the creation of knowledge together under the control of the circle guide. Preeti Soni provides an example of a collective voice of rural women that revolves around the theme of women's empowerment.

These cases make the point that in lifelong literacy provision, the shift from a psychological model of literacy (a set of absolute skills to be provided, which is in turn based on a deficit-model of education) to literacy-as-practice (literacy competence placed in the context of social-communication processes in which people operate) is extremely important. In other words, anchoring literacy understood as practice in activities undertaken in the community (however defined) sphere is seen as essential for the retention of skills. When learners modify their cognitive processes as a result of having to deal with transformed activities that have incorporated within themselves literacy practices, they are on the road to keeping themselves literate. But should a community practice be defined in terms of a limited geographical entity? Not necessarily, as the case by Kothari et al. seems to indicate. Given the reach of the media of mass communication, it should be possible to reach out to a dispersed community. What makes such a group of learners a community is the interactional possibility (much as an internet-based chat group might work or the feedback mechanisms—print primarily—devised by early distance education models). To this must be added a second possibility, an activity that will anchor the practice of the evolving literacy skills. One can think of a number of activities, ranging from *bhajan mandals* (since religious texts are often the only resource in many parts of the country) to readers' clubs and access points for literacy and to writers' workshops. The possibilities appear to be many. What needs to be recognised, however, is that there must be an awareness of the different uses to which literacy is put in different cultural contexts (Barton and Hamilton, 1998).

This concluding chapter has discussed certain general themes of relevance to literacy and educational policy making, which the cases in this volume illustrate. Taken together, these themes indicate that there is an urgent need to develop a lifelong literacy policy. Such a policy would need to be aware of the conceptual foundations of past thinking on literacy policy. It would need to put in place mechanisms to harness 'political will' for promoting innovation in lifelong literacy and linking literacy with basic schooling. The policy would also have to deal with the issue of literacy in multiple languages. Avenues for supporting well-planned research need to be opened up so that the practice of lifelong literacy can be better informed. New areas which policy making needs to address include the role of information and communication technology in lifelong literacy, and production of relevant educational material in the context of the mass media as directly educational media. Ultimately, such a policy needs to communicate sustainability of literacy skills as a relevant, feasible and attainable goal.

A favourable policy environment, however, is only one aspect of ensuring lifelong literacy. Creating public spaces for newly-literate people is an equally important task, a task for civil society. Such spaces—physical as well as conceptual—are essential if 'literate societies' are to emerge. One may begin by quoting from Michael Norton (this volume): 'We should give examples of how books and the written word can and have changed people's lives. We should be collecting together case studies and stories.' One reading of this quote is an expression of doubt about the public space that is available to people trying to become irreversibly literate. Can examples of how people's lives have been changed motivate the process of sustainability? Where are the 'literacy corners' or the 'internet cafes for neo-literates'? Is there an equivalent of the sign language news bulletin telecast for the hearing-impaired? We end with an extreme example from a very different culture. George Dawson died at the age of 103 on 5 July 2001 (*The Economist*, 14–20 July 2001, page 84). This would have been an unremarkable obituary notice, if it were not for the fact that Dawson was 'illiterate'—as conventionally defined—till he was 98. Up to that time, his name had just been X. He then learned to read and write, and 'Writing my real name was one of the greatest things in my life.' The fact that Dawson was born in Texas and lived his life in the United States is only incidental. That there are people like Dawson who fall through the cracks of the educational systems of a highly literate country is also not relevant. What matters is that Dawson—through his public appearances at schools and universities and on television, two honorary degrees, and a biography published in 2000—triggered off discussion on the various roles that literacy can play with respect to other issues like the educational performance of African Americans, learning in old age, the performance of the United States on the 'functional literacy' front, and so on. His story runs the danger of being dismissed as typical of the 'hype' that some cultures invest exceptions with. But it is important to note that there was a public space that the exception, and there is no doubt that Dawson was one, could occupy during the last five years of his life. Even if Dawson did not manage to build on his newly learned skills, his example serves to illuminate new directions in the debate on the literacies that are relevant for the future.

References

Arnove, R. F. and **H. J. Graff** (eds) (1987). *National Literacy Campaigns: Historical and Comparative Perspectives.* New York: Plenum.

Barton, D. and **M. Hamilton** (1998). *Local Literacies: Reading and Writing in One Community.* London: Routledge.

Bhola, H.S. (1982). *Campaigning for Literacy: A Critical Analysis of Some Selected Literacy Campaigns of the 20th Century, with a Memorandum to Decision Makers.* Paris: UNESCO and International Council for Adult Education.

Faust, D., and **R. Nagar** (2001). 'Politics of Development in Postcolonial India: English Medium Education and Social Fracturing', *Economic and Political Weekly*, 36 (30): 2878–83.

Foucault, M. ([1975] 1985). *Surveiller et Punir: Naissance de la Prison.* Reprint. Paris: Gallimard.

Gandhi, M. K. (1951). *Basic Education.* Ahmedabad: Navjivan.

Ghosh, S. C. (2000). *The History of Education in Modern India, 1757–1998 (revised and updated edition).* New Delhi: Orient Longman.

Government of India (1940). Report of the Adult Education Committee of the Central Advisory Board of Education 1939, Manager, Government of India Press, New Delhi.

——— (1979). Report of the National Board of Adult Education Committee on Post Literacy and Follow up Programmes. New Delhi: Ministry of Education and Social Welfare.

Guillaume, A.M. (2000). 'Learning with Text in the Primary Grades.' In R.D. Robinson, M.C. McKenna and J.M. Wedman (eds), *Issues and Trends in Literacy Education*, 2d ed., pp. 247–59. Boston: Allyn and Bacon.

Kemmis, S., and **M. Wilkinson** (1998). 'Participatory Action Research and the Study of Practice.' In B. Atweh, S. Kemmis and P. Weeks (eds), *Action Research in Practice: Partnerships for Social Justice in Education*, pp. 21–36. London: Routledge.

Kumar, K. (1991). *The Political Agenda of Education: A Study of Colonialist and Nationalist Ideas.* New Delhi: Sage.

——— (1996). *Learning from Conflict.* New Delhi: Orient Longman.

Lewkowicz, N.K. (1980). 'Phonemic Awareness Training: What to Teach and How to Teach it', *Journal of Educational Psychology*, 72 (5): 686–700.

Probe Team, The (in association with Centre for Development Economics) (1999). *Public Report on Basic Education in India.* Delhi: Oxford University Press.

Raban, B. (2000). 'Reading: Literacy and Beyond.' In B. Moon, S. Brown and M. Ben-Peretz (eds), *Routledge International Companion to Education*, pp.801-8. London: Routledge.

Rampal, A., R. Ramanujam and **L.S. Saraswati** (2000). *Zindagi ka Hisab.* Mussoorie: National Literacy Resource Centre, Lal Bahadur Shastri National Academy of Administration.

Rao, N. (1993). 'Total Literacy Campaigns: A Field Report', *Economic and Political Weekly*, 28 (19): 914–18.

Scribner, S. and **M. Cole** (1978). 'Literacy without Schooling: Testing for Intellectual Effects', *Harvard Educational Review*, 48: 448–61.

Shah, S.Y. (1989). *A Source Book on Adult Education.* New Delhi: Directorate of Adult Education, Government of India.

Sinha, A. (1998). *Primary Schooling in India.* New Delhi: Vikas.

Vijaya Sherry Chand, P.G. (1998). 'School Economy and Society'. Initiative for Building Research Capability in DIETs, Monograph 1. Gandhinagar: Gujarat Council of Educational Research and Training.

World Bank, The (1997). *Primary Education in India.* Washington: The World Bank.

About the Editors and Contributors

The Editors

Brij Kothari is Associate Professor at the Indian Institute of Management, Ahmedabad, in the Ravi J. Matthai Centre for Educational Innovation (RJMCEI). A winner of two international innovation awards for his work on literacy development through television, he has previously published several articles on literacy, primary education and local knowledge.

P.G. Vijaya Sherry Chand is Associate Professor, Indian Institute of Management, Ahmedabad (RJMCEI). He was previously Programme Manager and then Director of the Behavioural Science Centre, Ahmedabad. He has previously co-edited *Institution Building: An International Perspective on Management Education* (1999).

Michael Norton is Director of the Centre for Innovation in Voluntary Action (CIVA), a UK-based NGO. CIVA is a partner with the National Foundation of India in the NFI Innovation Fund, which makes grants for innovations in social action, supports the development of Youth Banks and runs youth volunteering programmes. CIVA has established a publishing initiative for the non-profit sector called Books for Change (which is now run by Action Aid India), as also supports a range of initiatives in Andhra Pradesh to encourage reading and the setting up of village libraries. Among Michael Norton's previous publications are *Getting Started in Fundraising and How to be a Community Champion: A Manual for Young Activists*.

The Contributors

Gitarani Bhattacharya is the District Programme Co-ordinator, Assam Mahila Samata Society, Morigaon, Assam. She has specialised in population geography and has worked with women's empowerment programmes.

Biman Borah is Lecturer in geography at Nonoi College, Nagaon and Honorary Assistant Programme Co-ordinator of the Society for Socio-economic Awareness and Environment Protection. He has specialised in social geography and has studied the social impact of many small-scale development projects.

Ashok Joshi has been Research Associate at the Indian Institute of Management, Ahmedabad. A Gujarati language expert, he has been closely involved in projects on literacy through media and popular culture in Gujarat.

Shalini Joshi is the editor of *Pitara*, a news and features magazine written in simple Hindi. She works with Nirantar, a resource group with a focus on women and education and advises NGOs on the production and publication of their own material. Nirantar's activities include curriculum development, innovative educational strategies, material production, training, documentation and action research.

Sarah Kamala is Associate Professor in the Department of Extension Education at the Acharya N.G. Ranga Agricultural University, Hyderabad, Andhra Pradesh. She has also worked as Senior Faculty at the Andhra Pradesh Academy of Rural Development, Government of Andhra Pradesh. She has been a consultant for various national and international organisations specialising in Panchayati Raj Institutions, gender issues, rural development and poverty initiatives, village libraries, child labour, adult literacy, training methods, and extension education. She is presently the area representative for the Centre for Innovations in Voluntary Action (CIVA), UK.

S. Madasamy heads the Department of Tamil, SBK College, Aruppukottai, Tamil Nadu. He has worked as district co-ordinator of the literacy campaign in Virudhunagar, and was associated with the production of study material *Vaasal* (a broadsheet) and a series of books for neo-literates. He has adapted folk stories, songs and sayings to the needs of neo-literate readers. He also served as President of the Tamil Nadu Science Forum and Director of Youth Welfare at MS University, Tirunelveli.

Sushama Merh-Ashraf recently retired as Professor, University of Delhi. Her professional work and interest include, science education, women's education and empowerment, environmental education, cinema in social education, non-formal education, extension for the disadvantaged, and tele-mediated communication and education. She is also involved in the translation of literacy and educational materials in Gujarati, Hindi and English. She has published several books and articles and participated in a number of national and international conferences. Twice she was a Fulbright Fellow to the USA and a CIDA/Shastri Fellow to Canada. Her other interests are theatre and vocal music.

Avinash Pandey started Base Research, a company that specialises in market research and data analysis. Presently, he is Assistant Professor at Birla Institute of Management Technology, New Delhi.

Rajani Paranjpe is Founder President of the Door Step School, an NGO working for the education of the urban poor in Mumbai and Pune. She was on the faculty of the University of Mumbai in the College of Social Work until 1988. In 1994, she became a member of the faculty at Shikoku Christian University, Japan, where she retired as Professor in international social welfare in 1997.

K.S. Ram is Project Director, Literacy, in Bastar District and Secretary, Van Dhan Mission. He has served as Lecturer in English at Sarada Vilas College, Mysore, and worked at the State Bank of India. He has also been Chief Executive of a cement manufacturing company in Jagdalpur (Bastar), Chattisgarh. He has translated into English the *dohas* (couplets) of Kabir and others, under the title *Dohavali*.

Anita Rampal is Director of the National Literacy Resource Centre, at the Lal Bahadur Shastri National Academy of Administration, Mussoorie. Originally a trained physicist, she has been involved in curriculum development and teacher training for innovative science programmes in rural schools. She has also taught and designed new 'Science and Society' courses for university B.Ed. and M.Sc.(Ed.) programmes. She is the co-author of the *Public Report on Basic Education (1999)* and has also authored other books and research articles. She has been on several national committees, task forces and the Planning Commission Working Groups on Adolescents and Adult Education. She is a member of the All India People's Science Network and the Bharat Gyan Vigyan Samiti, two umbrella networks of voluntary organisations that initiated the mass literacy campaigns in the country.

D. Janardhana Reddy is Director, Department of Adult Education and Co-ordinator, Population Education Resource Centre at the Sri Venkateswara University, Tirupati. He has authored five books, nine literacy primers for adult learners, and numerous articles. His areas of specialisation include training and material development for adult education, and evaluation of adult education programmes.

Saswati Roy is working with Swadhina, an organisation committed to the empowerment of women and children, with a specific thrust on the promotion of non-formal education in rural and disadvantaged areas. She has acquired considerable experience working with people in tribal areas. She is also involved in the peace movement as Section Representative of War Resisters' International, London, of which, Swadhina is a Section in East India.

Jayanta Kumar Sarma is Lecturer in geography at Nowgong Girls'College and Honorary Programme Co-ordinator of the Society for Socio-economic Awareness and Environment Protection. He has a specialisation in regional planning. He has also conducted several micro-level participatory planning exercises and developed resources for environmental education and literacy.

P.K. Sasidharan teaches English at ANJA College, Sivakasi, Tamil Nadu. He is President of the Tamil Nadu Science Forum and has been the district co-ordinator of the Literacy Campaign of Virudhunagar district. He has contributed to the production of many broadsheets and books for neo-literates and the strategic formulation of reading campaigns and training methodologies for campaign functionaries. He has worked as a consultant for the National Literacy Mission and as a member of the steering committee of a UNESCO-sponsored study of post-literacy campaigns in India.

Jaya Shrivastava is a developmental activist based in Delhi. For the last 25 years she has been working for the rights of children, women, tribals, Dalits, minorities and people displaced by development projects. She is the Director of Ankur: Society for Alternatives in Education, but mainly concentrates on Ankur's documentation, networking and training activities.

Preeti Soni works with Kutch Mahila Vikas Sangathan (KMVS), a village women's collective with a presence in over 150 villages of Kutch. Her interest in girls' and women's education stems from her own personal struggles. At KMVS she has been deeply involved in women's mobilisation and empowerment. Recently she coordinated a radio serial, drawing upon women's experiences in the panchayati raj.

Joe Takeda is Lecturer at Kwansei Gakuin University, Nishinomiya, Japan, in the Department of Social Work. He has also been a visiting faculty at the Indian Institute of Management, Ahmedabad.